Praise for *Every Spy a Traitor*

'[Gerlis is] One of the superstars of modern spy fiction'
   Daily Express

'Gerlis takes a gamble with a slower pace here than in his previous
works set in the second world war. It pays off handsomely'
   Financial Times

'Thoroughly researched and with a strong sense of place, the novel
is fast moving … A fascinating yarn set against a historical background and countries in turmoil… The overall feel is a pleasant
blend of John Buchan derring-do if lightweight adventures and
the more gritty Le Carré-like grey travails in the secret corridors
of power'
   Crime Time

'With this brilliant tale of a writer entangled in pre-World War
II espionage, Gerlis cleverly builds an ironic and darkly realistic
world that shows just how nebulous is the border between good
and evil, observer and participant, our inner and outer lives.
Richly imagined, meticulously plotted and chock-full of historic
details, *Every Spy a Traitor* is one of those rare books that gets
better with every page. One of the best spy novels I've read'
   I. S. Berry, author of *The Peacock and the Sparrow*

'Utterly gripping and startlingly compelling, *Every Spy a Traitor*
is an absorbing portrait of a world on the brink that disarms you
before it floors you'
   Tim Glister, author of *Red Corona*

'In this gripping historical spy novel, a young British writer finds himself entrapped by the Soviet NVKD as war clouds gather over Europe. Alex Gerlis is at the top of his game with clever plotting, rich detail, and a compelling story of a young man forced to become a double agent to survive in a world where friends become adversaries and no one can be trusted. *Every Spy a Traitor* will reward fans of Graham Greene, Charles Cumming, Frederick Forsythe and Alan Furst'

Paul Vidich, author of *Beirut Station*

'Set in the tense run-up to war and ranging across Russia, Germany, Brussels and England, *Every Spy a Traitor* is a gripping and immersive novel which is also immaculately researched. There are shades of Eric Ambler in Alex Gerlis's appealing hero, Charles Cooper, an ingénue novelist who finds himself inveigled into becoming both a Russian agent and a British spy. Gerlis's knowledge of espionage and attention to detail are second to none. Highly recommended'

Jane Thynne, author of *Black Roses*

Every Spy a Traitor

Alex Gerlis was a BBC journalist for nearly thirty years and is the author of nine Second World war espionage thrillers, all published by Canelo.

His first four novels are in the acclaimed Spy Masters series, including the best-selling *The Best of Our Spies* which is currently being developed as a television series. *Prince of Spies* was published in March 2020 and was followed by three more in the Prince series. His latest series is the Wolf Pack novels, with *Agent in Berlin* published in November 2021, with the second in the series due to be published in July 2022.

Alex was born in Lincolnshire and now lives in west London with his wife and two black cats, a breed which makes cameo appearances in all his books. Alex has two daughters and two grandsons and supports Grimsby Town, which he believes helps him cope with the highs and especially the lows of writing a novel. He's frequently asked if he's ever worked for an intelligence agency but always declines to answer the question in the hope that someone may believe he actually has.

Also by Alex Gerlis

Spy Masters

The Best of Our Spies
The Swiss Spy
Vienna Spies
The Berlin Spies

The Richard Prince Thrillers

Prince of Spies
Sea of Spies
Ring of Spies
End of Spies

The Wolf Pack Spies

Agent in Berlin
Agent in Peril
Agent in the Shadows

The Double Agent series

Every Spy a Traitor

ALEX GERLIS

EVERY SPY A TRAITOR

CANELO

First published in the United Kingdom in 2024 by Canelo

This edition published in the United Kingdom in 2024 by

Canelo
Unit 9, 5th Floor
Cargo Works, 1-2 Hatfields
London SE1 9PG
United Kingdom

A CIP catalogue record for this book is available from the British Library.

Ebook ISBN 978 1 80436 377 5
Hardback ISBN 978 1 80436 375 1
Paperback ISBN 978 1 80436 376 8

This book is a work of fiction. Names, characters, businesses, organizations, places and events are either the product of the author's imagination or are used fictitiously. Any resemblance to actual persons, living or dead, events or locales is entirely coincidental.

Cover design by Black Sheep

Cover images © Deposit Photos; Shutterstock

Look for more great books at www.canelo.co

Printed and bound in Great Britain by Clays Ltd, Elcograf S.p.A.

1

Main Characters

BRITISH

Charles Cooper	also known as: **Christopher Shaw; Frank Reynolds; George William Hobson** codename: **Bertie**
Marjorie Cooper	mother of Charles Cooper
Sydney Carter	solicitor in Birmingham
Archie	codename of British traitor
Francis Randall	publisher
Pamela Clarke	Annexe officer
Percy Burton	Head of The Annexe
The Hon. Milo Smart	British diplomat, Moscow
George Banks	MI6 officer, Moscow
Austin Branstone	Cambridge academic
Dr Paxton	Cambridge academic and MI6 agent

Phillips	MI6
Simpkin	MI5
Murray	assassin
Ronnie	locksmith
Douglas Marsh	also known as: Harry Moore

British Communist Party and Soviet agent

Cliff Milne	British Communist Party and Soviet agent
Sidney Dunn	assistant to Cliff Milne
Wright	Communist Party organiser
Maggie	British woman in Paris

RUSSIAN

Nikolai Vasilyevich Zaslavsky	OMS officer, Moscow
Emil	OMS agent
Osip	OMS *rezident* London
Misha	publisher at Goslitizdat Moscow

Ernst and Ida Maurer	OMS agents Berlin
Eduard Vladimirovich	OMS Berlin and Moscow
Ivan Alexandrovich Morozov	NKVD *rezident* London
Andriy Oleksandrvych Kovalenko	Soviet diplomat, Vienna and The Hague
Sergei Grigoryevich Volkov	Comintern official, Moscow
Nadezhda Nikolaeva Kuznetsova	Comintern official, Moscow
Yegorov	NKVD *rezident* Vienna and The Hague
Tarasov	NKVD at Ministry of Foreign Affairs
Belov	relative of Kovalenko
Lysenko	Soviet diplomat
Ivan	GRU officer Barcelona

OTHERS

Manfred	passenger on Hamburg train
Rita Marks	American communist in Moscow

Intelligence Organisations

Soviet Intelligence organisations

OMS: the International Liaison Department of the Comintern, the Communist International. As such, the OMS was the most secret department of the Comintern and heavily involved in illegal and clandestine matters abroad. Formed in 1921, dissolved in 1939.

NKVD: the People's Commissariat for Internal Affairs. Originally established in 1917, the NKVD was the main secret police body within the Soviet Union, but also had intelligence and counter-intelligence functions, both within the Soviet Union and abroad. Predecessor to the **KGB**.

GRU: the Main Intelligence Directorate of the General Staff of the Red Army.

British Intelligence organisations

MI6: the Secret Intelligence Service, also referred to as 'the Service' or 'Head Office'. Formed 1909. The main British espionage organisation. Operates primarily overseas.

MI5: the Security Service, formed 1909. Responsible for counter-espionage within the UK.

Special Branch: intelligence branch of the police service.

The Annexe: fictional organisation (as far as one knows…). Formed in 1931 to liaise between the above three organisations and to carry out clandestine and non-attributable activities on behalf of the British state. Dissolved 1939.

Prologue

He was aware of her stirring next to him and then cursing in her harsh New York accent as she knocked something over on the bedside table. When he asked what time it was, she said it was ten to three, what time did he think it was, and then it was his turn to swear – but in his softer, middle-class English accent – as she pulled the covers back and the cold hit him hard.

She stood up, her naked body silhouetted by the dim light in the room, lit a cigarette and put on her dressing gown before walking over to the window and peeking out of the curtains, carefully looking up and down Vorovsky Street five floors below, holding the cigarette behind her just in case anyone spotted its tiny red glow.

'All quiet?'

She didn't reply, moving round to draw on her cigarette before turning back to the parted curtain.

'Come back to bed, Rita; there are four million people in Moscow and a dedicated communist like you is one of the least likely they'll arrest. And—'

'It's *because* I'm a dedicated communist, Cooper. How many times do I need to tell you that, for Christ's sake? I sometimes think you're putting on this naïve act.'

There was a noise from outside, and he asked her what it was.

'City police. It's a raid. Christ.'

'There are hundreds of apartments on Vorovsky, I really wouldn't worry, I—'

She pulled the curtain tight and stood with her back to it and when he turned on the lamp she looked like a ghost.

'What is it?'

'They're coming into this building. Get dressed, Cooper. You know what to do.'

He said something about not being silly and there were dozens of apartments in this building, but she was ignoring him as they hurriedly dressed and now he heard people inside, slamming doors and shouting, footsteps heading up the stairs.

The accepted wisdom in Moscow was that the best thing to do when they came for you was to be as warmly dressed as possible because they took you away as you were. You wouldn't want to be transported to a camp in your pyjamas. Or die in them.

He tidied the bed, hoping no one would notice two people had been in it, and when he turned round, she'd opened the hiding place and told him to get in and when he said she should get in too she snapped and said he knew there was only room for one of them and she was the one they'd come for.

–

Whenever the time changed, word spread through Moscow faster than rumours of the arrival of chickens for sale at the market.

Somehow, people knew at what unearthly hour of the night the secret police would knock on the doors of those whose turn it was to be arrested. Hardly anyone openly discussed such matters, even with those they trusted most, though very few people in Moscow in 1937 trusted anyone else, even those close to them. In fact, especially those close to them.

Towards the end of 1936 the raids had been at around five o'clock in the morning, the end of the previous year more like midnight.

But once the secret police had chosen a new time to start their raids they tended to stick to that time for a few weeks – something to do with their shifts, apparently. The squads worked nine-hour shifts, arriving at the Lubyanka for their briefing before setting out, three hours allotted for the raids, and then taking the prisoners to Butyrskaya on Novoslobodskaya, an hour to book the prisoners in and take a meal break in the surprisingly pleasant staff canteen, followed by another two hours for the paperwork and possibly sitting in on the initial interrogation.

And then home.

And knowing the time mattered. It was vital information to have. If someone feared they were going to be arrested – and few people in Moscow were confident enough to feel that they were under no risk – then at least they wanted to be ready. The chances of escape were slim, but if you were awake and dressed and listening out then at least you had a chance. That rarely worked, of course, but occasionally someone may have a good escape route to evade the city police, whose job was to surround the building, and NKVD officers occasionally believed a woman who told them she'd not seen her husband for days.

In March 1937 they'd taken to coming at three in the morning and even a foreigner like Charles Cooper was aware of the time.

–

In the end she had to push him into the tiny hiding place and just before she closed it, she thrust a thick envelope into his hands.

'My American passport's in there: it expired a year ago, but I guess I'm still a US citizen. Go to the embassy on Mokhovaya Street and tell them I've been arrested. I doubt it will help, especially if they look at my file, but you never know. And then get the envelope to my folks in New York City, though they probably won't want to know about me either. And I—'

There was shouting now outside the apartment and banging on the door. She paused for a split second, during which he noticed her eyes fill with tears, and then she closed the panel to his hiding place and pushed the chest of drawers across it.

He squatted down, his forehead pressed against his knees, clutching his raincoat tight against his face in case they heard his panicked breathing or he sneezed or coughed and all the time he felt his body shake. The sounds from the apartment were muffled, but he could hear Rita speaking, at first in her broken Russian and then someone spoke to her in English and she replied, saying something about not knowing what this was all about and, if it helped, she'd be prepared to leave the Soviet Union immediately because as a loyal communist she didn't want to cause any trouble and—

Someone must have hit her or grabbed her because she cried out and then told them, 'There's no need for that,' and that was the last he heard from her.

For a moment there was no sound, but then he heard what sounded like two people moving around, opening drawers, and he tensed his body, expecting them to move the chest of drawers any moment and thought this was a crazy hiding place, it was never going to fool the NKVD and as they pulled open the drawers inches from him, he felt the unit knock against his hiding place and then he heard one of them say *nee kherà tut nyet* which he knew meant 'there's fuck all here' and the other one grunted in agreement. *Ladno, poshlee!*

'Let's go!'

Chapter 1

It had been a pleasant encounter in Paris and a happy coincidence in Lyon but here in Cannes it was, in fact, downright sinister.

The meeting would change the course of his life and in the long years that followed he occasionally allowed himself the indulgence of wondering what might have happened had he simply told the man to get lost, there and then. Perhaps not in those terms, something more polite, as would be expected of a young English gentleman. He could have said he was terribly sorry but he had no idea what he was talking about and there'd clearly been a misunderstanding and he really had to leave now. He'd have thanked him graciously for the drink and hurried off.

He'd have disappeared. And probably left Cannes that night.

But, of course, he didn't.

He'd spent enough time in the countryside to know a trapped animal only makes its predicament worse with futile attempts to extricate itself. He knew he'd little choice but to stay.

And in those brief few moments when his instincts told him it would be foolish to leave it was as if he somehow came to terms with the situation he found himself in.

Not only was he reconciled to it, but he understood this was the hand he'd been dealt and it would be best all round if he accepted that, made the most of it and didn't waste time thinking about what might have been.

However awful that may be.

When he'd left London on the first of September he couldn't have been in a more optimistic mood. Ahead lay five weeks of holiday before he was to start his first job. And not just any job: this was a prestigious one, one he'd achieved after a gruelling series of interviews and examinations. Despite his family connections, he liked to think he'd got this job on merit. It was, as his father had solemnly pointed out when toasting him at dinner the previous evening, the start of his career – one which promised to be quite glorious.

He was twenty-two and he no longer needed to worry about studies or exams and it was a delightfully warm Tuesday morning and France was just hours away. His mother, of course, had worried about the journey – *such a long way to drive* – and what he'd get up to in France – *so long abroad*!

His ultimate destination was Cannes, where the family of a friend from university had a villa in the town's reassuringly named English Quarter.

The MG Midget was his pride and joy, handsome in British Racing Green livery and he was confident it would make the long journey to the south of France a pleasure. It only had a couple of hundred miles on the clock and was a bargain at £145 and the mechanic who checked it out at his father's garage said it was in excellent condition as long as he kept a good eye on the water and oil levels and didn't drive it for too long at its top speed of sixty-five miles per hour.

He left his parents' house in Chelsea shortly after six and was in Dover in good time for the ten-thirty crossing. It was early afternoon when they docked in Calais and he couldn't decide whether to drive straight through to Paris, which he reckoned would be a good four hours, or to stop on the way, and then he realised he didn't need to decide yet, he could see how he felt and he relished the sense of freedom this gave him. For the first time in his life, it was up to him to do what he wanted and when.

In the end he decided to stay overnight in Amiens, where he found a pleasant hotel close to the cathedral, overlooking Parc de l'Evêché.

He left Amiens early on the Wednesday morning after sending a high-spirited telegram to his parents assuring them their eldest son hadn't drowned in the Channel or been abducted.

CROSSING FINE STOP EN ROUTE PARIS STOP

IF KIDNAPPED PAY RANSOM STOP

He spent the drive to Paris mildly regretting the telegram: his mother's reaction would be that he should grow up, especially now he had a career.

He arrived in the French capital early in the afternoon. He was staying at an apartment in the 8th *arrondissement* belonging to a nephew of his godfather. The nephew worked at the Paris office of Barings bank and was back in London for the week, but had been happy to lend him the keys to his apartment, which was located on Rue Montalivet, just round the corner from the British Embassy in Rue du Faubourg Saint-Honoré.

He wasn't expected in Cannes before the weekend – he'd promised to be there for lunch on Sunday – and his plan was to stay two nights in Paris and then allow a further two days for the journey south.

He rested for a while and showered and at around five o'clock left the apartment, heading across the Place de la Concorde towards the Seine, and on the corner of Quai de la Conference and Avenue Dutuit found an empty table outside a cafe. It was a warm evening and the city was still quiet, as if those who'd taken part in the August exodus had yet to return.

The dappled sunlight filtered through the trees onto the neat red-and-white-chequered tablecloth and he shifted his chair so he was under the shade of the awning. He doubted he'd ever felt more relaxed and confident, so much so that he removed his jacket and loosened his tie, emboldened by the sight of a pair of distinguished-looking men on a nearby table, both of whom had open-necked shirts and no sign of a jacket, not even across the back of their chairs.

A pair of girls walked by, barely past their teens – certainly younger than his twenty-two years. They giggled and watched him as they walked and they were followed by an older woman walking her dog and although she was considerably older than him – quite possibly in her forties – she also looked at him, smiling and raising her eyebrows. He knew he was attractive to women – he'd been told that – but here in Paris that seemed so much more obvious. He'd been told he looked not unlike Edward, the Prince of Wales, who was some fifteen years older than him, but he shared the same aristocratic bearing and what he'd once been told was a touch of arrogance, but he'd taken that as a compliment.

He sat up, straightening his athletic figure, and the sun caught his fair hair while a tired-looking waiter hovered close to the table as he decided what to drink, and he asked him in what he hoped was good French if he minded giving him a few minutes and perhaps if he had a menu...

With some luck, a long night lay ahead and the thought of it filled him with both excitement and some trepidation. His very good friend Charlie from college said his older brother had told him about a nightclub close to the Gare Saint Lazare, which he simply had to visit. According to Charlie, the club was so discreet it had no name, and although it wasn't a brothel as such, remember this is Paris, and there were lots of knowing looks and he wondered whether Charlie had actually visited the club, which he'd find in an alley close to the junction of Rue de Naples and Rue du General Foy.

The waiter returned with a menu and it was a bit awkward as he tried to explain that thank you very much but no, he didn't want to eat but rather wanted to see what there was to drink, and the waiter shrugged and it was then that he heard the man speak.

Until that moment, he was unaware of the person sitting on the table next to his, so close that their shoulders were almost

8

touching, yet the man hadn't been there when he arrived and he'd not noticed him take his place.

'In Paris, they would not expect a gentleman to ask for a menu for a drink, especially if it is not accompanied by a meal. At this time of the day, they would assume you know what you want to drink.'

As he spoke, the man shifted his chair towards him and now, he could see him properly: he was perhaps in his late forties, hard to tell his height but he was slim and had an olive complexion, which suggested he may be from Southern Europe, and he wore a cream suit with a blue-and-white-striped shirt and a dark tie and a white fedora with a wide brim and a band round it, the same colour as his tie. He had a large moustache, the type people sometimes called a walrus moustache, so it appeared he was speaking without moving his lips. He spoke in English with an accent he couldn't for the life of him place.

'Thank you. I couldn't decide what to drink. I didn't realise asking for a menu would be such a *faux pas*!'

The man laughed politely.

'How did you know I was English?'

The man shrugged in a manner to indicate it was obvious. 'At this time of the day you would be expected to order an aperitif or possibly a white wine. But there are no rules, other than it would be assumed you know what you want... without the assistance of a menu!'

'Actually, I was wondering whether I'd be committing another *faux pas* if I were to order a coffee? I've had a rather long drive and am going out later and—'

'In that case' – the man had now turned his chair round so that they were more or less sitting at the same table – 'may I suggest coffee and brandy?'

'In the same cup?' He tried not to sound too horrified.

The man nodded. 'Absolutely, though I imagine in London at this time of day you'd have a cup of tea?' The man laughed loudly.

'Or a beer!'

The waiter reappeared and the man told him to bring a black coffee with a large Cognac. He was certainly not a native French speaker.

'That way you can choose how strong to make your drink. It will fortify you for whatever plans you have for tonight.'

'I'm not sure I do have plans.'

'I seem to recall you saying you were going out and, in any case, a young man on his own in Paris… it would be a missed opportunity! *Voilà*, here is your coffee and Cognac. Try it. Pour some brandy into the coffee and if you find it agreeable, add the rest.'

He did find it agreeable and poured all of the Cognac into the coffee. The waiter watched him from the shadows under the cafe's canopy and when he finished came to ask if he'd like another one. He was undecided and replied maybe he'd just have a coffee first, with milk, please, and when he looked up the man at the next table had gone, as furtively as he'd arrived.

–

He left Paris on the Friday morning. It hadn't been quite the visit he'd hoped it would be. Despite Charlie's assurances to the contrary, the nightclub in the alley close to Gare Saint Lazare was quite obviously a brothel and certainly wasn't discreet, so much so that he did wonder whether he'd got the wrong place, though he wasn't minded to try and find out. There was a certain air of menace in the area around Rue de Naples and Rue du General Foy and when he did finally enter the building with no name he was told he'd need to pay four francs to enter in return for which he'd be entitled to one drink and when he asked what kind of drink he was ignored and he decided that was ridiculous because four francs was the price of a decent dinner in Paris and if that was what they were charging for a drink then he shuddered to think what they'd charge for whatever else they had on offer.

That cast something of a cloud over the rest of his stay. He wandered miserably around the city on the Thursday, regretting his caution of the previous night and even had an early night to prepare for a six o'clock start on the Friday morning.

Lyon was some three hundred and thirty miles south-east and the journey took eight hours, driving for two hours at a time – never at more than sixty miles per hour – before stopping at one of the frequent roadside garages to fill up with petrol and have the tyres, oil and water checked. French mechanics were, he found, altogether more obliging than those in England.

In Lyon he found a pleasant hotel suggested in his Baedeker in the Presqu'île, on a small road close to Place Bellecour and as it was still light after he'd checked in, he went for a stroll and ended up at a pavement cafe on Place des Célestins, in the shadow of the theatre and the neat trees surrounding the small square.

He was sipping a glass of cold *bière de Lyon* when he felt a tap on his shoulder.

'I see you no longer have the taste for coffee and Cognac.' The voice was familiar, though the accent was more pronounced than when he'd first heard it two evenings ago in Paris. Then it could have been a Spanish or Italian accent. Now it was harsher.

This time the man got up and sat in the chair opposite. He was dressed as in Paris, but looked as if he'd been in a hurry and was breathing heavily and wiping the perspiration from his brow and when he called the waiter over, he asked for a beer too.

'In weather like this, a cold beer is the ideal drink. Lyon is far closer to the Mediterranean than it is to Paris, you know? People say it is where the south begins.'

'Are you from France?'

The man sighed as if to indicate it was a long story. 'Not as such, no. I prefer to describe myself as European.'

'I never imagined meeting you here: what an extraordinary coincidence, in a country this size!'

'A happy coincidence, I hope?'

'But of course.'

'Then we must not allow the opportunity to be wasted. Come, finish your beer. You know that Lyon is the heart of French gastronomy? I will take you to a proper *bouchon*, which serves the local cuisine.'

Although he regarded himself as an assertive person, certainly no pushover, he was surprised at how he allowed himself to be led along by the other man, who on the walk to the restaurant said he could call him Emil, which he thought was a funny way of phrasing it, rather than saying 'my name is Emil', but then the man was clearly not speaking in his native language so one did have to make allowances and he told him his name and Emil said, yes, he knew, and he wasn't sure how he knew and mentioned that and Emil said rather quickly that he'd told him so in the cafe on Place des Célestins.

The restaurant was called Le Garet and was a rather informal place, more of a bistro than a restaurant, if the truth be told. But the food was excellent, even if some of the dishes weren't ones he'd have chosen had he been there by himself, but Emil insisted on ordering. They started with *salade Lyonnaise*, followed by pike, then a large plate of andouillettes sausage with tripe and dumplings and after that he felt he couldn't eat another thing, but Emil told him not to be ridiculous, at which point a large lemon tart appeared before them and once that was finished, they were presented with a plate of the local Saint-Félicien cheese. By the time they'd finished the meal they'd also drunk two bottles of Macon Rouge.

Later, he did try to recall just what they spoke about during the meal and it was hard to be precise because Emil had a habit of talking in a discursive manner and it was hard to follow his train of thought, but he was amusing at times with tales of his travels and a terribly risqué story about a woman in Milan and then he spoke at some length about the situation in Europe and how it was a time of turmoil and great change and though he occasionally paused to ask him his point of view, he rarely gave his own opinion and by the end of the evening he realised what an enigmatic character Emil was, appearing so open and clubbable and yet on reflection he knew little about him.

It was eleven o'clock when he said he had to leave because he had a long drive south the next day and Emil nodded and said it had been a pleasure to meet him and he wished him a good evening.

–

He left Lyon the following morning and drove as far as Avignon where he spent the Saturday night and arrived in Cannes in time for lunch on the Sunday, as he'd promised.

He was staying at a villa in La Croix des Gardes, owned by the grandparents of his friend Randolph, who'd been in the same college as him at university. They were minor aristocracy – the grandfather more minor than the grandmother – and perfectly pleasant but it was clear that other than joining them for dinner, he was very much on his own, which was tolerable enough as Randolph and a couple of other friends would be arriving later in the week.

On the Tuesday he walked down to the port and had lunch on Quai St Pierre and then walked through the Mount Chevalier district to Square Brougham where he ordered a coffee and Cognac and was amused when the waiter said in this part of France they often called it a *caffè corretto* and as he drank it he leant back to enjoy the sun, closing his eyes and adjusting the expensive sunglasses he'd bought in Lyon, and was feeling quite at peace and decidedly happy and that was the moment when he became aware of someone sitting next to him and although it took him a moment or two to focus, he somehow sensed it was Emil and the sense of peace and happiness he'd been enjoying now disappeared.

Emil waved the waiter away.

'What on earth's going on, Emil? I can put Lyon down to a coincidence, though you never did explain what you were doing in the city, but here in Cannes… have you been following me?'

'Do you think I have?'

'I don't know what to think, but—'

'Let's just say that we've had our eyes on you since before you arrived in Paris. Before you left London, in fact.'

Despite the sun beating down from a clear blue sky it felt as if a dark cloud had appeared over him. He asked Emil who 'we' was, but he waved away the question in the same dismissive manner with which he'd dismissed the waiter and said he'd do very well to listen because it was very important and that was the first moment when he thought about making his excuses and leaving but more than anything else he was intrigued to know what this was all about.

Emil spoke for the next half hour. It was a detailed and unerringly accurate account of his life: where he'd been born and when, his family, his education, his friends and his new job, one which few people knew as much about, for what were obvious reasons.

He did ask Emil what the hell this was all about and started to leave but Emil must have been expecting this because he told him to sit down and listen very carefully because his life may well depend upon it.

'You were at Oxford University, weren't you – Oriel College?'

He found himself nodding in reply.

'During your second term at university – in February 1927 – you attended two meetings of the Chaucer Group, which was a discussion forum for students from across the university who were interested in current affairs. It was also attended by some academics. Although it wasn't explicit, the group had left-wing leanings without being associated with any political group. You do recall this, I assume?'

He nodded. He sipped his coffee, but it had gone cold, and called the waiter over and asked for a Cognac.

Grand.

'You participated in the discussions, especially at your second meeting, and after that meeting you were approached by one of the academics, a man called Gilbert. You remember him – you look confused?'

'It's rather fanciful for you to seriously think I can remember everyone I met or bumped into at university: it must have run

14

into the hundreds. And you're talking about when, 1927? Four years ago!'

'Maurice Gilbert: of course, you remember him. You had two very long meetings, one running into the early hours in his rooms at his college, I'm told. You insisted that despite or possibly because of your privileged background you felt strongly that society is unfair and immoral and you told him no one should be surprised if the oppressed classes – your words – had no alternative but to resort to violent means to bring about a more equal and just society. You told him – and Maurice made contemporaneous notes – how much you admired the Russian revolution and that you felt a proletarian revolution in the United Kingdom would be – and I quote – "justified and desirable". Ring any bells?'

'Do you really take seriously the drunken ramblings of a student? I don't recall this specific conversation, but I may well have flirted with all kinds of politics at university: it probably felt exciting at the time, as if I was doing something daring. No doubt it was exhilarating, like when one's fox hunting. But it would have been no more than a passing phase. Maybe this Gilbert chap was one of those academics who enjoyed the company of good-looking young men like me, there were plenty of that sort around.'

'We traditionally take a dim view of intellectuals, especially those from a background as privileged as yours. The Marxist–Leninist view is that socialism will only emerge as a movement of the working class and the involvement of your class is best regarded as bourgeoise interference, as an indulgence, a passing phase – as you yourself put it – before you re-join the oppressor ruling class. Students are a very good example of this.

'Usually, such students fall by the wayside after a few meetings: they are excited by their brief flirtation with revolutionary politics but soon realise it is not for them, especially if it involves any kind of work or, worse still, interaction with the working class.

'Maurice Gilbert was very experienced and had a good sense of who fell into such a category and who was worth taking more seriously and according to his notes, he'd never met a student more serious about what he said and more sincere in his beliefs than you. We've had our eye on you since then and nothing has altered that view.'

'Well, jolly good for you, Emil, but as far as I'm concerned this is all a load of nonsense and now I—'

'You kept in touch with Maurice Gilbert and did as he instructed – that is, to eschew any apparent interest in and involvement with politics and in so far as you expressed any political views, they were ones which firmly reflected the interests of the establishment. In the first term of your second year – I'm told it is called Michaelmas – Maurice asked you to obtain copies of documents your father brought home from work and he supplied you with a special camera for this along with a tool to pick the lock to his study. Over the following twelve months you handed over to Maurice dozens of films, with photographs of a large number of documents. Some were invaluable to us. We were surprised the Foreign Office allowed its senior officials to take such secret material home with them. You showed a degree of commitment we'd never expected and a cool nerve and guile that was most impressive. Maurice always said you were the most promising of his recruits.'

Emil paused and beckoned the waiter over and ordered two Cognacs – *large please, of course* – and when he said he wasn't sure he wanted one, Emil told him by the time he'd finished he'd need one.

'A year after you started to pass on this information to Maurice, he died, didn't he? Natural causes, according to the post-mortem, and we have no reason to think otherwise: he wasn't a terribly healthy man, I think the word is obese, eh? I imagine you were worried as were we by what they may find in his room when they cleared it out. We shouldn't have worried, of course: like most of Maurice's life, his chaotic and disorganised manner was just a front. He wouldn't have left anything incriminating in his room. He had a room in a lodging house in the south of the city, which we also had access to – it was how we collected material – and he was meticulous about keeping everything of any importance there. It was all intact, including the latest undeveloped film you'd handed over to him not long before he died. If you did worry, you needn't have done. After that you heard nothing and probably thought such involvement as you had had gone with Maurice's death. A lucky escape, you probably thought, eh? But it seems not.'

This was the point at which he could have walked away but instead he remained sitting quite still, possibly looking impassive but feeling cold despite the blazing sun as it became apparent to him that from this moment on, every aspect of his life would be changed: his loyalties and his allegiances, every waking moment preoccupied by caution – no time for relaxation or carefree thoughts.

He could have been angry with himself but quickly realised that would be a wasted emotion. Certainly, it had been a youthful indiscretion, one motivated by a sense of injustice but perhaps more so by a deep resentment of his father and an opportunity to get back at him, as he saw it then.

He nodded and listened carefully as Emil explained what would happen. They were delighted with his new job: after Maurice had died, they'd left him alone to see what happened to him and it had worked out perfectly. In his job he'd be ideally placed to help the Soviet Union and—

'Hang on, hang on… the Soviet Union is the "we"?'

'Of course: who did you imagine it would be?'

Emil continued: they would expect little of him for a year or two, perhaps even longer. The plan would be to allow him to rise in the organisation he was about to join without a hint of suspicion around him. When the time was right, he'd be expected to start supplying information and undertaking various tasks.

'Even if you don't hear from us for a while, never make the mistake of assuming that we've gone away. And should you ever give even the slightest consideration to breaking off relations with us, I'm sure you'll remember that we have a treasure trove of incriminating material.'

He nodded and said he'd already worked that out for himself, which was why he was still here. He thought it was ironic that he'd always craved a life of excitement and even danger and now he'd most certainly got one. And the cause he was attached to – the Soviet Union – well, it wasn't a bad one, was it? At least he was on the right side.

'Remain here in Cannes for the rest of your holiday,' said Emil. 'Act normally, you'll soon get used to that. Return to London and start your job. At some point, you'll be contacted by a person who gives you my regards and asks if you'd like to join them for coffee and Cognac: you will do what they say. Do you follow me?'

The Englishman nodded, brushing his fair hair away from his eyes.

'The person who contacts you will call you Archie. That is how you'll be known to us.'

Part 1

Chapter 2

Castle Avenue was a long, unbending road and in the autumn the absence of leaves from its many trees meant you could see farther ahead and into the houses, or as much as their net curtains would allow.

Number 148 was about five minutes' walk from the Common and as he approached it most evenings Charles Cooper would spot a figure in the bay window on the ground floor, standing behind the curtain that had been pulled partially aside.

Moments later Cooper would open the gate to 148 Castle Avenue, making sure to close it carefully behind him, as instructed by his landlady. As he opened the front door – making a point of wiping his feet on the mat, also as instructed by his landlady – Mrs Carpenter would suddenly appear in the hall from her vantage point in the bay window, apparently taken quite by surprise at his arrival.

'Oh, good heavens, Mr Cooper, is that really the time? I didn't expect to see you just yet!'

She'd have removed the housecoat she normally wore during the day and there'd be a touch of fresh lipstick and a hint of rouge on her face.

'I believe it's around the time I normally get home, Mrs Carpenter.'

'I suppose it must be, Mr Cooper, but you took me quite by surprise.'

And if he wasn't being careful or if his guard was slightly down, Mrs Carpenter would mention a tap in the kitchen which was stiff, or bag of coal which needed to be moved or perhaps he'd care to come into her office, as she called it, for just one minute because she had to tell him what her friend had told her that very morning or…

That particular afternoon he was tired and determined to go upstairs to get changed and rest before supper. But Mrs Carpenter had already positioned herself at the foot of the stairs, as she was prone to do when she was particularly keen to have his attention.

'If you care to come into my office, Mr Cooper, then I think I may have something most interesting for you!'

He reluctantly followed her into her office, which was in fact a room between the dining room and the front room and the presence of a desk in it made it her office. The rest of the room was taken up with an armchair and walls full of shelves displaying pottery animals.

As he entered the room his landlady picked up a silver-coloured plate from her desk and held it in front of him. Nestling among the crumbs was a letter, addressed to him in a long white envelope. She'd taken to using the plate to present post that looked important to her tenants. Cooper assumed she'd seen it in a film. She held the plate closer to him, encouraging him to take it.

'Thank you very much, Mrs Carpenter, but you really needn't have gone to all this trouble. You could have left it on the hall table with the other post.'

'Well, I normally would, Mr Cooper, but have you seen the letter? It looks very important: most distinguished, I would say!'

He looked at the envelope and could see what she meant. The envelope appeared to be made of something far better quality than mere paper. It seemed to be partially made of cloth. He noticed the address was written in beautiful copperplate writing and there was a Birmingham postmark and he was as intrigued as Mrs Carpenter. She'd raised her head and was looking at him expectantly, clearly hoping he'd open it then and there.

'It does look most important, would you not agree, Mr Cooper?'

He agreed and thanked her very much for keeping it so safe and if she didn't mind, he'd head upstairs and he'd see her later at supper.

Mrs Carpenter's disappointment was palpable: he could sense it behind him as he climbed the stairs to his room on the first floor, aware she was standing at the foot of the stairs.

His room was small, but it served his purposes and it did have the merit of being at the back of the house, overlooking the garden.

He removed his shoes and jacket and loosened his tie and lay down on the bed, turning on the lamp on the bedside table to read the letter more easily. Inside was a single sheet of paper.

Hardy, Davis, Carter & Hardy
Imperial Chambers
Stephenson Street
Birmingham

Dear Mr Cooper

This letter is intended to reach you in the week of your twenty-fifth birthday, which I understand to be this coming Friday, 16 October. May I wish you many happy returns on this auspicious occasion.

The purpose of this letter is to ask you to attend a meeting with myself at my office at a date not before but as soon as possible after your birthday. May I ask you to contact my secretary, Miss Penelope Frost, to arrange a convenient time. Our offices are located less than five minutes' walk from New Street Station via the Stephenson Street exit.

I would also ask you bring with you your birth certificate and another form of identification, along with details of your bank account.

I can assure you that the matter to be discussed is very much in your interests and will be of significant benefit to you.

I would suggest that you keep the circumstances of our forthcoming meeting confidential, at least until it has taken place.

I very much look forward to meeting you.

Yours faithfully

Sydney Carter

Cooper lay back on the bed, quite awake now. He knew no one in Birmingham, he'd never been to the city and none of the names on the letter-head – Hardy, Davis, Carter or Hardy – meant a thing to him.

Then, in the abstract way that his mind wandered, he found himself thinking whether the two Hardys were related and if so how and then he re-read the letter and there was no denying that the penultimate sentence '…in your interests … of significant benefit to you…' meant that it was good news. Or at the very least, not bad news.

The suggestion he keep the meeting confidential was fine by him: it wasn't in his nature to discuss matters like this with anyone. There was no one he was close enough to with whom to discuss it. He could of course ask his mother whether she had any idea as to why a Birmingham solicitor may wish to see him – but it was some months since he'd last spoken to her and the way that conversation had gone on Boxing Day it would be many more months before he intended to do so again.

–

Charles Cooper was employed as reporter at *Designs and Drawings*, a magazine aimed at draughtsmen and designers and with a surprisingly high circulation. It was based near Fenchurch Street station and the editor was also the publisher, a perpetually tired-looking man called Charles Arthurs, always referred to as Mr Arthurs.

It was the morning after Cooper had received the letter from Hardy, Davis, Carter and Hardy and he was now standing in front of Mr Arthurs in his office, which was really a cubicle in the main office, windows on all sides enabling him to keep an eye on everyone.

'Which day next week, did you say, Cooper?' He was leafing through his diary, an enormous ledger-like book which took up much of his desk.

'Any day, Mr Arthurs, though the earlier the better: we don't go to press until the following week and—'

'I do know when we go to press, Cooper. Is it a medical matter, may I ask?'

Cooper said no, it wasn't a medical matter – it was something… something which had cropped up and which he'd like to deal with and—

'If it's an interview for another job, Cooper, I'd be most disappointed: only last month I increased your pay to one pound and fourteen shillings a week.'

Cooper assured Mr Arthurs it was not to do with another job: the pay rise had been most appreciated. It was more of a personal matter. They agreed he take the following Tuesday as annual leave.

–

He left the house on Castle Avenue at the normal time that Tuesday morning and the journey from Euston was very pleasant, though he was quite nervous and found it hard to concentrate on the copy of the *Manchester Guardian* he'd bought at the station.

Within fifteen minutes of his train arriving at New Street, Charles Cooper was facing Sydney Carter, who reminded him of Mr Arthurs with his unhealthy pallor and tired manner. Mr Carter had greeted him formally, asked him to sit down and then asked to see the paperwork Charles Cooper had brought with him, assuring him checking his identity was a necessary formality.

'So, it is indeed you: Charles Christopher Cooper!'

He had a broad smile on his face, revealing an array of gold teeth. Charles Cooper said yes it was him, and was going to say something about it being a long time since anyone used the 'Christopher' but by now Sydney Carter had stopped smiling and had adopted a more business-like manner.

'I hope you don't mind if I seek clarification on something before we proceed to the main purpose of this meeting?'

Cooper nodded.

'Your name is Charles Christopher Cooper, yet we understand your name was changed in 1925, I think it was to Christopher Charles Shaw. Is that correct?'

'It is, sir, yes: Shaw is the surname of my stepfather and when I was fourteen my mother decided I should adopt his surname. But I've never really used it, not least because I felt it would be disloyal to my late father. So, I suppose I have two names!'

'I see, one suspected as much. So, Charles Christopher Cooper it is then: I hope you will indulge me as I relate the circumstances that have brought us to this meeting?'

Cooper nodded. He wondered whether he should ask if he could take notes and thought of mentioning his short-hand, but the solicitor had now adopted a magisterial pose and turned on the angle-poise lamp as he opened a file on his desk.

'You were born Charles Christopher Cooper, in Dorset, on the sixteenth of October, 1911.'

He paused and Cooper said 'yes' and Mr Carter said to please let him continue and only interrupt if he said something factually incorrect, which he very much doubted would be the case.

'Your father was Christopher Alfred Cooper, your mother Marjorie Edna Cooper, née Travis. You were an only child. Your father was a schoolteacher in Bridport in Dorset. Sadly, your father was killed on active service in April 1917: the Battle of Arras, I presume?'

Cooper nodded.

'You would have been what – five, when your father died, eh?'

Cooper nodded again and steeled himself as a familiar wave of emotion launched at him. It happened whenever mention of his father's death cropped up unexpectedly. It made him think how different his life would have been had his father lived. He had no doubt how much happier and settled he'd have been and certainly less lonely.

'Your mother remarried in 1920, I believe, a Thomas John Shaw, a man considerably older than her.'

'And wealthier, sir, which I imagine is why she married him. He's no longer wealthy and he's quite unwell, two things my mother clearly resents.'

'And you moved to London upon that marriage. Tell me, Mr Cooper, do you get on with your mother and step-father?'

'I would say no, sir, I'm afraid. My relationship with my step-father has always been a distant one. He never had children and never adapted to having one around, even one as quiet as me. He prefers dogs. My mother and I... I think it is best to say that we do not see eye to eye on a range of matters. She certainly disapproves of me being a reporter. She says it's trade: she'd have liked me to work in the City, where my step-father has connections. She's never been terribly warm towards me. My memories of my father are remote, of course, but I've always remembered him as a terribly jolly character. We were always having fun.'

Sydney Carter raised a hand: he wished to continue.

'Your father had a paternal aunt, Mathilda Dorothy Cooper. Does that name mean anything to you?'

'Only very vaguely.'

'Has your mother ever mentioned this aunt to you?'

'Possibly in passing, sir, but as far as I know, my mother had little if anything to do with my father's family after he was killed.'

'Mathilda Dorothy Cooper never married and, of course, had no children. She lived in Birmingham, hence our involvement in this case – she was our client. She died in 1922, five years after your father. However, in 1915 Mathilda Dorothy Cooper had made a will leaving a substantial proportion of her estate to her nephew, your father. There was provision in the will that the money was left to your father *per stirpes*, which is one of those Latin phrases so favoured by my profession.

'In essence, Mr Cooper, this means that in the event of your father predeceasing Mathilda Dorothy Cooper, the money intended for your father would pass through the branch of his direct descendants. That is to say, you became the beneficiary.'

Sydney Carter knew to pause for a while to allow Cooper to absorb what he was being told.

Cooper wondered whether to ask how much he was likely to inherit but Mr Carter continued.

'But as is so often the case, Mr Cooper, matters are more complicated than that. In the case of your great aunt's will, there was the normal legal requirement that she should be of sound mind when making it. When she died, your mother contacted us and said that by 1920, which was the last time she'd seen Mathilda Dorothy Cooper, she was not of sound mind and according to her doctor, that was indeed the case. You'll note that your mother had kept in contact with your aunt: I suspect she was aware of her wealth and of the will. However, we were able to show that when the will was signed in 1915, Mathilda Dorothy Cooper was of sound mind.

'Your mother was having none of this and she most ill-advisedly brought a legal action against the estate of Mathilda Dorothy Cooper: she claimed that as she was not of sound mind the money bequeathed to your father should go to her, as his heir, rather than to you, as his direct descendant. We defended the action and I'm pleased to say that we won: your mother was not only extremely embittered at the outcome, but also considerably out of pocket, given the costs she had to pay for both parties. It was an expensive action: a two-day court hearing and the costs may well account for your step-father's diminishing wealth.

'There was one point though on which the judge found partially in her favour: the provision of the will relating to you

27

stated you would receive the inheritance on your twenty-first birthday. Your mother asked that this be altered to your thirtieth birthday. She told the court that she doubted you could be trusted with the money, even at the age of twenty-one. The judge held you would receive the inheritance on or after your twenty-fifth birthday.'

Sydney Carter leant back in his chair, studying the young man opposite him. 'You knew nothing of this, Mr Cooper?'

Cooper shook his head. 'This would have been, when?'

'The court case was in 1923. You'd have been around twelve years of age then.'

'Thirteen years ago, then: I know that the following year we moved from the house in Regent's Park to Cricklewood – from a largish house in a very smart area to a smaller one in an area my mother described as suburban. She made it clear she resented the move, but I was never sure why it occurred. Now it all makes sense. Rather serves her right!'

Sydney Carter smiled broadly, the gold teeth on display once more. 'Which brings us to why we are here today. You're probably slightly curious as to how much you are to inherit?'

Cooper said he was, if that didn't sound too—

'Too mercenary? Not at all: my finance clerk provided me with a detailed account this morning, as I'd requested ahead of our meeting, and here's a copy for you. The sum includes interest accrued over the years and is minus various permitted costs, all of which are itemised in the document I shall give you. The sum you inherit today is £357, Charles Christopher Cooper.'

As the solicitor had been talking, Cooper had thought the inheritance would be around £50, maybe somewhere between there and £100, but £357 was beyond his wildest dreams. Now he found himself unable to speak.

'That has clearly come as a surprise to you, no doubt, Mr Cooper?'

'You can say that again, sir: my salary as a reporter is some £86 per annum. £350 is what… more than four times my salary! I… it's more of a shock than a surprise.'

'You need time to think about it, Mr Cooper. My advice would be not to make any rash decisions: you don't look like the kind of chap who would, though. We will arrange for the money to be transferred to your bank account by the close of business tomorrow. I hope that is agreeable.'

Cooper said it was and he had no idea... well, he was shocked, and of course he wouldn't do anything rash and...

They chatted politely for a while and the solicitor said he hoped Mr Cooper didn't think it presumptuous of him, but he'd booked a table in the Grill at the Grand Hotel, which was near the station, and he'd be able to catch his train home after that.

–

Sydney Carter waited until they'd finished their main course before he spoke again of the inheritance.

'In effect, you've been a client of mine since 1922, though no more than a name on documents. Nevertheless, I was intrigued by you: your great aunt had been very fond of your father and I felt a quasi-parental sense of obligation towards you as well as a legal one, so much so that I wrote to your mother once a year around your birthday to enquire as to your welfare: on your eighteenth birthday I was able to allot some of your inheritance towards your university education.'

'My mother told me it was my step-father's generosity.'

'Well, there we are – now you know. I thought about you a lot over the years and your twenty-fifth birthday was something I very much looked forward to. I cannot tell you what a pleasure it has been to meet you today and give you such splendid news. I'm delighted you've turned out to be such a pleasant young gentleman.'

Cooper thanked him again.

'I hope you don't mind if I talk personally for a moment. I feel able to do so because as far back as 1922 I sensed your family life was a difficult one. After your mother lost the court case, I suspected she may take out her resentment on you. My advice

29

is this: you've inherited an awful lot of money, more than four times your salary, as you say, and it's free of tax. You are now a wealthy young man. You may be surprised to hear a solicitor in his late fifties say this, but despite warning you not to be rash, you should also try and enjoy the money. You're still young: if you have ambitions and dreams, maybe use some of the money to follow them for a while. Follow your conscience. Travel, eat good food, get drunk once in a while, maybe sow your wild oats for a year or two and when you do decide to settle down, do so with someone you love rather than someone it is expected of you to marry.'

Cooper looked in surprise at Sydney Carter. The older man looked emotional.

'I don't have terribly long left, Mr Cooper. At the end of last year, I was given a year at the most to live and my doctor assures me I'm on course for that, unfortunately. I shall stop work very soon. As soon as I was diagnosed, I hoped I'd still be around to have this happy meeting: it's been something of a spur for me to carry on.'

'I'm terribly sorry, I...'

'Please, Mr Cooper, you don't need to be. Hence my advice to you to enjoy your inheritance: use it to have a happy life. When I was much younger, I was told that the things one regrets in life as one gets older are the things you didn't do, rather than the things you did do, and I can promise you, with the benefit of hindsight and given my unfortunate predicament, that is very true. There are so many things I didn't do which I now regret. Promise me you won't end up in that position, eh? Just think of me once in a while and raise a glass: a large whisky – neat – was always my preference. The last few weeks I've just been tying up a few loose ends. You, Charles Christopher Cooper, were my final one.'

–

Cooper waited until the last Sunday in October before going to visit his mother. He turned up unannounced, because he found she was slightly less difficult to deal with if she was unprepared for him. And a Sunday afternoon was the ideal time because the nurse who looked after his step-father would have returned after her day off on the Saturday. His mother would have no choice but to give her son her full attention, not something she was well practised in.

Marjorie Cooper was suitably flustered when he arrived at their apartment in Belsize Park. They'd moved there three years previously, soon after his stepfather's second or third stroke, Cooper had lost count. It was, as his mother saw it, a more desirable area but the apartment was small and the atmosphere stifling.

It was tense as she led him through into the small sitting room, telling the nurse to keep an eye on Mr Shaw and if she could be so good as to bring a tray of tea.

Cooper noticed his mother glance at the clock on the mantel-piece, most probably calculating whether it was too early to allow herself a sherry. She had a rule that no alcohol was to be consumed before four o' clock on a Sunday afternoon, as if the apartment was licensed by the local authority.

'Were you really unable to call ahead of your visit, Charles? You know I like to know in advance when I have visitors.'

'I'm hardly just a visitor. I'm your son.'

'You know full well what I mean, Charles, it's not as if you reside here. I've not seen you since last Christmas, and apart from the odd card it's as if you've disappeared from the face of the earth!'

'It was Boxing Day, not Christmas.'

'You know full well what I mean.'

Cooper asked how his step-father was.

'You'll go and say hello before you leave: he sits in his room and listens to the transistor all day, though how much he takes in I'm not sure, and the nurse has to do everything for him apart from on Saturdays when that duty falls to me. If we were able to afford it, I'd hire someone to help me then, too.'

Cooper didn't reply but instead sat there quietly, carefully watching his mother, knowing she'd be disconcerted by the silence.

'You realise it was my birthday on the sixteenth?'

'I do: I was not sure whether given your silence you'd want to hear from me?'

'It was my twenty-fifth birthday, Mother.'

'Well, I never, makes one feel quite old! Happy birthday, Charles.'

He could sense she was stressed because her affected accent slipped and her more natural Dorset accent peeped through. She'd omitted the 'h' in happy.

'And you are aware of the significance of my twenty-fifth birthday?'

She raised her eyebrows, as if in surprise, but said nothing.

And then he recounted the circumstances of his visit to the offices of Hardy, Davis, Carter and Hardy in Birmingham and his meeting with Sydney Carter with whom he understood she was acquainted and how he'd been informed of her involvement in the inheritance – her attempts to have the money paid to her, and the subsequent court case, which meant it was only now he'd inherited what was, thankfully, a very large sum of money.

'May I ask how much, Charles?'

'You mean you don't know?'

She smiled sweetly. He noticed her fingers were laced so tightly together that her knuckles were almost as white as her face.

'It's enough for me to be very comfortable, Mother. To be truly independent. To follow my dreams.'

'It was all for the best, Charles, I want you to understand that.'

He remained staring at her, not replying. 'It was all for the best', in its various conjugations and tenses was her default phrase to cover a range of circumstances, invariably invoked in defence of some action of hers to which her son took exception.

'And may I ask, Charles, whether you have given any consideration perhaps to showing some small act of generosity to your mother as a result of your unexpected inheritance?'

He leant back and smiled, and she smiled too, possibly misinterpreting this as a gesture of consent.

'I'm afraid not, Mother: Mr Carter told me to travel, eat good food, get drunk and sow my wild oats and who am I to argue with a solicitor?'

His mother now looked shocked and furious.

'It's for the best, Mother.'

Chapter 3

Cambridge, England
January 1937

The heavy oak door swung open, revealing the equally heavy figure of the Provost, who stood framed in the doorway, breathing heavily as if the effort of opening it had been a bit too much. He glared at the younger man standing nervously in the waiting area.

'Were you not told to knock, Branstone?'

'I was, sir, and I did, but I don't think you heard me.'

'You need to knock hard. It's not made of paper, you know, Branstone. Come in.'

Austin Branstone followed the head of King's College into his study, a magnificent room on Front Court overlooking an immaculate lawn, which was unseasonably verdant below a hint of frost. The Provost sat behind his desk and pointed to a chair in front of it, and once the younger man sat down, the Provost stared at him, trying to make him out. Branstone was somewhere in his thirties, but with the thinning hair and stooped bearing of someone a good deal older and the innocent appearance of one much younger.

'I trust you had an agreeable Christmas, Branstone?'

'Yes, indeed, sir. Thank you...' Austin Branstone hesitated because he wasn't sure if he was now expected to ask the Provost how his Christmas was. One didn't want to be too familiar with someone so senior, but did he want to appear rude?

'Worcester, isn't it?'

'I beg your pardon, sir?'

34

'Where your family are: Worcester, I believe.'

'Yes, sir, Worcestershire, actually.' He could have kicked himself, appearing so pedantic like that with the Provost. The Provost took a cigarette from a silver box and proffered the box to Austin.

There was a friendly enough discussion about Branstone's work and the Provost said he didn't pretend to understand this form of art – equestrian paintings were his preference – but it was clearly an important subject and it reflected very well on the College to have a Fellow evidently so eminent in their subject – and at such a young age.

'Thank you, sir.'

'And I understand, Branstone, you have had an approach?'

It took him a moment to work out quite what he was referring to. 'In respect of what, sir?'

'An approach from the Soviet Union, Branstone. Perhaps you'd care to tell us all about it?' As he said this, the Provost glanced to his right, beyond Branstone, and when Branstone turned round he spotted a dark-suited figure sitting very still in the shadows at the back of the study. It was the first inkling he'd had that someone else was in the room.

'As you may be aware, sir, last autumn I was fortunate enough to be able to travel to Rome, where I took part in a symposium at Sapienza University on my speciality and was then able to spend a week in the Vatican studying their excellent collection of icons. It really was the most marvellous opportunity and I'm terribly grateful that the—'

'You may wish to get to the point, Branstone.'

'A French gentleman approached me in the Vatican and said he'd heard me speak at the symposium and indeed had read some of my papers and said he had excellent contacts in the Soviet Union. The collection of icons in the Kremlin in Moscow is beyond comparison with any collection elsewhere, including the Vatican. It is unique and remarkable, but since the Russian revolution very few people from outside the country have been

35

granted access to see these icons. It is something that any scholar in this subject would… well, give their right arm to see, sir. One could spend an entire academic career studying icons and writing about them without having an opportunity to see the Kremlin ones in person.'

'And this French gentleman, Branstone… what did he actually say?'

'He asked if I would be interested in visiting the Soviet Union to study the icons in the Kremlin. He said the authorities there were keen to have parts of the collection authenticated and catalogued by an external expert and that I fitted this requirement admirably. They're looking for someone to spend three months in Moscow from April to June and if I was interested then a letter would be sent to me to invite me formally and lay out the terms of the visit.'

'And I understand that letter arrived in… when – mid December?'

'Indeed, sir: it was sent from the Soviet Embassy in London, from the Cultural Affairs attaché who said they would pay for my travel to and from Moscow, my hotel and other costs, and in addition I'd receive a stipend of one hundred pounds.'

'I thought the communists don't believe in money?'

'Naturally I informed Professor Hatherley as soon as I received the letter and he said I should reply and say I was interested and to see what happened, and when I returned to Cambridge last week there was a letter waiting from Mr Fedorov saying they were keen to fix the dates and make the travel arrangements and that naturally there'd be no problem with my visa and please could I let them have my bank details so they could pay the first part of the stipend. I immediately showed the letter to Professor Hatherley, of course, and he said he'd have a word with you.'

The Provost's study was silent: few students were back at College and so there was none of the usual bustle of College life and Austin Branstone watched as the Provost glanced once more beyond him and nodded and the figure who'd been sitting in the shadows came forward and sat in a chair to the side of the Provost's desk.

He was a tall man, perhaps in his fifties, and he was wearing a bowtie, which he fiddled with as he looked carefully at Branstone, as if he too was trying to make up his mind about him. He seemed to be looking at Branstone's prominent ears. People were always doing that.

'Dr Paxton is at Gonville and Caius.' That was all the Provost said by way of introduction and Austin Branstone wasn't sure if he was to say anything in response: Gonville and Caius was the next-door college, and he thought of saying something about meeting neighbours but fortunately he didn't get the chance because the man introduced as Dr Paxton spoke.

'I understand you speak Russian, Branstone?' Branstone was relieved to hear a hint of an accent: one hard to place, but the man sounded grammar school rather than public school and that always helped him feel less intimidated.

'Yes, sir: when I started to specialise in the study of icons, I realised that a proficiency in Russian was desirable. I rather struggled with Latin and French at school, but I appear to have taken to Russian like a duck to water – an *utka*.'

'I beg your pardon?'

'An *utka* is a duck in Russian.'

'I see. I don't know if you are aware, Mr Branstone, but it is extremely rare for an invitation like this to be made.'

Branstone said it had struck him as odd, but before he could continue Dr Paxton raised his hand and Branstone noticed his fingers were improbably long.

'So rare, indeed, that the Provost discussed the matter with me. I would like to know, Branstone, whether you'd be prepared, prior to your visit to Moscow, to meet with some people I know in London and co-operate with them?'

'If it helps, Branstone,' said the Provost, 'then let me say this. If you are to take up this invitation then it requires my approval and my approval is conditional on you complying fully with Dr

Paxton's request. Can I add that if you do so then the College would view this most favourably. Should the visit be regarded as satisfactory then we would be prepared to grant you a paid sabbatical for you to complete your PhD.'

Austin Branstone watched both men carefully. Despite what some people thought, he was no fool. He was not naïve. The chance to study the Kremlin icons was too good to miss. He'd do anything to have the opportunity.

'That seems fair enough, sir: after all, what harm can come from meeting some people in London, eh?'

Chapter 4

France
February–April 1937

Charles Cooper handed in his notice at *Designs and Drawings* at the end of October and promised to work until the new year, so as to give them ample opportunity to replace him. He explained to Mr Arthurs that he'd unexpectedly come into funds and planned to travel.

Now it was the first week of February. Cooper had left England on a surprisingly warm Thursday, taking the night ferry boat train from Victoria station, leaving at nine o'clock that night and crossing the channel on the SS *Twickenham Ferry*. By nine o'clock on the Friday morning the train arrived in Gare du Nord in Paris.

It was his first time in Paris and he was overwhelmed by the city. It somehow felt as if he'd travelled halfway round the world rather than just some three hundred miles.

He booked a room for five nights at the Avenida Hotel on Rue du Colisée – he'd been presented with an extensive choice by the travel agent and this one had the merit of being close to the Arc de Triomphe and he was attracted by the rate of twenty-five francs for the five nights, including what they described as a plain breakfast. The travel agent assured him it was a bargain.

He enjoyed Paris, happily adapting to the role of the enthusiastic tourist, eating to his heart's content and pleasantly surprised at how good his French was. Each evening he carefully made a note of how much he'd spent. He'd allocated £50 of the £357 he'd inherited for this trip. His plan was to travel through Europe for as long as the budget allowed, which he hoped would take him through to the end of June, possibly early July.

Cooper's plan was to use the trip to begin writing his novel, which was very much in its early stages. So early, in fact, that he had no plot. Or characters. But he did recall reading an interview somewhere with an author who stressed the importance of allowing a story to evolve naturally and to take advantage of one's experiences. On his third day in Paris, he began to think about a story involving a young man – not exactly him, of course, but a similar age, certainly, possibly taller – who travels through Europe in pursuit of a mysterious woman who steals valuable diamonds in Paris.

–

He spent a week in Paris and then headed south, to the French Riviera, a far more natural habitat for the elegant and refined Louise, which was the name he'd christened her with. He had an idea about her meeting with a wealthy Italian at a rendezvous in Marseilles and she would then move east to Cannes and Nice to acquire more diamonds.

He spent the best part of a month in the south of France. He stayed in Marseilles for a few days and then headed into the Riviera, but was becoming increasingly conscious of the strains on his budget. Cannes was so eye-wateringly expensive that he found himself wondering about stealing a diamond himself.

It would be material for the book, at the very least.

Aware of the perils of life imitating art, he looked out for somewhere cheaper to stay and found a small, quiet port called Antibes just outside Cannes and on the tramline to Nice. The Hôtel des Aigles-d'Or on Rue Thuret became his base. The tram meant it was a good place for travelling from, but even better was the location of the hotel. From his room he had views of the bay, the light blue of the never-ending Mediterranean stretched out before him. He had a small desk by the window and he'd sit with a coffee and baguette from the cafe next to the hotel and he'd write.

They were just draft chapters at this stage, more backstory than anything else, but it was warm for most of the day and the breeze that blew in from the sea was gentle and seemed to help him to write.

He soon realised he couldn't stay in Antibes forever. For this novel to work, it needed to move on from his idyllic surroundings, to avoid being stuck in one place. And he asked himself what would Louise, his elegant jewel thief, do after her daring robberies in Cannes and Nice?

She was, he concluded, hardly likely to hang around the French Riviera, especially with the Englishman hot on her high heels. Even the French gendarmerie would be unlikely to miss a sitting target.

He spread his map of Europe out on the desk by the window, studying it and then the sea in front of him in case it provided inspiration.

Louise would head for Switzerland, he decided. The previous week he'd begun to think of Louise as being Swiss, with the ability to appear French, German and Italian, apparently effortlessly. And the enigmatic Louise would now head home. Surely Swiss jewellers would be as discreet as the country's bankers, asking few annoying questions about ownership and provenance as she negotiated a good price for her diamonds.

He'd head for Geneva, he decided, folding his map and looking out over the Mediterranean, which for the first time since he arrived in Antibes had taken on a green, disturbed appearance and he could see low clouds on the horizon rolling in towards the coast and in the way that the sea does, it was as if he was being sent a warning.

–

After spending a month in the warm Mediterranean air of the south of France, Switzerland was a shock to the system.

Geneva had a sharp Alpine bite to it, a cold wind sweeping into the city from the mountains and across the lake, managing to find him wherever he was, not least in the over-priced but very ordinary *pension* he was staying in in the old town. And there was a formality to the city that put him on edge. Every time he walked past a jeweller, let alone went into one, he felt he was a suspect, and he didn't help matters when he found a jeweller in an alley off Rue Diday near the theatre. He was greeted in a friendly manner by the genial owner, who wanted to know if he could help, and for the first time in Geneva, Cooper relaxed.

'Are you perhaps interested in purchasing diamonds as well as selling them?' He imagined Louise asking the question, pulling her long fur coat around her, smiling sweetly and possibly brushing her hand through her hair, an expensive scent surrounding her.

'I beg your pardon?' Now, the owner was no longer so friendly. He had that familiar, suspicious air about him.

'I was just asking out of curiosity, you see. I was wondering if you buy diamonds as well as sell them. In London, that is the case and I understand in Paris, too.'

The man paused, looking at Cooper, and then at his telephone as if he was considering summoning help. When he replied he spoke in an even slower and more deliberate manner than was usual in Geneva. 'Well, this isn't London. Or Paris. If you have diamonds to sell you will need proper paperwork to show you are the legal owner. You should visit a diamond bourse, not a man trying to make an honest living! You may wish to leave now.'

He left Geneva the next day, taking the train to Bern for no other reason than he felt he ought to visit it and then the next day travelled on to Zürich, where Louise would have another contact.

But Cooper felt strangely bereft after a few days in Zürich, which was even more formal and unfriendly than Geneva. He couldn't decide where the plot would go after that. What would Christopher the Englishman do now? Where would Louise go? He reckoned he had enough of a plot to cover a half a dozen disparate chapters at the most.

He decided he needed to clear his mind and headed south to Interlaken, where he'd spend a few days on long walks by the lakes and around the town and gather his thoughts. He was halfway through the five months he'd allowed for his European tour but had spent close to forty of the fifty pounds he'd budgeted. At this rate, he'd return to London far earlier than he'd planned, with his tail between his legs, a lot less money in his bank account and not much of a book.

To cheer himself up he stayed at the Beau Rivage on Höheweg, close to the River Aare. He justified the expense on the grounds that this was very much the kind of place where Louise would stay, perhaps to gather her thoughts after the unpleasant encounter with her contact on the Münsterbrücke.

And it was here that he did indeed find Louise.

—

It was early evening in the bar at the Beau Rivage and Cooper had found a comfortable armchair on a raised area which gave him good views over the room, and that afternoon he'd bought a new notebook with a soft, black leather cover in the hope that maybe this would help him construct a more interesting plot.

And so far, it was working. He made notes on fellow occupants of the bar.

Tall man, possibly Italian, heavy moustache, moves hands when talking, danger of spilling drink...

Young woman who could be Scandinavian, possibly German, blonde and very pretty... appears to be on own. Looks as if waiting for someone...

Two older ladies, perhaps seventies... both wearing fur shawls and plenty of jewellery...

Couple who appear to be arguing... in German... man has his arms crossed: woman red in the face.

Beautiful woman in her late forties, possibly... on her own. Drinking red wine and talking to barman...

It was as if they were all inadvertently auditioning for a part in the novel. He found himself imagining their stories, the couple arguing maybe because the wife has discovered her husband's infidelity, the two older ladies – sisters, maybe widowed, the beautiful woman at the bar unquestionably French…

She wasn't French. She was American and her name was Grace and he knew this because he watched as she left the bar and walked in his direction and asked if the seat next to his was free and he said he didn't know and then yes, of course, and she said he wasn't to act so flustered, she only wanted to sit down as she'd been walking all day and he said he had too and, yes, please do sit down.

Grace was impressed when he told her he was a writer and she told him that she was from Chicago in the United States and had accompanied her husband to Zürich and as everything to do with banking was boring she'd escaped and here she was!

Cooper said he'd been in Zürich and he'd found the city depressing and Grace said she did so agree, that was the right word, no wonder you're a writer!

She then asked Cooper if he minded her calling him Charles or was he one of those Englishmen who preferred to be addressed more formally and Cooper said no, Charles is fine, and Grace announced she now had an appetite and did Charles know the Adlerhalle on Harderstrasse, which she had heard was quite the best restaurant in Interlaken?

She asked few questions during dinner, other than his age, and she'd smiled when he told her he was twenty-six. She talked about her wealthy parents, her even wealthier husband, her children who were a similar age to him, would he believe, and he said he didn't, and she spoke of her main interest in life apart from supporting charities being travel, which was one of the very few rewards of being married to a man twelve years older and with little interest in her once she passed the age of fifty.

And at that point Grace stopped and placed her cutlery neatly alongside her plate and dabbed her lips with the napkin and looked directly at him and placed her hand on top of his and stroked it and he was so shocked he couldn't think of anything to say other than 'thank you', which came out rather high-pitched, and she laced her fingers in between his and leant close to him and spoke quietly.

'When we return to the hotel Charles, I am in room 720 on the top floor. If you wish, join me a quarter of an hour after we arrive back.'

It sounded more of an instruction than a request and when they returned to the hotel Cooper went to his room and nervously paced it, washing his face in cold water and changing his shirt and wondering if there was some perfectly innocent explanation for her inviting him to her room. He could stay in his room and have breakfast in it in the morning and check out early because he was so inexperienced with women that she would surely tell straight away and...

–

Afterwards she told him she'd been very pleasantly surprised that he'd turned up because her previous experience of Englishmen was that they seemed to have a problem behaving naturally with women and she'd very much hoped he wouldn't be like that because he was such an attractive young man.

'Thank you very much, Grace.'

'You really don't need to keep thanking me, Charles. I ought to be thanking you. You are a very satisfying lover.'

'Thank you, Grace, I hope it was...'

'It wasn't your first time was it, Charles?'

Cooper said, good heavens no, of course not, but he realised he was blushing and speaking too fast and Grace laughed and pulled away the sheet and said actually she rather hoped it was his first time because that added to the thrill and by the look of things, maybe he was now ready for his second time?

They remained awake for hours, naked in the bed, smoking and mostly Grace talking. Her husband didn't care, she said, and nor did she care that he didn't care because that meant that as long as she was discreet then it enabled her to have her own adventures,

45

though the one rule was that it never happened in Chicago, which was one of the reasons she liked to travel.

'Tell me what you're writing about?'

Cooper did his best to describe the book, feeling as he did so that it sounded not terribly gripping and Grace said as much herself.

'You're a bright young man, Charles. You're travelling around Europe yet you're not writing about Europe, are you, other than using some places as the setting for boringly similar diamond heists. We were in Europe twice last year and now this visit. We travel all over the place, we were in Berlin last week and then throughout Germany and France too. Something is happening in Europe, Charles. The Nazis in Germany… it's an unnerving experience to be there. And then the communists, they're all over Europe – it's all that the bankers talk about, I can tell you. Yet you're not writing about that, are you? You're writing another crime novel without an ending. You should become part of the story you're writing about.'

He left soon after that. It was nearly two o'clock and she said as tempting as it was for him to stay, he'd better leave, and Cooper thanked her again and she said there he was, ever the polite Englishman, and very well, he could stay for another half hour and by the time he did leave, closer to three o'clock, they'd not really spoken again.

He didn't sleep that night. He had a bath and then lay on the bed and thought about the extraordinary events of that evening and there was no question he was very pleased with himself. He'd always been quite shy with women and had worried about what would happen if the opportunity ever arose to be intimate and now it transpired there was no reason to have been worried.

And then there was what she said about Europe. Here he was in the heart of it, with the Continent apparently in turmoil, and he was writing about a woman stealing diamonds.

He would go to Germany and find out what was going on there. What was it Grace had said? *You should become part of the story you're writing about.*

It came as no surprise to find that Grace had checked out of the Beau Rivage that morning and his reaction was one of disappointment and some relief. As much as he'd enjoyed being with her, an affair with a married woman felt dangerous.

He decided to move on and make plans for travelling to Germany. He found a pleasant coffee shop in the grounds of the Kursaal and spent much of that day sitting on the terrace, watching the world go by and making detailed notes. His mind wandered easily, thinking about the night before and whether there was any way of working his encounter with Grace into his novel, and then he started sketching – not very well – the magnificent Jungfrau looming out of a remarkably clear sky to the south. He looked up and noticed an elderly couple had appeared at the table next to his who seemed altogether different from the other visitors to the town. It was hard to put his finger on it, but they seemed quieter and more modest.

He ordered another coffee and noticed the couple smiling at him and he smiled at them and nodded by way of a greeting and they did likewise and asked him in German if he was a visitor and Cooper replied in German and said he was indeed, from England, as it happened, and they asked where in England and he said London and they nodded, indicating they'd heard of it.

'And are you here on holiday?' they asked.

He explained he was and wondered whether to mention he was writing a novel but then thought better of it as technically he wasn't actually writing it yet and he didn't want to get into all that so he asked the couple where they were from and the two looked at each other and smiled, though he couldn't work out why, and replied that they were from Berlin. In Germany.

And that was how the conversation began. Cooper said as it happened, he was hoping to visit Germany soon and certainly intended to visit Berlin and the man – who said to call him Ernst – said to be careful because Germany was going through very dangerous times. Cooper noticed the woman placed her hand on her husband's as if to warn him he'd perhaps gone too far. She introduced herself as Ida and asked Cooper what he was doing in Switzerland, other than drawing mountains!

Ida had switched to speaking English – quite fluently, though with a strong accent – and she said he should join them, and Cooper found himself chatting away. He explained how he was in between jobs in England and found himself with some time so was travelling through Europe and they asked him where he'd been and seemed surprised that he'd only been to France and Switzerland. Cooper said he'd come to Interlaken looking for peace and quiet though, if he was honest, Interlaken hadn't been as quiet as he hoped. It seemed a rather busy town.

'You should try Brienz,' said Ida. 'Have you been there?'

'I haven't, no.'

'It's at the other end of the Brienzersee and is far smaller than Interlaken, much more peaceful. You can travel there by steamer from Interlaken, it is a most pleasant trip. And stay at the Schütze or the Steinbock: they're smaller hotels, a more agreeable clientele.'

–

Cooper checked out of the Beau Rivage the following day. The German couple were right: Brienz was a much quieter and calmer place and it was a short walk from the station to the hotels they'd recommended. He found a room at the Schützen and immediately decided he'd made the right decision. He paid extra for a view of the lake and the room had a desk by the window. Here he would write and for the next few days, he was prolific.

Every night he ate in a small restaurant on the next block from the hotel, always the same meal: veal escalope with traditional Swiss rosti and a delicious green salad, quite unlike any he'd ever had in England. He indulged himself with two glasses of Italian red wine and a slice of torte for dessert. The proprietor and his wife, he decided, would feature somewhere in the book. He even took to making notes about them, the choreographed way they moved around each other in the tiny kitchen area, the manner in which she'd mop his brow, him slipping a note from the cash box when she wasn't watching.

Cooper preferred to sit at the rear of the restaurant and was usually alone there, but on his fifth night in Brienz, he looked up from his notebook as a couple were being shown to the table next to his. In the gloom it was hard to make them out: it was only when they sat down that he realised it was the German couple he'd met in Interlaken, Ernst and Ida.

They seemed to be as surprised as he was at finding themselves at adjoining tables, again. There was much shaking of hands and saying 'fancy that' and 'well I never' and the three of them agreed it was a small world and Cooper thanked them very much indeed for recommending Brienz because he'd made considerable effort with his book.

'Please do tell us about it,' asked Ernst, and Cooper, against his better judgement, found himself recounting the plot, such as it was, realising as he did so that it sounded rather thin.

Ernst and Ida seemed to think the same.

'If I may say, Charles, I think your story lacks drama, there's not enough danger or suspense in it: your kind of book requires a sense of jeopardy.' Ernst looked apologetic.

'It sounds like a travel guide,' said Ida. 'You are setting your story in Europe yet it is devoid of politics. That is an omission. Politics consumes Europe at present. If I may make what I very much hope will be a constructive criticism: your story is set in France and Switzerland so far. And you are writing it here in Switzerland. But France is… well, France – fine if you're writing a romance but not a good setting otherwise for a novel. And Switzerland – well what do we have here? You're surrounded by mountains and trees and people are very smug – and it's really not a place to inspire a novelist. A writer needs to be interested and angry, perhaps even afraid. You won't be that in Switzerland. You need to be surrounded by life. You mentioned you planned to visit Germany. I suggest you now do so. You'll find your novel there.'

They spoke until long past closing time: Cooper noticed Ernst slip some cash to the owner and it must have been a generous amount because he brought over a bottle of sweet German dessert wine and insisted there was no hurry.

Ernst and Ida were interested in him: they insisted he tell them all about himself and he assured them there was really very little of interest, but they insisted, so he told them a version of his life story.

There was an awkward moment when they asked him about his politics and he had to admit he wasn't very political and Ida said of course he was, everyone is political, even if they don't realise it and he did admit to feeling strongly about poverty and injustice and he didn't like extremism and they asked him who he voted for and he said he'd only voted once and that was in 1935 when he'd voted Labour because he was a big admirer of Mr Attlee.

It was midnight when they agreed it was time to leave. As they were settling the bill – Ernst insisted on paying, it was their pleasure, he said – he added they were leaving Switzerland in the morning. It was time to return to Berlin.

Ernst handed him a piece of paper with their address written on it. 'You are to promise to visit us. Berlin will capture your imagination in a way novelists can only dream of. You'll find the ending to your novel there, my friend.'

'Ah, but will it be a happy one?'

Ernst and Ida went quiet and looked at each other, as if they'd been asked a difficult question. 'Only history can decide that.'

Chapter 5

'You will be contacted by a person addressing you as Archie who gives you my regards and asks if you'd like to join them for coffee and Cognac: you are then to do what they say.'

But Archie hadn't expected to wait more than five years to be contacted: he sometimes wondered if they'd forgotten about him, though in his heart of hearts he knew they'd catch up with him sooner or later.

What he didn't expect was that it would be a woman doing the catching up. It was a damp March afternoon and he was hurrying to Waterloo after work because they were going away for the weekend and as he reached the south side of Westminster Bridge a woman in a smart raincoat and a beret with a feather in it bumped into him and when he apologised, insisting it was his fault, she said not to worry and her friend Emil sends his regards and would Archie like to join her for a coffee – and Cognac?

They never had the coffee, or the Cognac. Instead, they had a brief conversation in the shadow of County Hall: he was to go to Austria and she gave him a book of matches from a Viennese cafe. That was the number to call: ask for August, he'll arrange to get you to Moscow.

'They want you there before the end of May. You'll be in Moscow for a week.'

He booked a week and a half's leave and told his wife he needed a break and was going walking in the Austrian Alps and said of course she was welcome to join him, which he knew full well she'd decline, as she didn't even like walking down to the village shop.

In Vienna, August gave him an Austrian passport in the name of Leopold Steiner and put him on a train to Budapest and, twenty-four hours later, he was sitting in a stuffy room in Moscow with Emil, who he'd last seen in France nearly six years before, and a man called Nikolai, who seemed to be in charge.

'You haven't aged at all, Archie.'

'Nor have you, Emil.'

'You still look like that man who was your king.'

'Edward – the one who abdicated?'

'Such a strange business: we never allowed our last tsar the chance to abdicate. But we need to get to work. Five days, Archie, that's all we need.'

'Is it really worth the risk? Surely all this could be done in Europe.'

'We are in Europe.'

'You know what I mean.'

'It is nearly six years since I recruited you,' said Emil. 'You were told then to start your new job and to concentrate on that for a few years so as to allow no reason for anyone to be suspicious of you. And that has been the case: we are delighted with how much you have progressed in your job. You are clearly very well thought of.'

'Which is why we now believe this is the time for you to move to the next phase of working for us,' said Nikolai. 'But there is so much to discuss before that can happen. You need extensive briefings on the kind of intelligence we need and how you should gather it and then how to pass it on to us. It is a complicated and perilous business and the briefings and training we need to give you cannot be done through dead letter boxes in London parks and a snatched hour here and there in a safe house. We need the time here in Moscow, believe me.'

By the end of the five days, he certainly did believe them. He'd been taken to a large and surprisingly well-furnished house surrounded by high walls in a place called Bordino, a suburb of Moscow, to the north-east of the city centre. A succession of men came, each to brief him extensively on what intelligence they were looking for him to supply to the Soviet Union.

The sessions were quite repetitive because he wasn't permitted to take notes and the strain of concentrating so hard was exacerbated by sitting in the dark at the rear of the room, with the men who'd come to brief him sitting in pools of bright light at the front. Such was the degree of suspicion that they couldn't risk any of them being able to identify him. Nikolai sat alongside him for most of the sessions and if he wanted to ask a question, he'd beckon him over and do it through him.

Then there were the sessions with the experts brought in to teach him what they called the tricks of the trade: how to secretly photograph documents as quickly and clearly as possible; how to leave – and receive – messages for and from his main contact in London; how to behave around a dead letter drop; how to ensure he was not being followed and how to behave if he ever came under suspicion.

And that session didn't mean being suspected of being a spy, because they said that, in all honesty, if it came to that then the game was pretty much up. For someone in his position to be suspected of being a Soviet spy meant they must have some evidence. What this session was so useful for was how to cope with being caught unawares – in other words, how to avoid ever being suspected of being a spy.

'In many situations, someone comes under suspicion not because they're actually caught spying but because they're doing something that is a bit out of the ordinary, which may cause eyebrows to be raised. Let me give you an example. Say you need to photograph a document in a colleague's office after everyone has left for the night and that person returns unexpectedly, possibly to collect something they'd left behind and finds you in there. How would you get out of that one?'

Archie said he wasn't sure, and it was certainly a tricky one and he couldn't think off the top of his head.

'You'd need to be prepared before you go in. How about you were to say your pencil was blunt and you needed a pencil sharpener because you'd lost yours?'

'That's a reasonable idea, I suppose.'

'So, what do you do?'

'I'm not following you.'

The man bathed in the pool of bright light sighed. 'You need to anticipate that possibility and be prepared accordingly. So, before you go into the office you make sure you have a very blunt pencil in your hand and also that you've concealed the pencil sharpener in your own office. Do you follow me? Or maybe have a note for them in your hand, which you can say you were about to leave on their desk: maybe inviting them for dinner at your club, that's what you do, don't you?'

'Do what?'

'Entertain colleagues at gentlemen's clubs?'

'Sometimes, yes.'

'And if you're in a part of London you don't normally frequent on your way to meet your contact and you bump into someone from work, what would you do then?'

'Turn the table on them? If I'm not expected to be in the area, then what are they doing there?'

'Possibly, but they'll have a good reason because they're not a Soviet agent, but you are. What excuse do you have up your sleeve?'

'Stamps, maybe? I could say I'm a philatelist and am meeting a fellow collector?'

The other man half nodded. 'Not a bad idea, but it's a bit convoluted. Show an interest in church architecture: find out the names of nearby churches and say you're on your way to visit one of them. We often talk of the importance of having a backstory but equally, we need a front story – anticipate a crisis and be prepared for it. You cannot eliminate risk, because espionage is, by its very nature, a most dangerous occupation. But you can minimise that danger.'

That evening a man who looked like a weightlifter turned up and joined Nikolai and him in a room overlooking the garden.

Nikolai explained that he worked for the OMS – the International Liaison Department of the Comintern, which was the organisation responsible for communist parties abroad. The OMS was its most secret section, responsible for subversion and espionage. Nikolai explained that the OMS was not to be confused with the NKVD.

'And Osip here, he works for the OMS in London. He will be your main contact.'

'And me?'

'You work for the OMS also.'

There was a long silence during which time Nikolai watched the Englishman carefully, but there was no sign of any reaction. He'd noticed this about him and was impressed with how calm and unflappable he was. Being enigmatic was a fine quality for a spy.

'You'll continue to be known as Archie.'

Archie had never liked Archie: it was the name of one of his grandfather's most vicious dogs, but he suspected that was going to be the least of his problems.

–

There'd been some propaganda too, as if he needed persuading he was on the right side. He managed to subdue any cynicism about these matters and was on his best behaviour as he was shown round what were clearly model collective farms and immaculate tractor factories full of happy workers.

On his fifth day in Moscow, he was taken to the Kremlin and to a special lunch in his honour in the Council of Ministers building overlooking Lenin's mausoleum. It was a strange affair, a minister of something or other present as a mark of how important he was, and he thought the whole business was most peculiar. Everyone else drank excessively but he remained sober. He'd learnt this on his first day in Moscow: the only way to survive was to feign some condition or the other which prevented him from drinking alcohol.

After the lunch, Nikolai and Osip both looked exhausted and said it would be another hour and a half before the car arrived to return them to Bordino. If he wished, he could wander around the Kremlin alone for an hour at the most, which he did.

And which was how he came to encounter the strange Englishman in the Secret Tower.

Chapter 6

Moscow
May 1937

'This Branstone chap—'

'The icon man who looks as if he should be in one himself?'

'Yes, thin, with ears that stick out, probably how Russian saints looked – when they had them, that is!'

'What about him, Milo?'

'The set-up seems rather... odd, as does he. There must be a bloody good reason why London is so keen for us to use him. You seem to be the one your Head Office trusts, George.'

They were in a secure room in the basement of the British Embassy on Sofiyskaya Naberezhnaya, just yards from the Moskva River in the heart of the Soviet capital and despite the time of year the remnants of the Russian winter still held some kind of grip on the city, reluctant to give way. George Banks was one of the British Intelligence officers based at the embassy; Milo Smart – the Honourable Milo Smart, indeed – was a senior attaché there and because the Foreign Office had an innate dislike and distrust of anything to do with espionage, part of his job was to have an oversight of his colleague's work. The awkwardness of the relationship was exacerbated by the fact that the two men – both in their late forties – had been at school together: Banks a year above Smart.

'It's a long story, Milo. Are you sure you have the time?'

Milo Smart glanced at his watch as if to demonstrate that he didn't really, but... 'Go on, George, but preferably not too long, please.'

George Banks settled back and adopted a demeanour indicating he wouldn't be rushed. 'The Service has a chap at Cambridge called David Paxton: he's a Fellow at Gonville and Caius, spots potential recruits to the Service – suggests names and does some checking on people who've been recommended to us. He has trusted contacts in most of the colleges and occasionally is approached if a matter that may be of interest or concern to us crops up. In January he was approached by the Provost of King's because one of his Fellows – Branstone – had been approached by the Soviets to see if he fancied spending three months in Moscow studying their icons, all expenses paid, plus a generous stipend. Branstone's regarded as an authority on Russian icons even though he's only in his early thirties. Apparently, the Soviets want him to help with authenticating and cataloguing their icons in the Kremlin.'

'You mean to say they don't have any experts of their own?'

'There's a very good reason why they want Branstone. There's a large collection of icons in the Tretyakov Gallery, not terribly far from where we are now. But there are a lot more icons in the Kremlin and since the revolution the Soviets have given the impression of caring little about them and, as a consequence, little is known about them. When Paxton contacted the Service, they were terribly interested and started to look into the matter. They asked our station in Paris to check it out and they discovered that the man who'd made the original approach to Branstone – a Marcel Lefèvre – is working with the Soviets running a black market in Russian icons.'

'Do you really mean to suggest that the Soviets – the bloody Communists – are selling icons on the black market?'

'Apparently so, Milo; our people in Paris got chapter and verse on it from their French colleagues. There are large Russian emigre communities in France and Switzerland with a number of very wealthy people keen to get their hands on medieval Russian icons. For the Soviets, it's a way of raising hard currency, which they desperately need, and they couldn't care less about the icons because they've abolished religion, haven't they? I'm told that a decent icon from the fourteenth or fifteenth century can fetch around fifty thousand French francs.'

'Which is how much?'

'A shade under five hundred pounds, Milo.'

Milo Smart let out a long whistle. 'Good heavens: it takes me six months to earn that!'

'And me slightly longer. Anyway, this is where our Mr Branstone comes in. The emigres don't entirely trust the Soviets and potential purchasers of icons need to be satisfied as to their provenance. What we understand happens is that when an icon is put up for sale by the Soviets, a buyer makes an offer by writing a letter claiming that very same icon was in their family for many years and they'd like it back and are prepared to pay a certain amount to cover expenses. This is all a bit of fiction, which enables the icons to be taken out of Russia and become the legal property of the purchaser.

'Up until last August, the all-important provenance was provided by a respected Swiss art historian called Bucher, but he died. There was a delay until the Soviets and the emigres could agree on another expert to provide the provenance, hence the approach to Mr Branstone.'

'And Branstone is aware of all this?'

'Certainly not, he was just thrilled to be invited. It was made clear to him that permission to come here would only be granted if he met with some friends of Paxton in London and co-operated with them. He subsequently met a couple of my colleagues from Head Office and, not to put too fine a point on it, was press-ganged into working for the Service. Hard to imagine a less suitable recruit, if you ask my opinion. Reluctant, sickly, nervous… you remember the type from school, Milo: the ones who were always homesick, preferred to spend their time in the library rather than playing sports. The ones I daresay we bullied.'

'Probably did them no harm, George.'

'One would hope so, but I sometimes shudder when I think about how we behaved. When Branstone arrived here last month

I had two clandestine meetings with him – by way of introduction and to pass on the secret camera. I have to say, it didn't raise my hopes. Told Head Office as much, he struck me as far too nervous to be of any use.

'I said if anything cropped up of particular interest then he could contact me by leaving a message with the concierge at the Moskva, where he's staying. And I received a message this morning: Branstone is very anxious to meet up. I'm seeing him tonight.'

'And do you think it's safe, George?'

'Thank you for asking, Milo: I'd like you to join me!'

Austin Branstone's meeting with colleagues of Dr Paxton had been held in a room on the upper floor of St Ermin's Hotel two days after his encounter with the Provost.

In front of him were a man whose name he was never given and Dr Paxton, who rather succinctly summarised the circumstances of the invitation to Moscow.

The man who'd not been introduced spoke with a soft Scottish accent. 'And I understand you're keen to go to Moscow?'

'I am indeed, it's an opportunity I never imagined I'd be afforded. The chance to see the collection of icons in the Kremlin is… well, I find it difficult to express how important that is.'

'And you speak Russian, I understand?'

'I do, sir.'

'But you didn't study it as an undergraduate?'

'No, sir: my degree was in Divinity, which is how I became interested in icons – they're religious paintings, I'm sure you're aware. Once I began to pursue this interest at post-graduate level, I decided that learning Russian would be most helpful. I seem to have an aptitude in the language, even if I say so myself.'

The room fell silent and Branstone watched as the two men glanced at each other and there was some nodding and then the Scotsman leant forward.

'Let me just say this, Mr Branstone: it is in the national interests of the United Kingdom to have a more informed and thorough understanding of what is going on in the Soviet Union. Although we have diplomatic representation in Moscow, it is nonetheless a very difficult country to operate in. Our officials at the embassy find their movements are restricted and are always followed around. Therefore, for someone such as yourself to be invited to Moscow and to be allowed into the Kremlin is an opportunity we cannot allow to pass.'

He leant back, not taking his eyes off him. Branstone wasn't sure how to react, other than to ask a lot of questions, but he wasn't sure if that was permitted.

'What we're asking,' said the Scotsman, 'is for you to work for this country while you are in Moscow. Obviously, you will do what the Soviets ask in terms of the icons, but we have a number of specific requests. Firstly, we would like you to provide us with as much detail as possible of what you see in the Kremlin: its layout, names on doors of offices, security arrangements, that kind of thing.

'We'll want the names and positions of everyone you meet. And perhaps most importantly, we want to know who else from this country is in Moscow. We know that there are dozens of British communists in the city, perhaps in excess of a hundred. Some of them we know about: a few of them are there under their own names, but not many. Most of them use assumed names. They're there for a variety of reasons, few of which are likely to be in the interests of this country, and we need to know as much about them as possible – where they're from; what names they're using; what they're up to in Moscow and what they look like...'

'What they look like?' It was the first time Branstone had spoken.

'You'll be given one of these, Branstone.' The Scotsman produced a small metal box from his pocket and held it up. It was about the size of a packet of ten cigarettes, possibly smaller, certainly slimmer. 'It's a camera produced by a company called Minox in Latvia. They began to produce them last year and they enable one to take photographs surreptitiously of documents, people and buildings. We don't believe that the Soviets will suspect you because they recruited you to go there. Nonetheless, you and all your luggage will be closely searched when you get there, so this will be passed to you when you're in Moscow. And don't look so worried – you'll get ample training.'

'That's not so much what I'm worried about.'

'What is it then?'

'Well, you're asking me to be a spy!'

'Don't think of it as spying, Branstone: that's the stuff of cheap adventure books one buys on station platforms. Think of it as gathering information to help out your country. You are a patriot, aren't you?'

'Well, yes… of course, I suppose I must be, Dr Paxton; I mean I—'

'Well then, there we are: it will just be a matter of keeping your eyes and ears open, remembering what you see and taking the odd snap here and there. Get whatever you can from inside the Kremlin and the more you can pick up on our fellow countrymen in Moscow the better.'

'What about if I were to have reservations?'

'What kind of reservations, Branstone?'

'For a start, I'm not the brave sort: I'm probably a bit of a coward, if I'm honest. And more to the point, I fear my academic integrity may be compromised. It somehow doesn't feel right. I'll be there as their guest, after all.'

The Scotsman made a snorting sound and rolled his eyes. Paxton replied.

'I'm afraid, Branstone, that when the security of this country is at stake, matters like that are irrelevant. If the communists get their way and take over this country then I can assure you there'll be precious little academic integrity or freedom: the likes of you and me will be lined up against a wall and shot or, if we're very lucky, sent to work in a mine for seven days a week. Do you fancy that? So that's why we're asking you to do this: to help your country out. The more we know what the Soviets are up to and who's helping them, the more we can protect this country from them.'

When the Scotsman asked Branstone if it was fair to assume he was 'on board', the young man said he was – though not with an enormous amount of conviction, it had to be said.

–

'Hardly first-rate agent material, Paxton.'

'I know, but he's in a unique position to pick up intelligence for us.'

'Do you think he's up to it?'

'He's a bright enough chap – and speaks Russian.'

'Doesn't make him an agent. We all know what that entails – agents need nerves of steel and with the best will in the world Branstone's made of more pliable stuff. And you're absolutely sure, are you, Paxton, about his politics – no chance he could be a secret socialist?'

'I've checked him out thoroughly: everyone agrees he's never shown the slightest awareness let alone interest in politics. He's got no links with any of those left-wing tutors or public schoolboys flirting with socialism. I'm absolutely confident on that score.'

'Very well then, we go ahead with it. What's the worst that could happen?'

–

Austin Branstone had a week of sleepless nights prior to his visit to Moscow. As much as he relished the opportunity to study the icons in the Kremlin, the thought of being obliged to act as a British spy had driven him to the edge of a nervous breakdown. All he could think about was being arrested and beaten up and probably tortured and being sent to one of the dreadful prison camps and he wondered how he'd cope with his asthma and no doubt the British Embassy would wash their hands of him, say they'd never heard of him before.

Two days before his departure he asked to see Professor Hatherley and informed him he wanted to pull out of the visit and when he asked him why he said the Provost would understand and within an hour Branstone was standing in the Provost's study like a pupil about to be punished.

The Provost made it clear that while they couldn't force him to go to Moscow, he should nevertheless understand that should he decide not to then there'd be consequences.

'By which I mean you'll be out of a job, Branstone, and I can assure you, you won't find another post at Cambridge or even Oxford, for that matter. I imagine you'll have to resort to teaching some subject no one else wants to teach at some minor public school and forgetting about your precious icons. Do you fancy that?'

'Of course not, sir.'

'Well then, Branstone, I suggest you pull yourself together and start packing your suitcase.'

–

But it hadn't been nearly as bad as he'd feared. The Russians proved to be hospitable hosts and couldn't do enough for him. They put him up at the Moskva Hotel on Manezhka Square and he had to say his room was a considerable improvement on his one at King's. For a start it was warm and there was no draught and he had his own bathroom with ample hot water and there was a very helpful lady behind a desk at the end of his corridor who looked after his room key and gave him towels and soap as he needed them.

For the first couple of days he was shown round Moscow and taken to visit a collective farm and a factory making machine tools, whatever they were, and Branstone had to say that it all seemed to be very efficient and neat and tidy and the ordinary people he met were rather charming and although they didn't have a lot to say for themselves, they did seem to be happy.

He was no communist, of course, but he had to admit that things were most certainly not as bleak or oppressive as he'd been given to understand they could be.

And then he began his work.

He was looked after very nicely by two gentlemen he nicknamed Big Boris and Little Boris who accompanied him all the time. Each morning one would be waiting outside his room at seven o'clock and then accompany him to breakfast in the hotel's vast dining room and from there to the Kremlin.

Once inside the Kremlin they'd walk to Cathedral Square, ringed by palaces to the west and churches to the east.

Most of the icons were in the three largest cathedrals; the Archangel Michael, the Annunciation and the Dormition, with more in the smaller Cathedral of the Twelve Apostles within the Patriarch's Palace. Branstone was based in the Terem Palace. He had a large room with an enormous table and icons would be brought for him to study one by one and after each one he'd dictate his report to a terribly obliging young man called Pavel whose English was excellent, and later that day the report would be brought for him to sign and although Branstone noticed some phrases had been altered and one or two sections added, he was happy to sign because it wasn't as if he had much time and there were an awful lot of icons for him to view!

In the evenings he'd eat in the Moskva with Big Boris and Little Boris sitting nearby. After a couple of weeks, they began to take him to restaurants in the city, though in truth he found them rather noisy and there was a bit too much drinking.

Usually, lunch was brought to him in his room at the Terem Palace but as April turned into May and it became warmer, he decided he'd ask if he could have a stroll at lunchtime to get some fresh air and Big Boris and Little Boris seemed fine with that, just as long as he stayed within the Kremlin and, more particularly, around Cathedral Square.

He realised of course that he wasn't entirely on his own: either Big Boris or Little Boris would always follow him.

And so, one day in early May he was on his lunchtime walk and this time he was being followed by Big Boris, who tended to move surprisingly slowly for someone whose job was apparently to follow other people.

As Branstone passed the Ivan the Great Bell Tower he noticed that Big Boris was now nowhere to be seen, so he decided to head on towards the Presidium of the Supreme Soviet and the Council of Ministers building, the two great edifices of the Soviet state, on the side of the Kremlin overlooking Red Square.

And that was where he saw him.

He spotted him as he left the Council of Ministers building, a little uncertain, as if he didn't know his way around as he emerged from the heavily guarded doors and made his way down the flight of steps, but he carried on and headed south in Branstone's direction and there was something about his appearance that alerted him.

The man walking towards him didn't look like the other men he'd become used to seeing walking around Moscow. At first, it was hard to put his finger on it, but as the man approached, Branstone realised what it was. The man was not quite six foot but looked distinguished, not unlike the king who'd recently abdicated, as it happened, and was dressed differently. His hat, his shoes, his smart overcoat and the suit visible underneath it was of an altogether superior quality to what he'd become used to seeing in recent weeks. He looked every inch a man dressed by the best of British tailors, shoemakers and hatters rather than by a Soviet factory rushing to meet their production targets.

If he was English that really was something because the Kremlin was such a restricted area and the Council of Ministers particularly so and Dr Paxton's colleague at that hotel in London had been quite insistent that they were most interested in anything he could pick up about his fellow countrymen in Moscow.

In itself, he wouldn't have thought much more than that, but there was something far more shocking as they walked past each other, just a yard apart at the most. Branstone was able to get a good look, because the man was looking to his left, towards the Supreme Soviet building and wouldn't have noticed Branstone – not that many people did. And there was something strikingly familiar about the man, though for the life of him he couldn't think what it was.

So he decided to follow him as he headed south, in the direction of the Kremlin Gardens. The man paused by the Kremlin Wall, looking around him in the curious manner one does in a place one is unfamiliar with. Austin Branstone kept his distance. There was still no sign of Big Boris behind him and as the man came alongside one of the towers on the southern wall Branstone held back until he entered it and then hurried along to enter it himself.

It was the Taynitskaya Tower, one he'd visited on a lunchtime walk the previous week. Its name meant 'the secret' tower due to its tunnel leading to the river, now bricked up. It was dark inside, hard to make out much more than shapes, but Branstone spotted the man, looking around and when he turned round Branstone decided to take the plunge. Showing a degree of courage and resolve that surprised him, he waited until the man walked past him and then – when the man was halfway out of the tower and his back facing him – spoke.

'I say, you wouldn't happen to know where the Komendant-skaya Tower is, by any chance? I seem to have been going round in circles!'

In English.

And the man immediately turned round. He'd removed his hat revealing his fair hair and now Branstone had an even better view of him and was even more convinced he'd met him before.

'I'm afraid not; I'm something of a stranger here myself. I imagine if you keep walking round the walls you'll sooner or later come to it!'

The two men chuckled for a moment or two and Branstone was about to ask what the man was doing there and introduce himself – he'd say his name was Charles West – when the man suddenly looked shocked, as if he'd only just realised he'd made a mistake by speaking in English. He turned around and hurried away.

Branstone began to follow him, but was soon spotted by Big Boris. It was time to return to the Terem Palace.

Now he had something to tell the man from the embassy.

—

'The best thing, Branstone, would be to calm down, have a drink, get your breath back and then tell us the whole story.'

George Banks – who Branstone knew as 'Paul' – was acting in an avuncular manner, a hand on Austin Branstone's shoulder and smiling pleasantly at him. Milo Smart – who'd been introduced as 'Peter' – was impressed. Banks was good at this. The arrangements for the meeting were most impressive.

After sending the message through the concierge, Branstone had told the two Borises he'd like to take up their suggestion to have dinner that evening at the Yar on Kuznetsky Most, not too far from the Lubyanka, as it happened. Meanwhile, Banks and Smart had arrived at the Ziyofat, a bleak Uzbek restaurant diagonally opposite the Yar, from where in an upper room they'd watched Branstone and the other two arrive and then at the agreed hour saw him emerge from a side entrance and hurry across the road before disappearing from view.

It was a tense couple of minutes. Milo Smart could hear his own breathing and felt sweat running freely inside his shirt and wondered whether he ought to have brought a pistol or, indeed, whether he ought to have been there at all, but Banks was very calm and must have sensed he was worried because he told him everything would be fine.

Moments later the door opened and Ruslan, the manager of the Ziyofat – and one of Banks's best agents in Moscow – showed Branstone in.

The young man was in such a state he could barely talk and his protruding ears were bright red and Banks told him to calm down and have a drink, which he did.

'What did you tell them?'

'I said I wanted to use the lavatory. When I return, I'll say I felt sick and needed fresh air and then got lost.'

'Very well, but we need to be quick. Ruslan will ensure you get out of here without being seen. What is it that's so urgent?'

Austin Branstone described the encounter in the Taynitskaya Tower.

'And you're certain he was English.'

'Absolutely, sir, no question whatsoever.'

'And you say he came out of the Council of Ministers building?'

'Definitely.'

'And you think you recognised him but couldn't place him?'

'Well, this is the thing, sir: at the time, there was something familiar about him, but I couldn't place him – wracked my brain over it. Then last night I woke up with a start and recalled where I was sure I'd seen him.

'I was an accomplished chess player when I was an under-graduate: I still play occasionally, but nothing like as much as I used to. I represented my college in my first year at Cambridge and in Easter term we travelled to Oxford to play a tournament at Merton College, though there were also teams from at least a couple of other Oxford colleges taking part.

'As far as I recall, we each played three games and in my last one I was up against a student who seemed a year or two older than me and was one of those upper-class, public-school types who act as if they owned the place. He was very arrogant – hardly exchanged a word with me and had a haughty manner about him, and what I'd describe as a sneering expression: very much the way people from that background acted towards what they took to be grammar-school boys. They still behave like that. Can I ask, do you know much about chess?'

George Banks shrugged and said a little, but he glanced at his watch and said he really ought to get a move on.

'Well, to cut a long story short, I trapped this chap with a four-move checkmate called the Scholar's Mate. It's really not a move an experienced player should fall for and it's somewhat humiliating to lose a game in that manner, especially so quickly. I remember that there were a few people watching and there was some laughter when I won with that move. My opponent was absolutely furious, presumably not just because he'd lost but more so at the humiliating manner of it. He got up and stormed off and didn't even shake my hand.'

Branstone paused and there was a broad grin on his face, presumably at the memory of a famous victory, and Milo Smart looked anxiously at George Banks who glanced again at his watch and told Branstone he needed to come to the point.

'This was the chap I bumped into in the Kremlin, you see – the chap I beat with the Scholar's Mate!'

'Really – you're that sure?'

'What you need to realise is that I've an excellent memory for faces: it's one of the reasons I can analyse icons so well, the figures in them are familiar to me. I spot recurring themes.'

'Even so, Branstone, we're talking about someone you saw, what… ten years ago? Quite something to recognise him here in the middle of Moscow and be certain of it.'

'I do realise that.'

'And he didn't recognise you?'

'He certainly didn't show any sign of doing so. In any case, my appearance has changed somewhat since my undergraduate days.' Branstone ran his hand over his bald head and smiled.

'And you say he seemed shocked?'

'As if he'd suddenly realised he'd made a mistake by speaking English. He rushed away then.'

'And you didn't get a photograph of him?'

'I didn't think it would be a terribly good idea to whip out my camera in the Kremlin, do you?'

70

That was the first and last George Banks heard of the mysterious, well-dressed Englishman in the Kremlin. He instructed Branstone to spend what time he could at the Lux Hotel on Gorky Street where the majority of western visitors stayed, but Branstone never saw him again.

London was most interested, of course. No one at Head Office needed telling how important the sighting was – an Englishman in the Kremlin, after all, and leaving the Council of Ministers building. Not just another communist getting drunk in the bar at the Lux.

But they got nowhere. MI6 looked into it as best they could, but drew a blank. Merton was a large college and, according to Branstone, there were two other colleges involved. They were talking about one of *thousands* of potential students. Of course, they did investigate the matter, but there were no records that were of any use, no lists of who'd played for the Merton chess team all those years ago and details of any tournaments.

As someone helpfully pointed out, it wasn't even as if they were searching for a needle in a haystack. They first needed to find the bloody haystack!

Chapter 7

Germany
May 1937

Cooper followed the route through Germany suggested by the Maurers. Munich seemed like a good place to start and when he studied his map of Europe the route made sense – a clockwise tour of Germany.

He allowed himself three weeks, taking a lunchtime train on a Tuesday from Zürich to Munich and staying on the first night at the Wolff on Arnhulf Strasse, close to the station. He'd stayed there because he'd arrived late and thought he'd move somewhere less busy, but there was something about Munich that immediately put him on edge and from the moment he arrived he felt he needed to be close to the station. Just in case, though he wasn't quite sure just in case of what.

There was an unquestionable military edge to the city, the station and the streets around it teeming with groups of armed men, most of which appeared to be Nazi gangs with their distinctive swastika armbands. It was little better when he checked in at the hotel. He was taken into a side room where his passport and the visa issued at the German consulate in Zürich was carefully examined by a man who never introduced himself and seemed to be unconvinced with Cooper's reasons for being in Munich. 'Looking around' sounded too vague, he had to admit, but he knew better than to announce he was a writer.

Cooper only went out during the day, never too far from the hotel, all the time feeling thoroughly miserable and nervous about making notes in public so doing his best to memorise his thoughts and then transcribe them in his room.

He did have a stroke of fortune, though, when he visited the Information Bureau at the railway station the morning after his arrival and discovered they were selling the new English edition of Baedeker's Guide to Germany. He spent a couple of hours going through it in a bar near the station, astonished at the amount of detail, even for relatively small towns. It would, he soon realised, be an invaluable companion.

He was a bit shaken though by the section on German history. National Socialism, it said, has 'systematically carried through the national revolution and eliminated both fruitless Parliamentarianism and the mutual clashing of economic and local interests'.

It didn't get any better. 'Simultaneously ... constructive work has begun on the abolition of unemployment, the reorganisation of agriculture as the backbone of the nation, the reawakening of race-consciousness and a corporative organisation of the classes.'

It seemed very political for a travel guide and he wondered whether the laws in Germany meant they'd been obliged to insert it. He had no idea, but it didn't feel like a warm 'welcome to Germany'.

–

The following morning, he was walking towards the river when he found himself on Prannerstrasse, where a slightly frayed Union Jack and a brass plate in need of a good polish announced the location of the British consulate and, for no obvious reason, Cooper decided to pop in: maybe the consulate had a library there where he could catch up on the English papers.

The consulate was reached through the courtyard of the building and on the steps leading to the entrance, a dozen people – mostly men – were waiting, each clutching a bag or a handful of papers and looking exhausted. Cooper joined the rear of the queue, but as he did so a man appeared from inside the consulate and approached him.

73

'Are you here for a visa?' He spoke in poor German with an English accent. He was tall and awkward-looking, with thinning hair and a pair of spectacles held together by white tape and had a harassed air about him.

'No, I'm British, actually. I was just passing and wondered if you perhaps had, I don't know, information for British visitors to Munich?'

'Do you have your passport with you?'

'I do, as it happens.'

'Very well then, you'd better come in, though I'm not sure what we can do to help. We're not a tourist office, you know.'

It was clear that the consulate was anything but a tourist bureau and was unlikely to be the home of an agreeable library where he could read the British papers in peace and quiet. Another dozen people waited in the foyer, some sitting, the others standing, all looking anxious.

The man who'd shown him in took him into an office and gestured for him to sit down and offered Cooper a cigarette. His desk was cluttered with stacks of files and at least three ashtrays.

'In other times I suppose we may have been of some help – places to visit, you know – that kind of thing. But not any more. We're overwhelmed here: all these Jews are looking for visas to get out of Germany. To get a visa to leave they need to be able to show an entry visa from a country that will take them in. The Jews say they're having a dreadful time of it under the Nazis, their lives are barely worth living, they tell us, which is why so many of them are trying to leave. But it's not that easy, we can't just hand out visas to whoever asks for one. London is very, very strict, you know, and I'm not altogether sure I blame them. One does have a degree of sympathy for the Jews, of course, but... you know...'

He paused, as if unsure as to how Cooper would react.

'I say, you're not a journalist, are you, by some chance? I ought to have asked first. I hope you realise this is all *entre nous*, it makes a change to have someone in this office who's neither pleading for their life or telling me what to do!'

'No, I thought Munich would be an interesting place to visit. And you don't need to worry, I'm just an innocent tourist.'

'Well, that's good to know. My name's Andrews, by the way.'

Cooper smiled again and gave his name and Andrews said he knew, he'd seen it on the passport, and chuckled, clearly pleased with himself.

'What I meant to say is that while one is not completely unsympathetic to the Jews one does occasionally have to ask oneself whether they may have contributed in some way to their situation, if you get my drift... I mean, whose side are they on, other than their own? Why are they always so unpopular, eh? I know we have to be cognisant of the Nazi threat and stability in Europe, but as I see it the communist threat is of greater concern to us and one does have to say that the communists and the Jews... well... they're often one and the same.'

Cooper was appalled, so much so he didn't react at all, but Andrews appeared to take this as some kind of agreement.

'If they stay in Germany, they'll just have to get used to being not so well off. And if they leave... well, that's what they've done for centuries. The wandering Jew, eh?'

Andrews laughed loudly, making a snorting sound as he did so as if something was caught in his throat, leant back in his chair and looked very pleased with himself.

Cooper stood up and said he really must get a move on and he could see how busy it was here.

Andrews escorted him to the reception area and wished him a good day. Before he left, Cooper stood in the entrance and paused. The people waiting there looked at him desperately on the off chance he may be there to help them and Cooper – not without a little shame – studied them for a while.

He was the writer now, searching for characters.

The old man with a stained tie clutching a framed certificate.

The couple in their early thirties each holding a small suitcase, possibly hoping they could depart that day.

The middle-aged man in an immaculately tailored suit trying to adopt a confident, military bearing but with trembling lips.

The woman in her twenties, a sleeping baby coddled beneath her coat.

Each one of them a character.

Each one of them a novel.

–

Cooper spent the rest of the day walking around Munich, trying to absorb the atmosphere but instead feeling polluted by it. On his way back to the hotel he stopped at the station to book a ticket. He'd leave for Stuttgart the following afternoon. That night he studied his Baedeker, planning where to go the following morning before his train departed.

'National Socialism originated in Munich in 1920; the party still has its headquarters here and the town is officially known as "the capital of the movement".'

As if spurred on by this, the next morning he found himself drawn to Brienner Strasse, where the Braun Haus – the headquarters of the Nazi Party – was located, north of the station, between Königsplatz and Karolinenplatz.

Cooper felt unaccountably calm as he approached the large building guarded by a dozen men in uniform. Perhaps it was the ticket in his wallet that would take him away from Munich in just a couple of hours, or maybe he felt less vulnerable being a foreigner or it could be that he was thinking now as a writer and seeking out experiences. But for whatever reason, he bounded up the stairs to the entrance and when he was stopped by a guard, acted put-out and said he was here to see… and it was at that moment that his confidence failed him and his German sounded decidedly hesitant as he asked if it was possible to see someone who could explain the situation to him and the guards looked at him as if he was mad as they surrounded him, and for a moment Cooper thought he was about to be beaten up, and then someone he couldn't see barked an instruction and a small man appeared as the guards parted and asked him who he was and what he wanted.

Five minutes later Cooper was in a windowless room in the basement of the Braun Haus, which would have felt like a cell had it not been so comfortably furnished, and he was sitting in an easy chair answering the questions from a man in a black suit that looked like a uniform.

He told them his name and where he was from and said he had no interest in politics whatsoever but he had heard much about Germany and some of it was… controversial… but he thought it best if he come to see for himself. 'Because you can't always believe what you read in the newspapers, can you?'

'No, you most certainly can't.' This was all in English because they'd already established that the man in the black suit that looked like a uniform spoke far better English than Cooper did German. 'And you say you're a writer?'

'After a fashion, I suppose.'

The man raised his eyebrows to indicate he was confused, and Cooper had to admit he couldn't blame him because it did all sound rather vague.

'I'd describe myself as an aspirant writer: I'm planning to write something.'

'An article?'

'A book.'

'About Germany?'

'And France too, possibly Switzerland. Maybe Italy and Spain and I daresay I'll try and visit Belgium and Holland, too. It's a novel, you see.'

Cooper tried to outline the plot and although it did all sound rather rambling the man seemed rather interested, especially when he mentioned the diamond thief and when Cooper described the woman he'd met in the hotel in Innsbruck and hinted at a theme of romance in the plot.

'And you've come to the Braun Haus… why? Do you think the National Socialist Party purchases stolen diamonds?'

The man's thin lips tightened, and his eyes narrowed, and now Cooper began to feel uncomfortable and wondered what on earth had made him come anywhere near this place.

77

'You see, Mr Cooper, we know you were in the British consulate on Prannerstrasse yesterday and we're interested to know what your instructions were? To find out what we're up to? See if you have any cells here? Borrow some files... get as many names as possible?'

Afterwards, when he left the wretched building, Cooper took the view that in the circumstances, he'd handled everything really rather well. He recalled his schooldays when he'd been somewhat shy and often fearful but coped intuitively by concentrating on being calm. And always smiling. A teacher had once told him that with his good looks and his smile, he'd get away with a lot. So, in that windowless room in the Braun Haus, he hadn't panicked, he'd managed to appear put-out without being too angry and, most importantly of all, came up with a plausible story which he stuck to.

That was the most important part of it, sticking to a story.

He was jolly pleased with himself. It was as if he had a natural aptitude for all this. He had an imagination and could think through tricky circumstances. Perhaps he'd be a writer after all.

He told them he'd gone into the consulate for any information they had for an Englishman at a loose end in Munich and they didn't have any so he had a brief chat with an official there – his name? Andrews – and then left. The place was full of people looking for visas.

'How many?'

'About a dozen inside and maybe a similar number queuing outside.'

'Jews?'

'I imagine so.'

'Did you speak with any of them?'

Cooper shook his head.

'Then how did you know they were Jewish?'

'I'm assuming they were. I was told they were applying for visas to enter Britain and I gather your Jewish citizens don't feel terribly welcome here. Look, I'm mindful that I've taken up a good deal of your time and so you must have work to do and I have a train to catch so if I could…'

The man stood up and said to wait. He closed the door and Cooper didn't hear a locking noise, which was reassuring, but he thought better than to check and he assumed he was being watched so he made a point of looking as calm as possible, leaning back in his chair and closing his eyes and toying with the idea of writing some notes on the encounter because this was really very good material but he thought that would look suspicious, so he just sat still.

It was two hours later when the man returned, standing in the now open doorway and saying he could leave and holding out his passport and his wallet and as Cooper took them, he said he was most sorry that Mr Cooper had missed his train, but he was sure he'd find another one.

Cooper smiled and said nothing as he was escorted out of the Braun Haus.

Missing the train was inconvenient, but more importantly, it was, after all, material for the book.

–

Cooper spent the next fortnight travelling round Germany, loosely keeping to the route suggested to him by the Maurers, because that seemed as good an itinerary as any. From Munich he travelled to Stuttgart, which his Baedeker assured him enjoyed 'the reputation of being the most go-ahead city in Germany', though there seemed little about it which could be counted as go-ahead. From there he took the train to Frankfurt, the birthplace of Goethe, whose poetry he'd studied at university and which he'd never really got on with. He visited the Goethe Haus on Grosser Hirschgraben near the Rossmarkt, but even then, the poetry failed to come to life.

And so, he continued, from Frankfurt into the Ruhr – Düsseldorf, Essen, Dortmund – which felt like one enormous factory, and he thought that maybe these politicians in Britain who talked about German rearmament had a point. But above all, it was the unremitting Nazi nature of the places he visited that made the greatest impression on him: the ubiquity of the men in uniform and the huge swastika flags draping down buildings; the all-pervading atmosphere of menace, suspicion and triumphalism.

It didn't feel like a nation that had been heavily defeated almost twenty years before. Quite the opposite, in fact.

It was summed up for him by a line in his guidebook on Essen, which he'd read as the train pulled into the station: 'Adolf Hitler Strasse leads from the main station to Adolf Hitler Platz'.

In Düsseldorf he'd had a haircut at a barber shop on Kaiser-Wilhelm Strasse where the atmosphere was cold and unfriendly, as if they suspected him of something and as a result Cooper was nervous and asked for *das üblich* – 'the usual' – which didn't seem to translate in the way he'd hoped. He spent a miserable twenty minutes staring at the framed photograph of Hitler in his eyeline and at the end was horrified: he'd been given a brutal, military haircut. The man watching him from the wall would have been amused.

–

He'd expected more from Hamburg. He'd travelled there on a night train from Münster because he was worried about his budget and decided he needed to economise. He ended up in a third-class compartment, but it wasn't too busy, and the few other passengers slept through the journey. The train stopped in Osnabrück, where another passenger joined Cooper's compartment, sitting opposite him, their feet touching. The man was in his early twenties, pale and weary, an unlit cigarette in his mouth, and when he got round to lighting it his hands were clearly trembling.

The train was held at Osnabrück for nearly twenty minutes and all the time the young man glanced anxiously out of the window.

He only relaxed when they noisily pulled away, but still clutched a leather holdall tightly to his chest and made sure his battered suitcase was wedged between his legs and the seat. Cooper smiled at his companion and wished him a good evening and the young man asked where he had travelled from and Cooper said Essen, but he'd been in a number of places before that, and the young man said his German was very good, but where was he from?

'I'm British,' replied Cooper, lowering his voice.

At that the other man leant forward and Cooper did likewise. Even in the dim light of the carriage he could see the man's eyes were bloodshot. They darted around the compartment.

'I am hoping to get to Britain.'

'Have you been before?'

He shook his head. 'I am afraid not, and my chances of getting there now are slim… I tried the British Passport Office in Berlin, but I had no chance. I'm not Jewish, and I have no contacts in Britain, which would have helped but… Are you here for work, may I ask?'

Cooper explained he was a traveller, someone who was interested in the world around him, and was visiting different places and possibly writing a book – a novel – based on what he saw.

'You speak French?'

'I do actually, yes.'

'Are you familiar with the poet Baudelaire?'

Cooper nodded. Almost as difficult as Goethe.

'He wrote of the *flâneur* – a gentleman who strolls the streets of a city, detached from the routine around him, but instead observing what is going on, not rushed or with an appointment to hurry to or a church or a museum to visit. The *flâneur* is the ideal person to makes sense of the world, to observe it from a casual yet objective point of view. I have always aspired to be a *flâneur*, but for now I cannot contemplate that luxury. But you, my friend, you're a *flâneur*, you're a very fortunate man.'

And then the young man leant even closer. He introduced himself as Manfred and Cooper shook his hand and Manfred grasped it eagerly, holding Cooper's hand with both of his and not letting go. He explained his family were committed Nazis but he was a socialist and he'd fled the family home in Dresden and moved to Berlin, which was still a liberal city despite everything, and there he'd fallen in love with a Jewish girl and as a result had been thrown off his university course and from his lodgings and then there'd been a fight – no more than a scuffle, really – with a member of the SS when he'd tried to protect another man who was being beaten up and although he'd managed to get away they knew who he was and there was a warrant out for his arrest.

'The papers I have' – he patted his jacket pocket – 'got me out of Berlin and I'm hoping they'll get me to Hamburg. Do you know Hamburg? It's essentially a socialist city, even now – though, don't get me wrong, the Nazis control it. But if I can get to the docks, I have a chance of getting on a boat. Ideally, I'll go to your country, but I'll go anywhere – Denmark, maybe? I have to get out of this cursed place.'

'I expect to be back in London in July. You should look me up.'

Manfred smiled for the first time, but when Cooper opened his notebook and began to write he reacted with alarm.

'It is too dangerous to write anything down. Tell me your address.'

They talked quietly for the remainder of the journey, punctuated by periods of silence during which both men closed their eyes, but sleep was never a companion on that train and when Cooper took out a roll he'd bought at Essen station he shared it with Manfred, who confided he hadn't eaten for more than a day. Cooper opened his wallet and handed Manfred a ten Reichsmark note.

'I can't, really. I have no chance of repaying it!'

'When you meet me in London you can take me out for a drink. Knowing you made it out safely is repayment enough for me.'

–

In truth, Hamburg had never stood a chance. He was well-disposed towards it because of what Manfred had told him, but these feelings disappeared soon after they arrived.

Dawn had broken as the train pulled into the station and he and Manfred walked alongside each other as they approached the barrier.

'Perhaps if you go immediately ahead of me, as you're a foreigner, they will pay you more attention and maybe let me through more easily.'

But it was a disaster. Cooper was quickly waved through, but he heard raised voices and shouting behind him and carried on walking until he could resist the urge to turn round no longer.

He saw Manfred being marched away, a man on either side of him, Manfred staring ahead of him, most probably doing his best to avoid looking anywhere in Cooper's direction.

And as he left the station and emerged onto Steintor Platz, he had the most dreadful thought: what if poor Manfred thought it was he who'd betrayed him?

–

Until Hamburg, Cooper had been a tourist. A reasonably well-informed and interested tourist certainly, a keen observer, a *flâneur*, as Manfred had put it, but a tourist nonetheless.

But now he was something different, though he couldn't quite put his finger on what that was. He was less wide-eyed and no longer so naïve about what he saw. It was as if he'd hardened up, mindful of a quote from the Old Testament he remembered from school about being a stranger in a strange land.

He wasn't even sure whether he wanted to remain in this strange land for much longer. Summer was approaching and maybe he could head to Italy for as long as his budget allowed and forget about the book and politics.

He remained in Hamburg for a few days, but his heart wasn't in it, despite the atmosphere being markedly less oppressive than elsewhere. He travelled from Hamburg to Hanover where

Baedeker informed him 'the purest German is supposed to be spoken' and stayed there for a few days.

And then he went to Berlin.

Chapter 8

Berlin
May–June 1937

Charles Cooper left Hanover in the final hours of May. By the time his train pulled into Lehrte station in Berlin it was a bright Tuesday morning. The station was already busy, with clouds of steam drifting along the platforms and the concourse as Cooper made his way to the ticket barrier.

He was waved through and couldn't help noticing there were more men around in uniform than anywhere else he'd been in Germany, including Munich. For much of his journey through Germany he wondered about visiting Berlin at all. For one thing, he was running short of money, and Berlin had a reputation for being expensive.

But, more to the point, he was unsure he wanted to see the Maurers again. They'd been pleasant enough in their own way and even quite interesting but there was something odd about them, something he couldn't put his finger on, and he was a bit ashamed to be feeling like that because it was quite possible that the problem was his English reserve, his reluctance to get too close to people. And the last few weeks travelling round Germany had certainly had an effect on him: he was now less inclined to assume the best in everyone and everything he encountered. He noticed how much more sceptical he'd become.

But he was sure the Maurers were just trying to be friendly and he really ought to learn to be less sceptical about people, he resolved. More trusting and open to other ideas and customs

– that was part of the purpose of his trip round Europe, after all. And, in any case, needs must: it wasn't as if he had much of a choice about taking up the Maurers' offer of hospitality. He had precious little of the fifty pounds he'd budgeted for this trip remaining.

Staying with the Maurers would help enormously.

–

He worried that six o'clock may be too early to call them, so found a cafe in Invaliden Strasse in front of the station and made a large mug of weak coffee and a jam roll last an hour and at seven o'clock rang the number the Maurers had given him. Ida answered the phone and said, no, of course it wasn't so early and he mustn't keep apologising and of course he was more than welcome to come and stay with them. In fact, they'd been expecting him.

–

The Maurers lived in Prenzlauer Berg and it took him just over half an hour to walk there, allowing him an opportunity to get a feel for the city. It didn't take him too long to be overwhelmed by Berlin. Munich, Frankfurt and Hamburg were large cities, but Berlin had a grandeur to it and an air of authority and confidence that came with being a capital city. London was like that, and he'd sensed it in Paris, too. But neither Paris nor London had streets teeming with armed men. Neither Paris nor London had their imposing buildings draped in enormous flags. Neither Paris nor London had a populace who moved around in such a subdued manner, glancing around nervously while avoiding eye contact with other passers-by.

Had Cooper put his mind to it he'd have guessed that the Maurers were solidly middle-class, perhaps professionals, so he was surprised when he arrived at their apartment block on Wörther Strasse. It was a few minutes' walk north of Senefelder

U–Bahn station, between Schönhauser Allee and Prenzlauer Allee and on the junction with Treskow Strasse, and while he wouldn't have described it as a slum – and he'd be the first to admit he wasn't familiar with how people lived in Berlin – it did all feel a bit rundown. The kind of area that had evidently enjoyed better times.

There were four apartments on each of the five floors, all reached off a central staircase, the air musty with a pervading smell of cooked cabbage. The Maurers were on the top floor. As he climbed past the fourth floor a dog barked loudly from behind a door, setting off a cacophony of noise from the block's other canine residents.

The Maurers were both there to greet him, standing in the narrow hallway, quite formally dressed, and they shook his hand in a formal manner. The apartment was small and sparsely furnished and his first reaction was that this was a predominantly functional place, more a house than a home, which he thought was a good line for his novel.

The apartment comprised a lounge, a small kitchen, a bathroom and toilet and the Maurers' bedroom. Next to it was a small room with a single bed in it and little else – there wasn't the space.

He was shown into the lounge and sat in an upright chair opposite the Maurers who sat next to each other on a sofa. There was silence for a while as they observed him, Ida Maurer studying him intently and unnervingly, Ernst Maurer smiling and fidgeting, possibly uncomfortable. The curtains were only half drawn and with the heavy net curtain the room was cast in a dim light, such sunlight as managed to get through catching specks of dust as they drifted through the gloom.

'It's very decent of you to put me up: I'm terribly grateful. My travels in Germany proved to be quite a drain on my funds.'

'But interesting, I hope?'

'Oh yes, most interesting, Frau Maurer.'

'You must call me Ida, please. And has your journey been worthwhile?'

'Indeed, though I…' He hesitated, unsure of straying into any area that could be regarded as political. He'd developed a sense of that on his travels: there were certain matters one did not discuss, at least not with people one didn't really know and he realised how little he knew about the Maurers. They were clearly very good at playing their cards close to their chests. The characters in his novel based on them would be described as enigmatic.

But he decided to be as frank as he dared. As interesting – and worthwhile – as his trip round Germany had been, he said, he had to admit it had been… and he hesitated but caught Ernst's friendly smile. 'Unnerving, I think that's the word.'

'In what way?'

He talked about what he called the excessive militarism and general atmosphere of suspicion and of always feeling one had to be on one's guard and he noticed both of the Maurers nodding so he talked about his visit to the British consulate in Munich and the Jews queuing there in the hope of getting a visa and the Braun Haus and how he was prepared to admit he'd been foolish going there, because he'd ended up being interrogated, and how the other places he stopped at weren't quite as intense as Munich but were nonetheless places he couldn't feel relaxed in.

'If you wanted to be relaxed you should have remained in Switzerland.'

'I do realise that, Ernst, and I keep reminding myself that I am after all gathering material for a book and I've certainly got plenty of that.'

And then he told them about his encounter with poor Manfred on the train to Hamburg, except that he decided to be cautious so said the young man's name was Paul, but soon realised his caution was pointless because if the Maurers were on the side of the authorities then he could soon enough be linked with the man arrested at Hamburg station.

He paused, thinking about Manfred and wondering what had become of him. He couldn't imagine it being anything other than something dreadful. He should have intervened at the time.

'What do you make of everything you saw; of the atmosphere you so neatly describe? Does it appal you or does part of you approve of it? After all, many people around Europe – not just in this country – approve of the order Hitler has brought to Germany and the way he is doing something about the economic and social chaos. They may not approve of all of his methods, but there is a sense that it is all worth it. And as for the Jews, well, many people feel that it is not a bad thing that they're being put in their place, likewise the communists and the socialists.'

'When I arrived in Germany, I imagined myself as an observer, a traveller who was able to view matters objectively and dispassionately. I'm told there's a French word – the *flâneur* – someone who wanders around apparently aimlessly, yet not without purpose, if that doesn't sound somewhat complicated. But while on the one hand I like to think of myself as a *flâneur* I've also come to realise that with the situation here in Germany, one cannot sit on the fence.'

He stopped and coughed and looked at the Maurers hoping they may give him some encouragement or at least a reaction, but they sat impassively, and the most he got was a brief nod from Ida Maurer to indicate he should carry on.

'I strongly disapprove of what the Nazis are up to. When my guide book speaks of "fruitless Parliamentarianism" and "the reawakening of race-consciousness", well... it offends my sense of fair play.'

He'd been staring at the threadbare carpet as he spoke, unsure of how they'd react and when he looked up, they gave the impression that he was to continue.

'So, there we are... I'm sorry if I've spoken out of turn, but then you did ask me what I thought. I do tend to ramble, though – eh?'

He'd surprised himself at how outspoken he'd been. He was normally so much more equivocal. He glanced up and smiled and to his intense relief so did the Maurers and Ida Maurer said she could quite see his point and it was interesting to hear an outsider's perspective and he was very welcome to stay with them to the end of June, if he wished.

'But a warning though, Herr Cooper: it is one thing expressing your personal opinions to us, but do not repeat them to anyone else you meet. Berlin is a very dangerous place in that respect.'

–

And so it was for the following week. It had been made clear he was expected to leave the apartment at a quarter to eight in the morning, at the same time as the Maurers. He was never sure what they did or where they went and he thought better than to ask because to do so would have felt intrusive. He'd plan his itinerary for the day the previous evening and would either walk to his first destination or go to one of the U–Bahn stations on Schönhauser Allee.

He'd aim to return to the apartment around a quarter past six in good time for dinner at six thirty and they'd always be there, Ernst invariably opening the door as he approached it, as if they'd been watching his arrival from their window.

The Maurers were pleasant enough hosts, but supper was usually eaten in silence. The meals tended to be frugal, plenty of potatoes, little in the way of vegetables and small portions of meat, always overcooked. There'd be a plate of black rye bread and sometimes a cake and while he didn't go hungry, Cooper always made the most of the food stalls around Mitte where he could feast on sausages and rolls.

The longer he stayed with them, the more intrigued he was at quite who they were. By now, his ear was finely tuned to hearing German and there was something odd about the way they spoke: it was as if they were rehearsed, a bit too practised.

One evening he returned far earlier than usual, closer to six o'clock. There'd been a storm over Berlin and he was drenched and was sure they'd understand his early arrival.

When he approached the front door of their apartment, he noticed it was ajar and when he pushed it open, he could hear them talking in the kitchen, at the end of the hall.

He couldn't make out what they were saying, but they were certainly not speaking German. He couldn't make out what language it was other than it wasn't English or French either. The conversation had an urgency to it, as if they were arguing. When he called out 'hello' they stopped abruptly, and Ernst looked flustered. Ida ushered him into the lounge and said he was to remove his wet shoes and jacket and she'd bring him a lemon tea.

After he'd been with them for a week, he was woken early one morning by the ringing of a telephone. He looked at his watch and saw it was six thirty. He couldn't hear the conversation, but by seven o'clock Ida had left the house. Ernst explained she'd been called to visit a sick relative. She'd be back soon.

It was three days before she returned and during that period her husband was clearly on edge, sitting close to the telephone or waiting by the front window, anxiously watching the road through the blinds.

And the final mystery was the one which gave Cooper most pause for thought. Returning to the apartment, he was walking up Schönhauser Allee when he spotted the unmistakable figure of Ernst ahead of him.

But there was something different about Ernst: he walked differently – more cautiously, as if he had a bad back – and kept stopping to glance around. Cooper dropped back and watched as Ernst removed his hat and put it and his raincoat in a canvas bag he was carrying and then turned suddenly into a side street and as he did so quickened his pace, as if hurrying for a tram.

Cooper crossed the road, from where he had a good view of what happened next. Ernst stopped by the entrance of an alleyway where he was joined by another man who'd emerged from its shadows. There was a brief conversation and the man handed an envelope to Ernst who then held open his bag for the man to take out the coat and put it on himself.

And then they continued their separate ways: the man back down the alley, Ernst turning sharply to head home. Cooper only just managed to avoid being seen by him.

Later that evening he heard them in their room on the other side of the thin wall from his bed. Snatched lines of urgent conversation in the other language again. It was a hard language, its tones unfamiliar.

He decided that night it was time to move on from the Maurers. He had plenty of material from Germany and in particular from Berlin. One only needed to walk around the city to absorb the enormity and gravity of what was happening there. Perhaps the diamond thief first encountered in Paris could emerge now in Berlin, maybe she could be involved in smuggling jewellery and other valuables out of the country on behalf of people desperate leave but prohibited from taking much in the way of valuables with them.

The Maurers' conversation ceased, but Cooper found it hard to sleep. He looked through his notebook and the places he'd noted in Berlin that would make good settings for the novel.

A possible meeting in the Tiergarten.

A secret rendezvous at the back of a cafe on the Unter den Linden.

A love affair consummated in the Adlon hotel.

Heartbreak on the banks of the Wannsee.

An alley of Schönhauser Allee.

The following morning, he informed his hosts that he'd decided to move on. He wanted to visited Dresden and possibly Poland too before returning to England. He was very grateful for their hospitality and, as Ernst had promised, he'd certainly found his novel in Germany.

'And the ending, Herr Charles – have you found that in Berlin?'

Cooper replied, not quite, but he hoped…

'You can't leave your novel unfinished, my friend.'

'Unfinished? I haven't begun it yet, Ernst! I have a plot and a structure of sorts and a whole cast of characters and a few sections sketched out, but I want to visit a few more places and then go home and actually write it.'

'Perhaps stay two more days?' It was Ida, making it sound like an instruction rather than an invitation, her demeanour brittle as usual.

–

The following evening he returned after a day spent walking around the Tiergarten to find a man sitting in the front room with Ernst, smoking a cigarette of the strongest tobacco he'd ever experienced.

The man stood up as they were introduced: he was called Eduard and younger than the Maurers, perhaps in his early forties, and very tall with a confident air. He seemed very interested in Cooper – *ah, the man I've been hearing all about!* – and when he spoke Cooper could tell he wasn't a native German speaker.

They ate well that night, the four of them crowded around the small table, which tonight had a crisp white tablecloth and for the first time since he'd been there Ida Maurer served three courses, including a whole roast chicken for main course and an extravagant cake for dessert.

After dinner the Maurers said they'd tidy up and Eduard suggested Cooper join him in the lounge and the two of them were there alone for the next two hours, long after the kitchen should have been tidied up. Eduard wanted to know everything about Cooper.

'I wouldn't know where to start, to be honest!'

'You're an interesting chap: I'd like to know more about you.'

Cooper felt more relaxed in Eduard's company than he did with the Maurers and was happy to talk. He described his journey through Germany and some of what had happened during it and he gave his impressions and Eduard moved the conversation along very skilfully, a little prompt here, the right question there and while never giving his own opinion he was more encouraging than the Maurers had been.

After that Cooper found himself being frank with Eduard in a way he couldn't recall having ever been with anyone else. Eduard had a way of looking at him that was almost hypnotic. He appeared so interested that, in spite of himself, Cooper talked not just about Germany and his novel but also about himself: his mother, the grief he felt for his father, the inheritance, his lack of confidence and how he was determined to write and… even Grace, the older woman at the hotel in Innsbruck.

It was late when Eduard said he had to leave, but if Cooper was able to spend an extra couple of days in Berlin, then he'd like to have more time with him.

—

Two days later they were in the Kleine Tiergarten when Eduard suggested they sit down on a bench set some way back from the path.

'You have told me much about your book. I think it has potential. But you're a novice, you've never had anything published. You need help. I have contacts in publishing who can help you.'

Cooper said he was very grateful and, of course, any help he could give would be very much appreciated.

'My contacts are in Moscow. I can arrange for you to visit there, if you so wish.'

Cooper was unsure how to react. He'd never thought of going to Moscow. How would he even get there?

'You seem hesitant: let me tell you, as well as getting help you will also find much material for your novel in Moscow. The greatest novelists are all Russian and the modern novel was invented in Russia after all!'

'Are you Russian?'

Eduard shrugged and said if Cooper was interested then he could make the necessary arrangements. 'If you're not interested, Charles, then I quite understand, but in my opinion, you'd be foolish to turn down an opportunity to visit Moscow.'

'Perhaps if I could think it over for a couple of days?'

Eduard shook his head. 'I would need to make the arrangements, so I really need to know now. But, of course, if you'd rather not, I quite understand.'

'How long would it be for?'

'I would suggest a fortnight.'

'And excuse me asking, but is it expensive to travel to Moscow? And what about hotels?'

Eduard said not to worry, he'd take care of all that and all his expenses would be covered, but what he really wanted to know now was whether Mr Cooper was going to turn down such a wonderful opportunity and Cooper found himself saying no, because it seemed to be a good example of what the solicitor in Birmingham had meant about regretting things one didn't do and after all, what harm could a few days in Moscow do?

It was only later – much later, when it was far too late – he realised that notwithstanding what Mr Carter had told him in Birmingham, what one does can be the cause of far greater regret than what one hasn't done.

Chapter 9

Moscow
July 1937

One week after the conversation with Eduard in the Kleine Tiergarten Cooper was in Moscow.

Eduard had come to the Maurers' apartment the night before
his departure and presented him with a dark green passport from
the Irish Free State.

'It's better for you to travel under an Irish passport than a
British one,' said Eduard. He leant over and opened it.

'George William Hobson, same date of birth as your own –
sixteenth of October, 1911. You're a protestant, which will hopefully account for your accent. You have an address in Rathmines,
which is apparently an area where many protestants live. If you get
into conversation with people, you should be as vague as possible.
Volunteer very little, but we find it is helpful to allude to the fact
you've moved around.'

When he was satisfied Cooper understood the travel arrangements, Eduard hesitated before speaking in a quieter voice.

'Maybe I can give you some advice? The Soviet Union is
completely unlike any other country, certainly nothing like your
country. There is no scope here for discussion, for questioning
what people ask you to do. Assume if someone asks you to do
something or makes a suggestion, then it is an instruction. There's
an old Russian saying about never regretting arriving at your
destination: if you regret it, you should have never started out
on the journey.'

'Maybe that works better in Russian, Eduard, I'm not too sure I understand.'

'You will do, believe me.'

—

He arrived in Moscow and a car was waiting to take him to the Lux Hotel on Gorky Street.

A man in a dark suit was waiting in the foyer for him. He shook his hand and signalled for a porter to take his case and ask 'Mr Hobson' to follow him into his office.

He told Cooper his name was Grigory and spelt it out carefully in English and said his job was to look after important foreign guests staying at the Lux, and Cooper laughed — more out of sheer relief than anything else — and said that was very nice but he didn't think he counted as important, but Grigory waved his hand and said nonsense, of course he was important.

'You are Mr George William Hobson from Dublin.'

He smiled and nodded and Grigory said 'good' and he would be addressed as 'Comrade Hobson' and Cooper said 'very well', though by now he was utterly confused and apart from anything else, he had no idea he was anyone's comrade and, if he was honest, it sounded quite ridiculous.

'Let me explain about your stay, Comrade Hobson. The Lux Hotel is reserved for special guests of the Soviet Union. The hotel has four floors, your room will be on the second floor. You will need this pass.' He handed a card to Cooper.

'It is called a *propusk*. You need to show it to the guard on your floor. You are only to use the elevator, do not use the stairs. You are not to go to any other floor in the hotel, and only the common areas on the ground floor. Do you understand?'

Grigory paused and watched Cooper, waiting for acknowledgment, so Cooper said yes, of course, he understood.

'The cost of your stay here is covered. We have a cafe on the ground floor called the Filippov: you will need this other card to be able to eat there. Breakfast is served from six to eight and the evening meal from six to seven thirty. If you want to use the cafe at other times you will need to pay. Do you have foreign currency with you?'

Grigory leant forward as he asked the question, furrowing his brow and it felt like he was being interrogated.

'Yes, I do… I'm afraid I didn't realise that I—'

'What foreign currency do you have?'

'Mostly British sterling – some German marks and French francs, not many though as I was…'

'You will give me all your foreign currency, Comrade Hobson. In return you will be given Russian roubles. If you have any remaining when you leave it will be exchanged back for you. I should warn you that our exchange rate is non-negotiable.'

It took ten minutes to sort out the currency and then hand over his Irish passport and in return he was given a passport-sized card with his photograph on it – he thought better than to ask where they'd got it from.

'We are almost done. You are in the centre of Moscow, Comrade Hobson: it is important to remember that parts of the city are restricted areas. As a general rule I would advise sticking to the area around Gorky Street and Red Square. The Kremlin is a restricted area. The Bolshoi theatre is on the next block: they have an impressive repertoire of ballet and opera. I strongly recommend you go to at least one performance.'

'Thank you – and would it be possible to get a street map of Moscow?'

Grigory shook his head. 'That is not necessary: our concierge desk will give you all the information you need. I am told that you are expecting a meeting, regarding a book you wish to see published?'

'Yes, that's right – I'd been told that I'd meet someone in Moscow but I was rather hoping there'd be a message for me here or something.'

Grigory nodded and gathered up the papers on his desk. 'That is correct, a gentleman will meet you here. In the meantime, you have a few days to look around Moscow. I think you call it sightseeing.'

'And the person who'll be meeting me... how will I know when he's here?'

Grigory paused sorting out the papers and looked carefully at Cooper. 'Don't worry, Comrade Hobson: you'll know.'

–

July was known to be Moscow's warmest month and also its wettest one, which made for a consistently oppressive and muggy atmosphere. People who'd never been in one – that is, virtually the entire population of Moscow – said the city felt like a jungle.

Cooper was singularly ill-equipped for a Moscow July: he had his raincoat with him all the time and was forever taking it on and off and he wore his dark suit as that seemed more appropriate because he saw no men on the streets of Moscow wearing light brown suits like the one he had with him and which was more suited to hot weather. But the dark suit was quite heavy, and he was constantly hot and although he did sometimes remove the jacket that seemed to draw attention, which he wasn't too keen on.

It wasn't that people in Moscow were well dressed. Their clothes were clearly mass-produced and cut from cheaper materials, but there was a conformity about them. And the people seemed so exhausted and so quiet, quite unlike anywhere else in Europe.

Because of the language barrier he did a lot of pointing and people seemed to know he was a foreigner, eyeing him suspiciously, and he got the impression that however friendly he was, however much he smiled, people knew better than to be seen around him.

He made sure to stay in the areas advised by Grigory: up and down Gorky Street and the other shopping areas, though to describe them as such was overstating it. He walked around Red Square countless times and by the river too and enjoyed the ice-cream stands which seemed to be everywhere. He went to the Bolshoi one evening, on Grigory's advice. It was a Soviet version of a well-known Italian opera and although Cooper knew next to nothing about opera, he suspected the original version didn't include a detachment of Red Army troops marching across the stage in step with the orchestra, observed by a kindly looking Lenin peering at them from behind bright white clouds on the painted backdrop.

But if people on the streets appeared suspicious, that was nothing compared to the attitude of his fellow guests at the Hotel Lux.

For a start, all the guests were, as far as he could tell, foreigners. The lobby area and the Filippov cafe were like offshoots of the Tower of Babel. He could only make out a few of the languages: Italian certainly, some Spanish, English, French and a lot of German, along with plenty he didn't recognise.

Guests congregated in small groups comprised of others speaking the same language. They eyed anyone else suspiciously, usually falling silent or lowering their tone when someone came near.

Cooper had trouble thinking of himself as George William Hobson and he was nervous about being drawn into conversation with other guests. He did his best to keep to himself and frequented two other public areas of the Lux other than the Filippov cafe.

There was a library behind the reception area, a somewhat bleak room with high ceilings and a threadbare carpet, warm and stuffy, but a quiet place and the chairs were surprisingly comfortable and one could sit there surrounded by the high bookcases replete with works in different languages and framed portraits of Marx, Lenin and Stalin.

The tables between the chairs were scattered with a selection of newspapers, magazines and pamphlets: some in Russian and others in different European languages.

There were copies of two English newspapers: the *Moscow News*, which was produced in Moscow and was invaluable reading if you wanted to keep up to date with the latest five-year plans or were a bit behind on Stalin's recent speeches – all faithfully reproduced verbatim. And then there was the *Daily Worker*, the newspaper of the British Communist Party: unswervingly loyal to the Soviet Union, a poorly edited study in sycophancy and the most recent copy at least a fortnight out of date. But it did have one or two merits: a summary of sorts of British news and the football results – though, strangely elitist for a communist newspaper, only those from the English First Division.

And then there was the bar, which was as chilly as the library was hot. It was also brightly lit, with customers purchasing a voucher at one counter and then going to the bar to redeem it and collect their drinks before sitting at a wooden bench on one of a number of long tables.

Cooper got in the habit of eating in the cafe at around half past six – a solitary experience at his own table, and then a few minutes in the library, a stroll round the block followed by a drink in the bar.

He'd nurse his large glass of Zhigulevskoye beer, sitting at the end of a table, away from other drinkers and taking in as much as possible. It was as if he was conducting an audition for characters in his novel. There were the noisy Germans, up to a dozen of them, who exchanged news on which of their comrades in Germany had recently been arrested and then speculated on how long Hitler would last and then it would be a matter of time before they became increasingly maudlin – not quite tearful, unlike the Italians at the table in the far corner – and burst into song, usually something funereal.

His plot was progressing well, though there were large gaps: a storyline was emerging about people trying to smuggle valuables out of Moscow and the ideal courier was surely here among the residents of the Lux. Where his diamond thief fitted in, he wasn't sure, and he wasn't sure either what the Russian publisher – should he ever actually meet them – would make of the plot because he had an inkling that the subject matter may not altogether meet with the approval of whoever approved books in the Soviet Union.

There were two groups of English speakers, who sat clustered at either end of a long table. One group was Americans, four or five of them, mostly women, and they hardly exchanged a word – though plenty of glances – with the British group at the other end of the table.

Cooper was intrigued with this group, for obvious reasons. It was usually a slightly larger group than the Americans. There was little notable about them: he could have been sitting near such a group in any pub on any evening in London and not cast them a second glance, but here they took on an air of mystery.

One of them did intrigue him: a tall, thickset man with bushy, almost owl-like eyebrows who sat slightly apart from the rest of the group, as if both part of it and yet separate to it at the same time.

On his third or fourth evening in Moscow, Cooper was five minutes into his stroll when he became aware of someone walking alongside him.

'Do you mind if I join you?'

Cooper looked over and recognised the man from the English group in the bar, the one with the bushy eyebrows, and said of course.

'Harry Moore, but the Russians have already given me a nick-name: Sova – do you know what that means?'

Cooper shook his head and the man pointed to his eyebrows and winked. 'It's Russian for owl!'

They shook hands and Cooper said he was George Hobson.

'I know. From Ireland. Whereabouts?'

'Dublin.'

'A city I know well! And where in Dublin?'

Cooper slowed down and inhaled deeply. 'Rathmines, just south of the city centre.' That was the sum total of his knowledge of where he came from and he was conscious that his accent betrayed not a hint of Irish to it.

'I know Rathmines well! I stayed for a while on Grosvenor Square. And where do you live, George?'

'I beg your pardon?'

'Where do you live in Rathmines?'

'Well, I've not lived there in a while, Harry, and when I did, we were forever moving.'

'So where are you living these days?'

'I was in London for a few years and then Birmingham and recently I've been in Berlin.'

Harry nodded as if to show he understood.

'And I'm guessing by your name and your accent that you'd have gone to the Church of Ireland School on Beech Avenue?'

'Many, many years ago, yes! And may I ask where you're from, Harry?'

'And I bet you know the Lantern public house on the Leinster Road, eh?'

Harry Moore laughed as he asked that, and Cooper joined in and said 'of course' and asked him once more where he was from but, by now, they'd walked round the block and were close to the entrance of the Lux and Moore stopped and was facing him.

'You're not from Rathmines or Dublin for that matter any more than I'm from Bulgaria. There's no Lantern pub on the Leinster Road and the Church of Ireland school isn't on Beech Road, not least because there's no Beech Road! Let's go and have a drink.'

They found a quiet corner of the bar and Harry Moore brought him a large vodka and a glass of Zhigulevskoye and told him that everyone at the Lux had their secrets.

'We all have something to hide – something to be furtive about – otherwise we wouldn't be here, would we? For all you know, I may not be Harry Moore. But the point is, for whatever reason you're here, you have got to come across as more... plausible. I've been watching you, others have too: whoever you are and whatever you do, you've got to be more confident and more convincing. Don't walk around looking so nervous. Whose idea was it to give you an Irish identity?'

Copper didn't reply.

'Don't tell me, in fact, don't tell me anything because the less you know here the less dangerous it is. But I do think they can be terribly amateurish at times, throwing you into the deep end like this.'

Chapter 10

Moscow
July–August 1937

On the evening of his fourth day in Moscow there'd been an odd incident. By then Cooper had come to realise that despite Grigory's instructions not to use the stairs, most people did so because the lifts took so long and frequently took breaks between floors.

He was using the stairs to get to his floor when he heard a 'psst' and turned round to see a slim, short man with thick black hair standing in the doorway to the first floor.

'French?' Cooper explained he wasn't French, but spoke the language. The man did too.

'Can you help me? It's a misunderstanding and not a big problem but, to be honest, I could do without even a small problem. Can you go and get the key for your room from your floor lady, open the door and then go back and distract her so I can get into your room? I'll explain.'

Before he had an opportunity to ask any questions Cooper found himself pushed through the door to the second floor and once he had the key and unlocked his door he went back to the floor lady and made a fuss about a new towel and some soap, too, and when he returned to the room the man was sitting on his bed.

He got up and introduced himself. His name was Amadeo Moretti from Turin and a senior member of the Italian Communist Party. And he was in trouble.

'We have a saying in Italy that every member of the communist party is his or her own faction and as a result we squabble all the time and of course Mussolini is our enemy, so leading members like me are here in Moscow – and the squabbling continues: we're like children!

'The problem is that I come from a family that has nobility in it and therefore some of my compatriots here distrust me. Tonight, there's been an argument: they are accusing me of being a fascist agent and a Trotskyite and an embezzler and anything else they can think of. But tomorrow Togliatti arrives in Moscow. He's the party secretary and he's aware of my loyalty. When he arrives, it'll be fine... but until then, I've no idea what could happen. So if I could sleep on the floor and maybe borrow a blanket and one pillow, I'll be eternally grateful!'

He and Amadeo Moretti talked into the early hours. The man certainly had an aristocratic bearing, but he was also by far the most likeable person Cooper had come across in Moscow. He felt a real affinity to him and liked the fact that the Italian didn't pry: he let Cooper tell him as much as he wanted to – which wasn't an awful lot.

He wasn't sure what to say.

–

When he came down to breakfast the following morning Eduard was at his table, already halfway through his meal.

'How are you enjoying Moscow?' Eduard was lighting a cigarette as he spoke, in English, the first time Cooper had heard him speak it.

'It's certainly different: very hot and muggy. And it seems that there are only certain areas I'm allowed in, it makes strolling around rather difficult.'

'Is there somewhere in particular you'd like to visit? I can arrange it.'

'Not really, it's just that I don't know my way around, if you get my meaning. I did ask Grigory for a map but...'

Eduard waved his hand as if to indicate he should forget about a map: he wasn't here to talk about tourism. 'I promised to help you find a publisher. I decided it would be rude not to make the introduction in person, hence my presence in Moscow. This morning we'll go to meet a publisher who's interested to meet you. Finish your breakfast first.'

–

Cooper was unsure of where he was being driven to. They seemed to cross the river twice and the building they stopped at seemed to be somewhere off Lenninskij Prospekt. The publisher's office was in an enormous building that looked as if it had seen much better days, which he was coming to realise was a description that could be applied to much of what he'd seen of Moscow. The exterior and the common areas inside were dirty and such paint as had been applied – many years before, evidently – was peeling.

Cooper followed Eduard up endless flights of stairs and the two of them stood together on a gloomy landing, pausing to catch their breath.

'In here.' Eduard paused and pointed to a door a few yards ahead of them. 'You'll be introduced as Charles Cooper, by the way.'

Cooper followed Eduard through one door, down a corridor and into a reception area, which in contrast to the rest of the building was very pleasant: bright and airy with paintings of mountains on the walls next to ones of Stalin and Lenin and boxes of books stacked on the floor. A young man – early thirties, possibly – was waiting for them, greeting them with a broad smile and enthusiastic handshakes and a deferential nod to Eduard, who he gave every impression of not having met before.

He took them into an office swathed in sunlight, slightly too warm, and as a consequence Cooper was particularly uncomfortable, his clothes itchy and clammy, not helped by the plastic chair.

The meeting was conducted in English. Eduard explained how he'd had the good fortune to meet Mr Cooper in Berlin

– 'quite by chance, you understand' – and they'd discussed literature among many other matters and he found Mr Cooper to be an intelligent man with many interests, so imagine his delight when he discovered Mr Cooper was writing a novel and given how sympathetic Mr Cooper was to the ideals of the Soviet Union he'd undertaken to do what he could to help him, so he'd arranged his visit to Moscow and here they were!

Cooper nodded at what he took to be the right points, though his sympathy for the ideals of the Soviet Union was news to him.

The young man looked impressed and said his name was Misha Mikhailovich Abramov, at which point he stood up once more to shake hands again and Cooper realised that Misha was quite nervous, glancing anxiously at Eduard, giving the impression he didn't want to say the wrong thing.

'I am an editor here at Goslitizdat, or the State Publishing House of Fiction, as it is also known. We specialise in publishing fiction as is apparent from our name, but we also look to publish works of fiction by foreign writers. We are always on the lookout for new writers – unpublished elsewhere – and recently we have decided to explore the possibility of a list by foreign writers being published first in Russian, as opposed to being published in their own language first and then in translation by us. We also work with some foreign publishers and look to publish simultaneously in Russian and in the language of the author. In fact, we do have an informal partnership with a London publishing house. I hope this all makes sense.'

Cooper replied that it did, though he wasn't too sure.

'Perhaps you would be so good as to tell me about your novel?'

Cooper started to describe his novel, though he soon recognised he was making something of a hash of it. He was, in his defence, dreadfully uncomfortable: he was far too hot, sweat was flowing freely under his clothes and from his brow and he was desperate to remove his jacket and his tie too, but from what he'd seen this was not the done thing. He spoke about his novel, how it was planned to be read at different levels, as a crime novel following a diamond thief around Europe but also using her journeys as a way of describing – commenting on, if you like – the political situation on the Continent as she found it. He spotted Misha's eyebrows rise at this point, as if to indicate he was interested, so Cooper warmed to his theme of politics and described in some details the unpleasantness of what he'd encountered in Nazi Germany, hoping that at the very least he'd be on safe ground there. He realised he'd left out his own role in this, the narrator, the *flâneur*. He'd keep that up his sleeve, as he would her visit to Moscow.

'And this Louise, I think you called her, the diamond thief... what is her role in Nazi Germany? I'm a bit unclear.'

'I see her as an observer, someone used to working in the shadows, if you like, particularly alert as to what is going on around her and she is appalled at what she sees and is—'

'She's an anti-fascist?'

'Absolutely, Eduard, yes.'

'So, the anti-fascist heroine of your novel is a thief, is she?' Eduard sounded put-out.

'I do see what you mean, but in English folklore we have a very popular character called Robin Hood who is said to have existed some five hundred years ago and he robbed from the rich to help the poor. I would see Louise as very much in this mould and—'

'You're writing a children's book, then?'

'No, not at all.'

An awkward silence fell over the room and Misha lit a cigarette and removed his jacket and loosened his tie and Cooper did likewise, at last feeling more comfortable. He explained how the novel was still in its very early stages and he was sorry if his description of it was not as clear as he'd have liked and Misha said, no... not at all, it was actually very interesting indeed and he waved his hand expansively, his cigarette moving like a conductor's baton and a trail of smoke tracing its path.

'I would agree with you that your novel is lacking in structure and is still clearly what one would describe as being in its very early stages, but that is understood. I am suspicious of any author who presents the idea for a book as if it is the finished article. A book needs to evolve, characters need to come to life as it is written and as they do so, take the story in different directions in accordance with their own characteristics. But I like the ambition of your novel, the scale of it. Do you follow me?'

'I hope so, it's terribly nice of you to say so.'

'You know, it reminds me in many ways of some of the great Russian novels: the fact that it is rooted in realism and doesn't avoid or skirt round important political and social issues and also, as I said, the planned scale of the novel: it almost has the feel of a saga. I'm thinking of Tolstoy and Pushkin and... How old are you, Mr Cooper?'

'Twenty-five.'

'Dostoevsky had written two novels by the time he was twenty-six. In some cultures, your youth would be seen as a disadvantage, but here... not at all.'

They talked for another hour, during which time a bottle of vodka was brought in and this was used for various toasts, ranging from literature in general to Cooper's own book and to peace in Europe and the defeat of fascism and then Eduard added in a toast to socialism and this being the only way of defeating fascism and bringing about peace and by now Cooper had drunk half a dozen glasses of vodka and, as small as they were, he was thinking that it was not such a foul drink after all and he found himself surprisingly emotional and continued Eduard's theme by promising that his novel would certainly promote that theme.

Eduard announced that the meeting was perhaps nearing its end.

'You have some concluding remarks, I believe, Misha Mikhailovich?'

'Yes, yes, of course...' Misha looked a bit flustered, as if trying to remember his line, and seemed to be searching for some paperwork on his desk. 'We at Goslitizdat would like to work with you, Mr Cooper. We realise your novel is still at a very early stage, but we think the concept has undoubted promise. We believe it would be a sign of goodwill on both our part and yours if you were to sign this document – it simply states that we now have a relationship and we have the first option on your novel.'

Misha held up a document and passed it to Cooper, who leafed through its eight pages, all but two of which were in Russian. For something which apparently simply stated that Goslitizdat had an option on his novel it appeared quite extensive. The Russian pages in particular were densely typed.

'The English section will explain what the Russian says: simply that you will produce a novel and share it with us through our English partners, and if it helps, I think this is their kind of book, in any case. Their details are on page four, I believe.'

Cooper turned to page four, where the name and address of the publisher were underlined:

Francis Randall

Chairman

Francis Randall Books

Store Street

London WC1

'Do you know of them?'

'Not off the top of my head, no… one doesn't really pay much attention to the name of a publisher, does one?' Cooper read through the English text. 'And there's a reference here to an advance?'

Misha glanced over to Eduard who waved his hand as if to indicate this was a trifling matter. 'It's simply a gesture on our part to show our intent and also to acknowledge that authors do need financial support while they are writing a book. Once you sign the document we will transfer that money to your bank account in London, which I believe is at Martins Bank Limited?'

Cooper was about to ask how he knew who he banked with but worried that could sound ungrateful so he said, 'thank you very much' and asked how much money they were talking about?

Misha shrugged. 'The sum we would advance to you is fifty pounds: I know that is not a lot but—'

'It's an awful lot considering I've not started the book yet.'

Eduard stood up at that point and handed a pen to Cooper.

'Sign here – and write your full name and date of birth and today's date underneath your signature and then sign the bottom of each page.'

Cooper hesitated. 'You want me to sign pages in a language I don't understand?'

'I think Misha Mikhailovich has explained matters most clearly: please sign now.'

–

It would be an exaggeration to say that Charles Cooper immediately regretted signing the document, though it would be fair to say he had his doubts about it. He'd be the first to admit that he knew little about the business of publishing, other than it was not easy for a first-time writer to get published, especially one who had not even written the book yet.

And on top of that, this was a Moscow publishing house being surprisingly generous with their money – to the extent that they were able and willing to advance a not inconsiderable sum equivalent, more or less, to six months of his previous salary.

And then there was the whole matter of how they knew his bank account details.

But as the evening wore on Cooper decided this was all just another example of his excessive caution. He knew he needed to relax more, to take advantage of good fortune that came his way, as it had with his inheritance.

He was a lucky man and he really ought not to question it.

But he woke up the following morning with an appalling hangover: the previous night Eduard had taken him to an

Armenian restaurant at which there'd been more toasts and a large platter in the middle of the table with delicious pieces of lamb on top of an enormous pile of rice and they both helped themselves and then wine was served and at some stage he was aware of being helped out of the restaurant and into a car and he couldn't recall how he'd got into his room, yet alone into his bed, but that was the least of his worries as he staggered into the bathroom and threw up.

When Eduard knocked on his door it was just after ten o'clock. He took him down to the cafe where he poured him a very strong coffee and said they had another meeting and Cooper must have groaned because Eduard said not to worry, the person they were meeting was coming to the hotel, but maybe it would be a good idea if he had a bath first and put on some clean clothes.

The meeting took place in an office in the basement of the hotel and as Eduard led him along the sloping corridor, Cooper began to have his doubts again, though they had still not turned into what one would call regrets.

They were to come.

–

The room in the basement had a low ceiling and a notably thick carpet, with three low sofas arranged in a circle in the middle of the room. A tall man in a smarter suit than he was used to seeing in Moscow stood up as he entered and smiled and gestured for him to sit down on one of the sofas. Eduard sat on the other.

As he sat down the light caught the tall man's face and he appeared to have a darker complexion than most people in Moscow did – less pallid, less Slavic, perhaps. He looked at Cooper as if taking everything in and glanced at Eduard and nodded, apparently in approval, and then spoke in good English.

'I'm very pleased to meet you, Mr Charles Cooper.' He made 'Charles Cooper' sound as if it was one word: 'CharlesCooper'.

Cooper nodded.

'Eduard Vladimirovich has told me much about you. And I have read your file, of course.'

He paused and patted a large folder on the sofa next to him and Cooper desperately tried to gather his thoughts because the reference to a file sounded ominous.

'It is in my nature to be very blunt. I like to come straight to the point and avoid any misunderstandings. Yesterday you entered into a relationship with the Soviet Union. From now on, you will be working for me.'

He paused, and Cooper felt the room tighten round him. The man was silent, allowing time for what he'd said to sink in.

'Are you aware of the Comintern, Mr Charles Cooper?'

Cooper shook his head.

'The Comintern is the organisation based here in Moscow that looks after relations with communist parties abroad. Within the Comintern we have a section called the International Liaison Department, more often known by its initials – the OMS. The OMS is one of a small number of state agencies which gathers information – some people would call it intelligence – on behalf of the Soviet Union. We find that by knowing what is happening within foreign governments we can help ensure peace in the world. We need to be constantly vigilant as to what our enemies are up to as they seek to undermine the Soviet Union. I am a senior official in the OMS.'

'And... I don't think I understand where I fit in with all this? I'm a writer, Eduard took me to meet a publisher yesterday and he—'

The man held up his hand for Cooper to stop and opened the file and took out the document Cooper had signed the previous day at the publishers. It was now that Cooper began to have very serious regrets about the whole business.

'I'm sure you'll consider that our methods may seem somewhat underhand, but that is how we operate – it is how all agencies in our field operate, Mr CharlesCooper, even those in your country – especially those in your country. This document means you are now working for the OMS. You will be one of our agents. Should you have any doubts about that, don't forget we have this document – and this morning the sum of fifty English pounds was transferred to your bank account in London.'

Cooper looked round the room: there were just the three of them in there and the other two men looked relaxed and were smiling and Cooper glanced at the door, as if he could just get up and walk out and away from this whole business, but he knew he was trapped. He'd been extraordinarily foolish – allowing himself to be brought to Moscow and then so naively signing up as... well, a Soviet spy.

There was no other way of describing it.

He'd be a traitor.

He decided to react as calmly as possible and go along with this nonsense and as soon as he returned to London he'd report this matter, before any harm could be done.

The man walked over to him along with Eduard and he was aware he'd stood up to join them and the man shook his hand warmly and put an arm round his shoulder and said he wouldn't regret this.

'And allow me to apologise for not having introduced myself, Mr Charles Cooper. My name is Nikolai Vasilyevich Zaslavsky.'

Chapter 11

Moscow
September 1937

Charles Cooper remained in the tiny hiding space in Rita's apartment on Vorovsky Street until six thirty that morning, three hours after the apparent departure of the NKVD. He'd been frozen with fear, terrified it could be a trap: for all he knew, they could be waiting in silence outside the apartment.

He kept glancing at his wristwatch, a battered memory of his father, his initials engraved on the back: CAC. He could imagine his father peering to read the dial. The watch would have been one of the last things he looked at before he was killed in 1917. It was a very tangible connection to him and in the dark, almost airless hiding space he'd wrapped his right hand round his left wrist, clutching the watch. Even in good light it was hard to make out the time: he ought to have replaced the scratched glass years ago, but Cooper couldn't bring himself to do so.

At six thirty, he pushed the panel and the chest of drawers moved just enough to allow him to crawl through the gap into the main room of the tiny apartment. He lay on the floor, breathing hard and stretching his limbs. Because he'd been hunched up for so long, his legs had gone numb, but now he was in agony as their circulation returned. It was a good ten minutes before he felt able to haul himself up.

The apartment had been ransacked: all the drawers were open, along with cupboard doors and their contents spilled out, the bedding dumped on the floor.

The curtains were still drawn and Cooper stood behind them, gingerly opening enough of a gap to look down into Vorovsky Street, first in the direction of the Garden Ring and then towards the Boulevard Ring. But there was no sign of anything unusual on the streets, no police wagons parked or groups of NKVD officers in doorways or city police on the corners.

All he could see was the start of the morning commute to work, tiny figures wrapped against the chill of the early morning, their heads covered, hurrying along the pavement, most of them in the direction of Arbat Square and its many tram stops.

Cooper knew this rush to work would build up over the next hour, reaching its peak around a quarter past seven, which would be the safest time to join the crowds.

He stood in the tiny kitchen area surveying the apartment. The bookcase was still standing but its contents had been swept to the floor, the three volumes of *Das Kapital* had fallen together, neatly laying side by side and in the correct order. Scattered all over the floor and on the table were pamphlets, most in English but a few in Russian, even though Rita couldn't read Cyrillic. By the window was a box full of copies of a pamphlet she'd written and of which she was inordinately proud. She'd made him read 'Socialism and The Class Struggle in the United States of America and Canada' after their first night together, as they lay in bed. It was densely written, long sentences, which should have been paragraphs, a notable lack of editing and a pretentious, far too confident style.

She'd laid next to him as he struggled his way through its badly printed pages on cheap paper. It was like trying to make progress through a clayey ploughed field, the heavy phrases clinging like mud. At certain points she'd become visibly excited, stroking his chest with one hand and pointing to a passage with her red-painted nails.

'Here, read this out loud, Cooper.'

'You mean this?'

'Go on, yes.' Her breathing quickened and her eyes flashed as they had when they'd made love the previous night. Cooper cleared his throat and read out loud.

'By applying a true Marxist–Leninist dialectic approach to analysing the class struggle in the United States and the imminent crisis in capitalism it is possible to anticipate the inevitability of the forthcoming overthrow of the ruling classes and their replacement by the working class led by the Communist Party of the United States and the Communist Party of Canada and the most brightest…'

Cooper paused and cleared his throat once more and Rita looked up at him and asked why he'd stopped.

'There's a double superlative there – "most brightest".'

'So?'

'So, it's not correct: did anyone edit this, Rita?'

'An Austrian did.'

'Well, there we are then. And what's all this about Canada? You barely mention the country yet seem convinced their working classes are about to rise up?'

She made a snorting noise and said he didn't understand and certainly didn't need to sound so cynical and, in any case, the Communist Party of Canada had promised to distribute thousands of copies.

He heard a noise outside the apartment, a door closing and then footsteps, but they were clearly descending the stairs and he relaxed and decided to make a tea, because he was tired and cold and, in the tin, next to the gas ring, with the painting of a tractor on the lid, he found some of the small cakes Rita had baked and he sat at the table, sipping the tea and eating the cakes, thoroughly miserable and absolutely petrified.

–

He'd met Rita Marks a month earlier, in early August in the library of the Lux. It was a pleasant summer's evening, not as clammy as it had been and there'd even been a breeze that day and he was quite relaxed, if not bored, as he read a copy of the *Daily Worker* from the end of July and looked up to notice a woman staring at him, holding a long cigarette in her hand at a downward angle. What he noticed most about her were her bright red varnished nails, which was unusual in Moscow where women – even the western ones like those at the Lux – didn't appear to go in much for cosmetics.

And her looks, he noticed them too. She was older than him: had he been asked to guess there and then he'd have said she was maybe fifteen years older than him, so perhaps forty. Later, she told him she was fifty, which astonished him – she looked so much younger, with the way her black hair fell over her shoulders and her eyes flashed in the most extraordinary manner and her face seemed perfect in every way, her lips painted red, matching the colour of her nails.

She came over and sat next to him and took the *Daily Worker* away from him and asked if that was really the most interesting thing a good-looking young man like him could think of doing and he spluttered something about maybe not and she asked if he was English and he said 'of course' and then added that actually he was Irish.

'So, if you're English or Irish you should have excellent manners? And excellent manners mean a man introduces himself to a lady, do they not?'

Cooper replied that absolutely they do and he was terribly sorry and his name was George Hobson from Dublin in Ireland and she just smiled and said her name was Rita, Rita Marks.

'From New York City. In the United States. Of America.' She held out her hand in an almost regal manner, as if he was expected to kiss it, but he played safe and shook it but she didn't let go, holding his hand as they spoke, her thumb resting on his wrist.

'And what is George Hobson from Dublin in Ireland doing in Moscow, in the Soviet Union?'

He'd laughed and felt relaxed in her presence, reassured by her and so comforted by her warm hand and the flashing eyes and the hint of perfume that he felt like replying that he'd been tricked into coming to Moscow and now – would you believe, because he was finding it hard to – was in the process of becoming a Soviet spy, of all things!

'Oh, you know... looking around, educating oneself.' He shrugged, hoping she'd change the subject but instead she leant closer and he could feel her warmth when she spoke.

'But you must be an important man if you're staying here at the Lux. I would guess you're a guest of the Comintern.'

He blushed again and said he wasn't important in the great scheme of things and then he remembered his manners and asked what brought her to Moscow.

'I am a senior member of the Communist Party of the United States of America and came here with my husband Michael a year ago because we wanted to learn how to progress the cause of socialism in our country, but Michael couldn't take the Russian winter and he missed his mother and he took exception to me having a... relationship with a member of the Central Committee of the Soviet Communist Party. We agreed that Michael didn't have the makings of a true revolutionary, so he's gone back to New York and his mother, and I'm here with my Central Committee member, when he can be bothered to see me. However, he has found a small apartment for me near Arbat Square and I'm moving in there in two days. I write pamphlets aimed at educating the proletariat in the United States, even though they have no idea they're members of the proletariat.'

After that she invited him to invite her into the bar where they both drank Zhigulevskoye and she lectured him – that was the only word for it – on how well the Soviet system worked and the genius of Stalin and how misunderstood he was, certainly elsewhere in Europe, and as for the United States, that was almost a lost cause were it not for its impending crisis of capitalism.

She spoke in her animated New York accent, frequently pausing and looking at him with her eyebrows raised, inviting him to respond, and he'd nod in apparent agreement, hoping she didn't ask him questions because it was all getting a bit above his head. As far as he could tell, capitalism in Britain and indeed in the United States was doing just fine and showing no signs of imminent collapse. But he was in Moscow now and he knew better than to say that and, in any case, he didn't think Rita was the kind of person with whom disagreeing would be a comfortable experience.

When she'd finished her lecture she told him to order them a vodka each and then they'd go upstairs and he'd said nothing, confused as to what she meant.

'Do you want to come upstairs with me?'

'Well, I'm not sure... I mean, yes, of course... but...'

'But what. Do you like women?'

'Of course I do! But—'

'Good. I'm in room 313 on the third floor. Give me ten minutes and come up.'

'But don't I need a *propusk* to get onto your floor? I thought I was only allowed on my floor.'

'Don't worry; the floor lady will let you through.'

—

The night he'd spent with Grace in Interlaken in April had prepared him well. He no longer felt nervous or inexperienced, which was just as well because Rita was an enthusiastic lover, almost aggressive, and she had an energy and an appetite which quite belied her years.

Afterwards they lay in bed and she said she was glad he was an experienced lover because there was really no excuse for inexperience and then she looked at her watch and said it was nearly midnight and this being Moscow it meant that there'd be enough hot water for her bath so he could leave now, and she'd pulled back the covers for him to get out of bed and he asked if they could meet again.

'You English are so formal! We'll see. Aleksei is out of town this week and I move into the apartment later in the week. I'll leave a note for you.'

Three days later there was a note waiting for him in his room. He was to meet her outside Arbatskaya metro station the following afternoon.

She said nothing when they met, just a nod and a quick instruction to follow her but to keep his distance. He followed her onto Vorovsky Street and then to the fifth floor of an apartment block and waited on a landing until she entered the apartment and then re-emerged and signalled he should come in.

She hurriedly undressed and told him to get a move on and they didn't exchange a word until nearly two hours later as they lay breathless in the bed and she told him about the apartment.

'Aleksei is a member of the Central Committee of the Communist Party. Above that is the Politburo and above that is Stalin. The Central Committee is important and has more than one hundred members. Some of his colleagues have been disloyal to Stalin and have paid the price for being enemies of the people, but Aleksei is close to Stalin and is a hard worker and he hardly drinks, which distinguishes him from most of his comrades. He's out of town a lot these days though. That's why he got me this place.'

'And am I safe here?'

'Probably not! But this is the Soviet Union, Cooper; people don't behave in the same way as in your country or the United States. People don't own each other, there's more personal freedom.'

Cooper didn't respond because whenever Rita talked it was with an utter conviction that she was right and that Comrade Stalin was beyond reproach and that in the Soviet Union they'd created a near perfect society. All the rumours of people being arrested were an exaggeration, she insisted. There were some arrests she conceded, but these were of enemies of the people and therefore quite justified.

Cooper was uneasy though about sleeping with the mistress of a member of Central Committee: he reckoned that qualified him as an enemy of the people. But there was something about Rita that made it almost impossible for him to forget about her, which his instinct told him he ought to do.

—

After his recruitment by the OMS – they called it recruitment, Cooper thought of it as his entrapment – he spent most days with Nikolai Vasilyevich.

Compared to Eduard – who he saw occasionally – Nikolai was charming and friendly and did his best to be reassuring. Each day Cooper would be picked up at the Lux and driven in a car with curtained windows to a building around a quarter of an hour's drive away and from the basement garage taken up in a lift to a floor apparently high up in the building and into a room which always had its curtains drawn and there Nikolai Vasilyevich would brief him on how to operate as an OMS agent.

'You will return to London and by all means write your novel; apart from anything else it will explain your travels around Europe. But you are not to mention the Soviet Union in it and try to avoid anything that could be construed as political. Do you understand?'

'But what about Goslitizdat and everything that Misha said about wanting to publish me?'

Nikolai Vasilyevich moved his hand as if swatting away a fly. 'Forget about that, Cooper: the State Publishing House of Fiction has no intention of publishing your novel. Under no circumstances should there be even the slightest trace of a connection with us, do you understand? Write your book, by all means, and try and find a publisher in London, should you wish. But your priority in London is to start a new career. You are to apply for jobs in government departments which are of interest to the Soviet Union, those connected with foreign affairs or defence.

You should also consider the possibility of applying for training as an officer in one of your armed forces.

'But the important thing is not to rush: it takes time to be recruited to the right post and once you're there you need to allow yourself time to become established – and also to be beyond suspicion. We view agents like yourself as long-term prospects: it could be a few months before we start to call on your services.

'We've been thinking of a codename for you: we've decided you'll be Agent Bertie. From now on, we refer to you by that name. Do you like it?'

Actually, Cooper didn't like Bertie one bit: it reminded him of Wodehouse's eponymous character, which he struggled to think of as anything other than stupid. But he knew now that it was best not to dissent.

After that, Nikolai Vasilyevich conducted a series of briefings: a few hours in the morning, a short break for lunch and then another session in the afternoon before he'd be driven back to the Lux on Gorky Street.

Nikolai explained in detail the kind of information they were after. He'd give him lengthy documents and tell him to go through them and write a summary of the salient points and he was to do this in a short space of time and at first Cooper was hopeless, but under Nikolai's guidance soon learnt what kind of information to look for and how to summarise it.

There were sessions on encoding the information and how to leave it at a dead letter box and how to contact the person in London who'd be collecting the information and providing him with instructions.

At least three days were spent on what to do if he came under suspicion or was in danger. Nikolai was surprisingly reassuring.

'If they have evidence against you then they'll arrest you, but that only happens when an agent is careless, and we are training you not to be careless. But if they suspect you, that means that they have general suspicions maybe about your department or about a group of people, but they have no evidence. Are you following me?'

'I hope so.'

'No evidence means no arrest and you must therefore exploit that. If you are ever questioned, you need to act offended – angry, even – that your loyalty is being questioned. That is how an innocent man behaves. We will train you on that, don't worry.'

There were days of interrogations and he learnt how to come over as offended but innocent and how to cope when confronted by seeming contradictions in his story.

He was taken to an area on the outskirts of Moscow and given training on how to ensure he wasn't being followed and to get from A to B in the least suspicious manner.

Then there were sessions on what Nikolai described as perhaps the most important part of information gathering, which was the nurturing of unwitting contacts within an organisation – people who had access to secret information and how to get them to unwittingly share that information with him.

'Find out about their lives: find out what problems they have, what worries them, what makes them happy – anything that can get you closer to them and encourage them to trust you. Maybe do them a favour, tickets for the theatre, money you're happy to lend, an offer to pick up a piece of work for them if they're overwhelmed. Become their friend, and possibly a confidante, and remain a friend, possibly for years before you try and prise intelligence out of them. May I make an observation about you, Bertie?'

'Go ahead.'

'You possess certain innate qualities I consider to be essential in an agent. You're clearly intelligent and intuitive, and while those are essential qualities, they're not unique ones. But what you do have is a certain charm and charisma, I think you're the kind of person who people like and, more to the point, who they don't find threatening. And at the same time, you're somewhat enigmatic: it's hard to know what to make of you, the kind of person who fits more naturally into the background rather than the foreground. You cannot train people to be like that, they're rare and innate qualities. It's what alerted us to you in the first place. My advice is to exploit your charm, Bertie, always be confident in the knowledge that people will be well disposed towards you. Keep that in mind with the sources you cultivate, the ones I was talking about earlier.'

–

Cooper left Rita's apartment on Vorovsky Street at seven fifteen and walked to Arbat Square on the Boulevard Ring. He hoped he'd pass as a local; he was wearing the *ushanka* fur hat and a long overcoat he'd bought the previous week when there was a notable chill in the air and Nikolai told him he could get a special discount at the state store reserved for senior party members and their families.

He adopted the demeanour he'd observed among Moscow's residents: tired and resigned, slightly stooped and in a hurry. At Arbat Square he caught a cream-and-dark-brown-coloured tram and remembered his training:

Never go straight to your destination… travel to a point beyond it and then walk back, perhaps taking a circuitous route.

He took the tram to Red Square and then headed north, pausing outside the Moskva Hotel to ensure he wasn't being followed and onto Mokhovaya Street, past the Lenin library and as far as the United States Embassy, at which point his plans went wrong.

Rita had pleaded with him to go there and get help, but the embassy was closely guarded by Soviet police. There was a checkpoint on the pavement before the entrance and people were being searched. It would be impossible to get into the embassy. He walked past it and down a side street running along it, just in time to see a side gate open and a tall man hurry out. From the way he was dressed, he hoped he was an American diplomat.

He followed him as far as the Pushkin Museum, when the man stopped on the pavement to cross the road and Cooper stood next to him.

'I need your help.'

The man looked surprised but acted calmly, a brief nod and a discreet look around.

'A lady I know – an American lady living here in Moscow – she was arrested last night – well this morning. A few hours ago. She needs your embassy to help her.'

They were crossing the road now and Cooper had to hurry to keep up with the man. When he spoke, he was looking ahead of him.

'Not here, it's dangerous. Go to the embassy.'

'I can't. Look, take this.' With that he slipped Rita's American passport into the man's coat pocket and hurried off.

He felt guilty after that, though he was not sure what else he could have done.

When he returned to the Lux, he had just enough time to get changed before the car came to collect him. It was only when he was putting his jacket back on that he realised the envelope Rita had given him was still in his jacket pocket.

...get the envelope to my folks in New York City, though they probably won't want to know about me either.

He opened the envelope and tore its contents into tiny shreds, feeling even more guilty but he knew he had to be ruthless. If he was caught with it, he'd be in trouble. He promised himself that he'd do something to help her when he was back in London.

That assuaged his guilt, but not very much.

–

At the end of September Nikolai took him to a dacha outside Moscow for the weekend and it was clear that his training was coming to an end.

It was a peaceful, bucolic setting and there were just the two of them there, apart from a housekeeper and two guards.

For two days, the Russian said little as they walked along the lanes and he explained the names of the different trees and plants and they ate well and Nikolai told him how impressed he was with him because he recognised that there had been some subterfuge involved in his recruitment but his attitude had been commendably positive.

'We have another agent in London, someone in a similar position to you, though he has been with us longer. We cannot tell you much about him, other than that he is already very highly placed and we believe he is on course to go to the top of his organisation. In time your role will be to support him.

'At some point in the future you will be approached by our main contact in London. You will know it is them because they will approach you and ask where is the best place in London to see a collection of plants, and you are to reply that it is Kew Gardens and then they will ask which is the best entrance to use and you say the Lion Gate and then they will thank you. The next day you should enter Kew Gardens through the Lion Gate at the same time of the day as when this person approached you on. They will find you there, do you follow me?'

Cooper said he did and thought it was all rather ironic because he'd always intended to visit Kew Gardens but had never got round to it and now here was the opportunity, though not in the circumstances he'd envisaged.

At dinner that evening Nikolai told him they'd be returning to Moscow the following day and the day after that he'd begin his journey back to Berlin. He gave him his instructions for the journey and how to retrieve his passport in Berlin.

'May I mention something to you, please?'

The Russian stared hard at him, his eyes narrowing. 'I know what it is, Bertie, and I advise you not to: no good will come of it. It is about the American woman, is it not?'

'How did you know?'

Nikolai Vasilyevich laughed. 'Do you think we're fools? Of course we knew, but we decided it would be a good way to see how you behaved when acting in a clandestine manner, visiting her apartment and so forth. You were good, we were pleased: you took precautions and I have to admit that on one or two occasions we almost lost track of you.'

'Is that why she was arrested, because of me?'

'The NKVD arrested her because her lover, Aleksei Matveyevich, was arrested the night before she was and has been declared an enemy of the people, assuming he is still alive. If not, he's a former enemy of the people.'

'And Rita, what can I do to help her?'

'There's nothing whatsoever you can do to help Comrade Rita Marks. Forget about her. Let her fate be a warning of the consequences for those who fall out of favour with the Soviet Union, no matter how loyal and obedient they may have been. It is worth keeping that in mind, Bertie.'

Chapter 12

Cooper left Moscow on a bitterly cold morning, the first Monday in October.

His last night at the Lux Hotel had been a sleepless one. He'd convinced himself that raising Rita's fate with Nikolai had been a fatal error and he'd never leave the Soviet Union. He'd shown he wasn't to be trusted, that he too was an enemy of the people: unreliable and therefore disposable. He thought of the knock-on effect of one arrest: Rita's lover from the Central Committee was deemed a traitor, therefore Rita was too through her association with him and – inevitably, it seemed – he too through his links with Rita.

Cooper couldn't deny he was unreliable, as far as the Soviet Union was concerned: once back in London he had no intention whatsoever of spying for them or indeed for anyone else.

If he ever got back to London, that was – which, in the sleepless hours in the Lux Hotel, felt quite unlikely.

It would be so easy to make him disappear. There was no record of a Charles Christopher Cooper ever having been in the Soviet Union or indeed anywhere near it. His British passport was, as far as he knew, somewhere in Berlin.

When he nervously went down to the hotel lobby at six o'clock a guard from the dacha was waiting and took his case and when he got to the car Nikolai was sitting there and asked if he was all right.

'Fine, thank you, why do you ask?'

'You look pale, as if you've not slept all night.'

'I never sleep well before a journey.'

'Don't worry, Bertie, you'll have plenty of time to sleep on the train. Let me go through the details.'

–

When the car pulled up outside Belorussky station on Tverskaya Zastava Square Nikolai said he wouldn't come into the station because he always got tearful at railway stations and he laughed and Cooper now began to relax.

A man built like a boxer carried his case and Cooper followed him through the crowded station and towards the platform where the six-thirty train for Minsk was waiting impatiently, already noisy with bursts of white steam coming from the front and rolling across the carriages towards the concourse.

His escort pushed through the ticket barrier and took him as far as a carriage at the front, at which point he handed him his case and gestured to the open door. He was travelling in a 'special' carriage reserved for Party officials and those on state business, which of course wasn't to be confused with first class, because the Soviet Union no longer had a class system.

–

The train pulled out of Belorussky at a quarter to seven and crossed the Dnieper River and pulled into Smolensk station just after one o'clock. Six and a half hours later they arrived at Vilenski vakzal station in Minsk.

'You'll stay overnight at the Livadney Hotel on Koydanovskaya Street, which is close to the station. I've written it all here on this piece of paper: if you show this to someone, they'll point you in the right direction. Your room there is reserved and paid for. The train will leave Minsk at five tomorrow morning.'

He re-joined the train half an hour before its departure and dozed for much of that morning. They arrived at Tsentralny station in Brest and soon after that crossed the Bug River, where the train pulled to a noisy halt. The next station was Terespol, Poland.

The Polish officials – there were three of them, all in different uniforms – were polite but clearly in a hurry and passed the Irish Free State passport among themselves and seemed relieved when he asked in German if everything was in order and one of them replied that it was and stamped his passport.

–

The Deutsche Reichsbahn train left Warszawa Główna at eight thirty that Tuesday evening.

The border crossing at Frankfurt an der Oder was surprisingly straightforward; the German officials seemed more preoccupied with checking the papers of the Polish passengers.

First light had broken as the train entered Berlin and with it Cooper felt once again the sense of fear he associated with the German capital, the feeling that he must be under suspicion, the all-pervasive menace in the air.

At the platform at Zoologischer Garten station he paused, recalling the instructions Nikolai had given him: out of the station and across Kant Strasse, down Ranke Strasse and then Achenbach Strasse and into a cafe, up the flight of stairs at the back and Eduard was waiting there, framed in the doorway, glancing at his watch as if to indicate he was late and he briefly nodded by way of a greeting and said 'Bertie'.

–

There was no small talk from Eduard. Instead, he pointed to one of the two chairs in the sparsely furnished room and when they'd sat down, he said he didn't have long.

'You need to leave Berlin as soon as possible. Ernst and Ida Maurer were arrested at the weekend – we only found out yesterday and had we known earlier, you wouldn't have come on this route. Your British passport is here.'

132

He passed a brown envelope to Cooper. Inside it was his British passport and twenty-five pounds and around ten pounds' worth of Reichsmarks.

'That will be more than sufficient money to get you back to England and to cover the money you were required to exchange in Moscow. Give me the Irish passport.'

Eduard checked it and slipped it into his jacket pocket and then stood up and walked over to the window, making sure the blinds were drawn properly.

'It is fortunate they weren't looking for a George William Hobson, but even so you must act as if you're in danger, who knows what the Maurers will reveal in their interrogation. You'll travel to Hamburg this morning and then to Rotterdam and from there to London.'

Cooper noticed that Eduard was no longer as composed and in control as before. He seemed tense and as he lit a cigarette his hands weren't quite trembling but they certainly weren't steady. He ran his hand through his hair and glared at Cooper, waiting for an answer.

'You follow me?'

'I think so, I—'

'Think so? That's not good enough, Bertie. In your new life in the service of the Soviet Union you need to be more decisive: never hesitate. I will explain once more. Walk to Lehrter station through the Tiergarten. Take the first train to Hamburg, the journey takes around three hours. When you arrive in Hamburg, do not leave the station: take the next train from there to Rotterdam. Are you still with me?'

Eduard sounded impatient and exasperated, drumming his fingers on the table and lighting another cigarette even though the previous one was still lit.

'Stay overnight in Rotterdam – find a hotel near the station – and then take the train to the Hook of Holland and from there the steam ship to Harwich, if that is how you pronounce it. From there I understand there is a regular train service to London.'

Eduard stood up. Their meeting was clearly over.

'It is now seven thirty. Try and get on a train as soon as you can, the earlier ones are more crowded, more people for them to check.'

He held the door open for Cooper and when the Englishman was on the tiny landing placed a hand on his shoulder.

'It is most probable we shall never meet again. I wish you luck in your new life: notwithstanding the circumstances of your joining us, be assured that you are serving a fine cause. My advice to you is never to forget that and not to allow any occasional fears or doubts prevent you fulfilling your mission. To even contemplate that is a foolish indulgence: never forget, the arm of the Soviet Union is long and penetrating. Agents who think they can fade away and be forgotten about never get away with it. If you hide, you will always be found. You need to go now.'

Chapter 13

London
February 1938

Long before he arrived back in London in the October, Charles Cooper had devised a plan.

An early version of it had begun to be formed almost as soon as Nikolai Vasilyevich informed him back in August that he was now an agent for the OMS, the intelligence branch of the Comintern, and Cooper realised immediately that he'd been tricked into becoming a Soviet spy and therefore a traitor and as far as he was concerned that was ridiculous, totally out of the question. At the same time, he realised he needed to act normally, to be as agreeable and co-operative as possible while in Moscow.

He thought about what to do in some detail on the long journey back from the Soviet Union. His original plan – the one devised as he lay awake on the humid summer nights in his room at the Lux Hotel – was that as soon as he arrived back in London he'd go to the police and inform them that he'd been tricked into going to Moscow where he'd been approached to be a Soviet spy, which, of course, he had no intention whatsoever of doing and please could he speak with someone in authority because he was sure they'd be interested in what he could tell them and they'd be assured of his fullest co-operation. He'd admit to naïveté, foolishness perhaps, but certainly nothing more than that.

But by the time it came to leave Moscow, Cooper realised how much he'd changed.

He was less amenable now, more calculating and whereas previously he could be accused of being something of a scatter-brain, now he was much clearer in his thinking. He'd developed an ability to prioritise matters and his priority now was to avoid trouble at all costs. And so somewhere on the long train journey home it began to occur to him that his original plan wasn't nearly as clever as he'd first thought. There was still no question of course that he had any intention of working for the Soviet Union, but turning up at a police station and announcing he was a would-be Soviet spy now felt flawed. He had no evidence to present in support of his claim, just a few names that were most probably false ones and a meeting at a publisher that may or may not exist and training undertaken in a building for which he had no idea of the address.

Of course, he could mention the other agent Nikolai had told him about – the one already highly placed in London and how his role was to support him, and then there was his main contact in London, who'd approach him and ask about the best place to see plants and how they'd end up in Kew Gardens.

But he had no names, not even a description, it all sounded so vague and the more he thought about it the more he doubted they'd take it seriously. In fact, they were most likely to treat him as deranged or charge him with wasting police time and if they did choose to believe him then he'd probably be marked down as a trouble-maker, a communist agitator.

He'd be put on one of those lists meaning it would be hard for him to get a job. Life would be difficult, even more so than it now appeared it was going to be.

It was in Rotterdam that he refined his plan. He stayed overnight at the Leygraaff hotel on Westplein, another sleepless night in another overheated hotel room, and it was there that he decided on a different course of action. He still had no intention whatsoever of working for the Soviets but he concluded that in effect turning himself in to the British authorities was a bad idea.

This new plan, he concluded, was a good example of the intelligence and intuition of which Nikolai spoke.

Cooper was nine when his mother married Thomas Shaw.

He'd never been close to his step-father and their relationship could best be described as distant and formal. He wasn't an unpleasant man – just someone who'd never come to terms with living in the same house as a child. But the marriage did at least mean that he and his mother no longer lived on the edge of poverty and the move to London ensured they lived in a nicer house and he went to a good school.

When he was fourteen his mother informed him that had it not been for her husband's kindness and generosity, this would have been the age when he would have had to leave school and get a job as she wouldn't have been able to afford to keep him on.

You ought to show more appreciation to your step-father, she informed him. And one way of showing this was to take on his surname – in fact, she'd been to see a solicitor and all the paperwork was in place.

Cooper had been stunned at this announcement: it had always been understood that he would retain his father's surname and changing his name seemed to be a betrayal of his father, a fallen hero from the Great War.

She presented him with the papers, but thanks to a clerical error his given names had been transposed: Charles Christopher Cooper became Christopher Charles Shaw. And then the school informed his mother that she should have informed them well before the start of the academic year of the change of name, which meant that for the rest of that school year – and indeed for the remainder of his school career – he remained Charles Cooper.

And he remained Charles Cooper while he was at university and thereafter. He kept all the paperwork for Christopher Charles Shaw, though.

You never know, he'd tell himself, one day it may come in handy.

He stayed for his first week back in London at a hotel on Sussex Gardens, close to Paddington station. The day after his return he began to put his plan into action. Mr Arthurs at *Designs and Drawings* had kindly let him store his possessions – a couple of cases and three or four boxes – in the basement of the magazine offices near Fenchurch Street station and the first item he retrieved was his Christopher Charles Shaw paperwork.

And thus, it was a Christopher Shaw – he decided to drop the Charles to help further protect his anonymity – who rented a small but very pleasant flat on the top floor of a Georgian house on Dorset Square, which was off Gloucester Place and close to Regent's Park and well placed for both Marylebone and Baker Street stations.

He moved in at the start of the third week of October and took stock of his situation.

He visited his bank to assess his financial situation. He'd inherited £357 in October 1936 and the balance when he began his trip to Europe in February was £369. He'd spent the best part of £70 on his travels and had calculated he'd have a balance of around £299. But it was higher: he'd received seven separate payments of amounts from £5 to £12, all from different bank accounts, and the payments made at different dates over a six-week period starting in late July.

They totalled £50.

It was the money from the Russians.

On paper the payments didn't look suspicious, but he had no doubt that if Nikolai wanted to use these deposits to threaten him, he'd not hesitate in doing so.

He'd been tricked into going to Moscow and with these payments, he was trapped.

He withdrew one hundred and seventy-five of this in cash and used it – along with what remained of the twenty-five pounds Eduard had given him in Berlin – to open an account in the name of Christopher Shaw at a branch of Barclays Bank in Baker Street.

The paperwork his mother had so helpfully organised more than ten years before proved to be more than satisfactory.

He registered at a local doctor's surgery and at a library – all in the name of Christopher Shaw – and applied for a passport in that name.

By the end of October, he was living as Christopher Shaw. Charles Cooper still existed, though very much in the background. The important thing was he no longer needed to worry about being a Soviet spy because to all intents and purposes, there was no trace of Charles Cooper. He tried to avoid being complacent and he was mindful of Eduard's warning when they parted in Berlin: 'the arm of the Soviet Union is long and penetrating. Agents who think they can fade away and be forgotten about never get away with it. If you hide, you will always be found.'

But that applied to people who were careless, people who lacked his intelligence and intuition. It wouldn't apply to someone as clever as him, who'd been fortunate to have such a good new identity so readily available.

He'd just need to be careful for a few months, during which time the Soviets would probably either forget about him or give up on him.

Who knows, he thought on one of his pleasant strolls through Regent's Park, in a year or two it may even be safe enough for Charles Cooper to reappear!

–

By the February of 1938 Cooper – now Christopher Shaw – was quite settled.

He'd visited his mother a few weeks after his return and made an effort to be as agreeable as possible. Indeed, he made a point of visiting her and his step-father in Belsize Park every two or three weeks. He indulged her need for attention and played the dutiful son, even taking her out for lunch a few times, painful occasions as she barked at waiters and complained about the food and drank a fraction too much.

But Marjorie Shaw was clearly delighted with what she took to be her son's evident contrition and his improved behaviour. He told her he was having some trouble with Mrs Carpenter, his previous landlady. There'd been a petty dispute over how much notice he'd been obliged to give, so much so that she'd retained solicitors and was threatening to sue him and so if anyone ever approached her enquiring after him, she should say that as far as she was aware her son had travelled to the Continent the previous year and was still there.

'But you're here?'

'Obviously I'm here, Mother...' Cooper paused, trying hard not to sound too exasperated. 'The point is, I really do not want to become involved in a legal dispute so I'd be grateful if you could tell anyone who enquires about me that I'm abroad. Perhaps take their details and promise to pass them on in the event of you hearing from me. Perhaps hint at an estrangement.'

She said she understood and had never liked the sound of his landlady and why on earth had he chosen to live south of the river: hadn't she said it was bound to end in tears?

With that sorted and Charles Cooper consigned to oblivion for the time being, there remained the matter of what to do with his life.

He did, of course, have a book to write, but he was finding it hard to apply himself to that. His problem was that he had little motivation: his funds were sufficient to allow him to live comfortably for some while without needing to work and this resulted in a sense of inertia. He had days when his writing went quite well – there was one day in January when to the accompaniment of near torrential rain beating rhythmically on the window over his desk overlooking Dorset Square, he wrote one thousand words and felt Louise really come to life, as if she was lounging on the sofa behind him, dictating her dialogue.

There were other periods – often three or four days at a time – when he was overcome by a mixture of depression and fear. Fear that he'd either be unmasked as a Soviet spy – maybe by someone who'd seen him in Moscow – or found by the Soviets themselves. And this would throw him into a depression, in which he struggled to get out of bed and when he did, he kept the curtains of his apartment drawn and he didn't leave his home, convinced that as long as he remained there, he was safe, after a fashion.

But then he'd snap out of it, telling himself that he was allowing his imagination to run away with itself and he really needed to be more disciplined. As long as he was careful, he'd be fine. He enjoyed being a *flâneur* in his own city, walking into the West End or taking the bus to different destinations and wondering around for hours on end – his pace leisurely, enabling him to take in all around him. He persuaded himself it was all material for the book and certainly he'd have some chapters set in London, though in truth he wasn't too sure how they'd fit in with the plot. Louise was the kind of person who'd stand out in London, a glamorous and colourful character in the dull monochrome of the city.

The most obvious course the story should take was to set much of it in the Soviet Union: his experiences there were far more dramatic than anywhere else, including Nazi Germany.

But that presented a number of flaws. The heart of the Soviet Union was not a very fertile setting for a foreign jewel thief; in Moscow she'd be quite the most conspicuous person in the city. One solution was to change the subject matter of the book altogether: instead of it being about a diamond thief, it could be a thinly fictionalised version of what he'd seen in Moscow, the terror of the purge, the story of Rita, suitably disguised. Maybe a young Englishman visiting the city who becomes embroiled in espionage... Eduard and Nikolai would make perfect characters... and the Maurers in Moscow.

By February he was no nearer deciding what the book was about and recognised that he was actually quite bored. There was a limit as to how many days he could spend walking the streets of London.

And then, he took a wrong turn.

—

It was a Tuesday afternoon and he'd decided that London Bridge and the area north of it in the City of London would be an interesting setting for a chapter, with its narrow streets and colourful names like Threadneedle, Leadenhall, Minories, Mincing Lane.

But when he emerged from Liverpool Street station a thick smog had descended on the city and by the time he was halfway down Bishopsgate it was as if he was battling through a heavy snowstorm. Visibility was dropping by the minute and he was having trouble seeing more than a few yards in front of him and the acidic air made it hard to breathe.

He decided to turn round and head back to Liverpool Street station. When he arrived home, he'd write up that experience. The smog would be the perfect backdrop for a mysterious encounter.

But he was completely disorientated and when he turned a corner spotted the familiar red and blue of the London Underground roundel and the welcome sight of Aldgate underground station.

Standing on a corner were a man and a woman, shoulder to shoulder against the elements, one holding copies of the *Daily Worker* and the other a stack of leaflets. In front of them was a large placard: *Learn the TRUTH about the Soviet Union!*

Cooper paused and smiled. He doubted this pair knew the truth about the Soviet Union but he wasn't minded to discuss it with them and turned to enter Aldgate station, but they'd spotted his smile and obviously taken it as a sign of approval because when the woman spoke it was in a friendly voice.

'Are you interested in the Soviet Union?'

'I'm interested in world politics in general,' he replied.

'That is encouraging to hear,' she replied. She was well spoken and although she looked exhausted, when she smiled her face lit up. 'We simply want people to know the truth about the Soviet Union, not the lies the capitalist press repeat about it, day in day out.'

Cooper paused, unsure how to reply. When he was to look back on this encounter – months later – he realised at this point he ought to have walked away and continued his journey. He ought to have remembered that his priority was to avoid trouble at all costs. But for some reason he hesitated and wondered whether he should tell them about Rita and how she was as unswerving as them – perhaps more so – in her loyalty to Stalin, yet had been arrested in the early hours of a Moscow morning and he doubted she was still alive? Should he recount how he'd hidden in a cubby hole for hours as the secret police searched her apartment?

'Do you believe all the nonsense they write about the Soviet Union and the exemplary leadership of Comrade Stalin?' The woman pushed a leaflet into his hand.

'On Thursday night there's a meeting at The Golden Heart, it's around the corner from here. There'll be a speaker who's actually been to the Soviet Union and he'll be telling the truth about it. All the details are here.'

Cooper took the leaflet and found himself nodding and when the woman asked if he would come along, he found himself replying that he certainly hoped so, though he had no intention of doing so.

But on the journey home he got thinking. It could be interesting. He doubted he'd agree with very much if anything of what he heard, but he was bored and it would be an opportunity to do something.

And after all, no harm could come of it.

–

The meeting was a crowded and noisy affair in a large room at the top of the pub. Behind a trestle table on a slightly raised dais was a large banner for the Communist Party of Great Britain, Whitechapel Branch, slightly faded red with a large hammer and sickle in yellow.

The meeting was chaired by a man with a monotonous voice of which he was clearly very fond. He went through some party business and appealed for funds and for people to help sell the *Daily Worker* and Cooper stood against the back wall and noticed the pretty girl he'd encountered outside Aldgate a few days before and she raised her eyebrows in pleasant surprise when she noticed him and smiled and then it was time for the main speaker.

He was introduced as Larry and Cooper didn't catch the surname. Larry had a cockney accent which occasionally slipped – more so the longer he spoke – to reveal a middle-class voice, even one which could be described at times as posh.

Larry, it turned out, had last been in the Soviet Union in 1934 but that didn't stop him delivering the party line with the fervour of a street preacher: the lies being told about the country and especially about Comrade Stalin were those one would expect the capitalist system wished us to believe.

A good deal of the speech was then devoted to some of those achievements, which mostly comprised reading out long lists of industrial and agricultural targets being met at an improbable pace. He talked at length about a steam turbine plant he'd visited where he'd never seen people so happy and hard-working.

There was polite applause at the end, such enthusiasm as there was probably due more to relief that the lecture had come to an end. The chairman did invite questions and Cooper tentatively raised his hand because he wanted to know what Larry had to say about the news of all these arrests in the Soviet Union and he wondered whether he dared follow that up by talking about his own experiences, but the chance never came because the only two questions were about the achievements of Stalin and why Trotsky was a class enemy.

Cooper was relieved to leave the turgid atmosphere of The Golden Heart. It was not yet nine o'clock and he headed back to the station and halfway down Commercial Street he passed The Ten Bells pub and decided to go in for a drink.

The place was gloomy with dark wooden furniture and quite busy, though the noise was broken up by the layout of the pub – lots of small areas and snugs across its three floors. There was a small bar at the rear of the second floor and Cooper settled down with a half pint of bitter, watching the clientele and wondering if any of the older ones – those in their sixties and older – would have any memories of the murders and maybe in time he could seek to interview them.

At first, he didn't notice someone join him at his table. When he looked up it was the woman from Aldgate, the one he'd seen at the meeting. She lit a cigarette and asked him if he wanted one and then asked what he thought of the meeting.

'It was certainly long!'

'You can say that again! I thought you were being polite when we gave you the leaflet, I didn't expect you to come along.'

'You persuaded me.'

'Do you know much about the Soviet Union?'

He said a little – he read about it – and she introduced herself as Pamela and asked how come he was so well informed and Cooper talked from the heart about the turmoil in Europe – he told her about his travels in France and Germany, there didn't seem to be any harm in that – and he was worried about how unstable the Continent was and it was important for all people to be as educated as possible about different countries. She asked whether he was concerned at the rise of Nazis in Germany and he said of course he was and he could talk about it for hours if she wished and she said that would be interesting, maybe on another occasion.

'I thought the audience at the meeting tonight was very enthu-siastic about the Soviet Union, but it's not all they may wish it to be, you know.' He was unsure how she'd react because it was clear that communists didn't tolerate any criticism of the Soviet Union but she looked interested at what he'd said.

'I'm not sure I follow you. I didn't catch your name, by the way.'

Without thinking he told her it was 'Cooper' and the only reason he could think why he'd said that was that he was disconcerted, which was probably due to being in her presence and the earlier encounter with the communists. He moved on quickly, explaining that from what he understood – from what he'd read – there were a lot of arrests in the Soviet Union, with even loyal and long-standing communists disappearing, and Pamela place her small hand on his arm and said he ought to lower his voice and maybe this was not the kind of place where one should express those views too loudly.

Cooper did briefly wonder why she'd warned him not to express these views too loudly but it came across as friendly advice and, in truth, he was rather taken with her. Now that he could see her close up – even in the dim light of The Ten Bells – he thought she was close to his age and when she smiled and her face lit up as it had in the fog earlier in the week, it was quite captivating. She'd allowed her hand to remain on his arm for a while before sliding it down, over his hand, quite slowly, all the while smiling and then she said he must tell her more about Germany because she'd heard dreadful things about the country and Cooper spoke for quite a while, even telling her about Manfred, the man on the train who was arrested at Hamburg station by the Gestapo.

He'd made the mistake of giving Manfred's actual name but thought that didn't matter terribly as it was quite a common name, but he did exaggerate what had happened at the station, telling her he'd intervened on Manfred's behalf and a Gestapo officer had pushed him to the ground and how he was sure if he wasn't English, he'd have been arrested.

'Is that a bad thing?'

'Is what a bad thing, Pamela?'

'Being English: some people are ashamed of it, you know.'

'Well, I'm very proud of being English – British: there's nothing wrong with being a patriot. I'm not sure if the Communist Party of Great Britain approves of that!'

Pamela nodded and glanced at her watch. 'I really must get going. It's been a pleasure to meet you Cooper. Perhaps we'll meet again?'

'I certainly hope so.'

'There's another Communist Party meeting, a week on Friday. It's on Scientific Marxism and the speaker is a terribly bright academic, far more interesting than the man tonight. Will you be there?'

'I'll certainly try.'

'Can I give you some advice?' She was looking down at the table, her hand patting his arm as if what she was about to say was a bit awkward. 'Perhaps at the meeting you don't attempt to say anything or ask any questions? Sometimes it's best not to express one's views: in my experience a newcomer to Communist Party meetings should be like children in Victorian households, seen but not heard.'

–

The speaker was fluent and even cracked a few well-timed jokes, but by the end of the talk Cooper was little the wiser as to what was meant by scientific Marxism, other than that it described a world full of certainties, where Marxism–Leninism was correct in its analysis of society, the economy and political events and that to question it – and therefore to question both the Party and especially the Soviet Union – was to question scientifically proven fact.

Cooper almost admired the man's ability to be so sure and unerring in his beliefs, not unlike the religious studies teachers he'd encountered at school.

He was disappointed not to see Pamela at the meeting but not terribly surprised: the idea that she was interested in him as he'd rather hoped – and frankly the only reason he'd gone to the meeting – was most probably a fanciful one and perhaps it was for the best. He wasn't interested in communism and as far as the

Soviet Union was concerned, it would be a good idea to put as much distance between him and Moscow as possible.

He decided to focus on the novel and toyed with the idea of a British politician somehow being involved in the plot, which meant a visit to Westminster and from there he walked along Millbank towards the Tate Gallery, which he'd always meant to visit. It was a bright Tuesday morning, a pleasant change from the last few days which had been unremittingly wet and miserable. There was a fresh breeze from the river as he walked through Parliament Square and he passed two or three agreeable-looking pubs where he could stop later for his lunch and Cooper was pleased with himself.

There was a clatter of her high heels on the pavement behind him and a slightly breathless 'good heavens, fancy meeting you here!' and because a bus had been passing at the same time he'd not recognised her voice and so it was only when she came alongside him that Cooper realised it was Pamela and he felt conscious at his rush of excitement, certain she'd spot he was blushing.

'And I could say the same about you!'

'I'm meeting some comrades in Kennington. And you?'

Cooper said he was visiting the Tate Gallery, which by now they were opposite.

'Do you know, I've never been there? Isn't that shocking, I've always wanted to visit it! I may join you.'

'But what about your meeting?'

'They can wait.'

—

They spent an hour at the Tate Gallery and Pamela walked a bit too fast for someone who'd always wanted to visit the place and by the time they finished she said it was too late for her to go to Kennington so how about they head to Vauxhall Bridge Road where she knew a cheap place to eat.

Pamela was perfectly friendly, but quite inquisitive. She wanted to know what he'd really made of Europe and was curious about which countries he'd been to and when and in order to conceal the three months he'd spent in Moscow he made up a story of a romance with a woman called Inge he'd met in Berlin and with whom he'd travelled to Switzerland and he drew heavily on his experiences with Grace in Interlaken and Rita in Moscow, so much so that Pamela looked a bit embarrassed at one point and Cooper said he hoped she'd understand when he said he'd rather lost track of things for a while.

She continued to push him though, probing what he really made of what he saw in Nazi Germany and asking him about the civil war in Spain and what he thought of the political situation in this country and at this point he said it all felt a bit like a job interview!

'I'm interested in your views, that's all. Tell me though – you introduce yourself as Cooper. Why don't you use your first name?'

'I'm not sure: I'm invariably called Cooper – it's mononymous, you know, that's when a person's referred to by just the one name.'

'I did know that, but thank you very much for explaining.' She smiled and then placed her hand on his arm and said yes, she had been asking an awful lot of questions and he must excuse her but that was her way.

'I'm the curious type, you know. But I find you interesting. I like the idea of someone who's a writer, who's less than conventional. I'd love to chat more, Cooper, but I need to go. Look, are you free on Thursday night?'

'I think so, yes... no plans.'

'There's a restaurant on Chiltern Street, just on the corner with Paddington Street – not far from you. How about we meet there at half seven?'

–

When they'd parted on Vauxhall Bridge Road that Tuesday afternoon Pamela had pecked him on the cheek and held the back of his head as she did so and he'd caught the aroma of her perfume and was quite smitten, so much so that he gave little thought to Pamela's line of questioning.

Had he thought more carefully about it he'd have wondered at her remark that the restaurant on Chiltern Street was 'not far from you', because he couldn't recall telling her where he lived, but it really didn't seem to matter because he had rather talked for England and who knew what he'd said.

That Thursday afternoon he had a haircut and a shave at the barber's and even bought a new shirt and tie and when he turned up at the restaurant, he was clutching a bunch of tulips he'd bought outside Marylebone station and his heart was beating fast. An elderly waiter bowed his head and said to follow him and when he was shown into a room at the back, Pamela was waiting to greet him, and it was only when she stepped back from the doorway that Cooper saw they were not alone.

Sitting at the table was a man old enough to be Pamela's father and, in the way that Cooper's imagination worked in situations like this, he assumed this was indeed Pamela's father and there was going to be some kind of showdown and why on earth had she brought her father along anyway?

'Please, sit down, you're making me feel nervous standing there like that.' He was leaning back in his chair, a well-groomed man with silvery-grey hair and a very smart tweed jacket – tailored, much like the kind his step-father used to wear on a weekend – and a red silk handkerchief drooped out of the top pocket in a slightly rakish manner. He languidly held a lit cigarette away from his body and at shoulder-height.

He pointed to a chair opposite him for Cooper to sit down. 'May I clear up something?' He'd just inhaled from his cigarette so when he spoke puffs of smoke came out at the same time. Cooper expected the man to ask what his intentions were towards his daughter.

'Your name is Charles Christopher Cooper, yet your lodgings in Dorset Square are in the name of Christopher Shaw – which is the name associated with your recently opened Barclays Bank account – and yet you still have an active Martins Bank account in the name of Charles Christopher Cooper.'

He pointed the cigarette towards Cooper, a stub of ash dropping on the tablecloth and he raised his eyebrows in anticipation of a response and when Cooper just sat there, he added an, 'Eh?'.

Cooper was so shocked it took him a while to answer. 'I don't think I've broken any law, have I?'

'I'm not suggesting you have: it's just I'm curious as to why a journalist gives up a perfectly decent job, travels around Europe for the best part of eight months and when he returns assumes another identity.'

Cooper's first thought was to ask the man who the hell he was and why this was any of his business, but he went ahead and answered the question.

'I... I inherited some money, from a great aunt. I used that towards my travels and now I'm back I'm writing a novel and I thought I'd do so under a *nom de plume*, hence the Christopher Shaw, and I felt it would help my writing if I lived as Christopher Shaw for a while. You see, I already had that name through my step-father—'

'Thomas Shaw, yes... married your mother in 1920, wasn't it?'

Cooper nodded. He was now beginning to doubt this was Pamela's father and had no idea how the man knew all this about him, but he was pleased with his explanation about the two names: it had come out really rather well.

'My name is Percy, by the way: Percy Burton. I'm a colleague of Miss Clarke's – Pamela. We can eat now, if you want, and then I can talk or vice versa, but I wouldn't suggest we do both at the same time, eh? Miss Clarke, perhaps you...?'

Pamela nodded, stood up and smiled briefly in Cooper's direction and then slipped out of the room and Cooper was about to ask what on earth was going on when he realised he was still clutching the tulips, but the man called Percy spoke first.

'I ought to tell you at the outset that I represent an organisation connected to the British government and our function is of a highly confidential nature, what some people would term 'top secret'. If you feel uncomfortable about this and wish to proceed no further with the conversation then of course one quite understands. We can have our supper and talk about the weather and cricket if that's your game and then never need see each again, no offence taken and no harm done. On the other hand, if you wish to know more…'

The man who'd introduced himself as Percy Burton was holding his fork, pointing it in Cooper's direction. Cooper smiled and the man asked if that meant he wished him to proceed and Cooper wanted to say he'd rather not because he had an awful sense of *déjà vu* and the last thing he wanted was to appear to be open to whatever the man was going to suggest because 'highly confidential nature' sounded both ominous and familiar. But on the other hand, he was intrigued by what the man had said and wondered whether he could possibly know something about him and the Soviet Union and if that was the case it was better he knew what was going on. He must have nodded some form of assent because the man was now talking.

'The organisation I represent is a branch of British Intelligence, one which most people are unaware of – even those people who are normally well-informed on such matters.'

Percy was watching Cooper carefully through a thin screen of cigarette smoke. His eyes were half closed in concentration and he was very still, like a hawk on the lookout for prey and Cooper didn't say anything, partially because he had no idea what to say but more out of shock. It was now clear that the man was about to reveal they knew all about his trip to Moscow the previous year – about the Maurers in Berlin introducing him to Eduard, the journey to Moscow, Carl Gustaf Jansson, Nikolai, the meeting at the State Publishing House of Fiction which he thought was off Lenninskij Prospekt.

Cooper wondered if Percy's prolonged silence was a deliberate pause to allow him to confess and he decided that may be for the best: he'd explain that he'd avoided all contact with the Soviets since returning to London and point out that changing his name and assuming another identity was surely proof that he'd never had any intention of working for them.

'I perhaps, um… ought to say that I was—'

'In a moment, please, Cooper, in a moment. I'll cut to the chase: we've been on the lookout for people of a certain calibre who we think would make good agents for us and you certainly seem to fit the bill; you're smart, you've travelled and there's nothing we can discern from your past that would suggest you're anything other than a patriot – and believe me, we've looked very closely into your background. We know you inherited some three hundred and fifty pounds from Mathilda Dorothy Cooper and used some of that money to travel in Europe. We even know about this novel you're writing – which, incidentally, we're quite happy for you to proceed with, gives you a decent cover story. You'll need to undergo training, of course, and Miss Clarke would be working closely with you. We very much hope you are interested: you will of course be properly remunerated.'

Cooper's overwhelming emotion was one of utter relief. They clearly had no idea he'd ever been anywhere near Moscow. Evidently, there was no hint of suspicion about him. He was so relieved he thanked Percy profusely for the opportunity to serve and Percy had stood up – he was quite short, actually – to shake his hand and then he clapped and Pamela came in and patted him on the shoulder and soon after that a waiter appeared and they had a delicious meal.

It was long past eleven o'clock when they parted on the corner of Chiltern Street and Paddington Street, with much shaking of hands and Percy gripping him by the elbow and Pamela giving him another peck on the cheek and brushing her cheek against his and her scent lingered on his face.

He assured them he understood his instructions: he was to meet Pamela – Miss Clarke – at this very spot at eight o'clock on Monday morning and she would escort him to where he'd start his new role. And, yes, he quite understood his orders: he was not to breathe a word of this to a soul.

It was only over the weekend that he fully appreciated his predicament. He'd been so relieved they'd not known about his link with the Soviets that he failed to ask more questions and for time to think about things. After all, he didn't even know the name of the branch of British Intelligence which according to Percy most people are unaware of and which he'd now rather too hastily signed up to.

It was bad enough that he'd been recruited as a Soviet agent. But now he was a British spy too. He'd read about double agents, but he doubted he was even one of those. His situation was considerably more complicated than that.

Double agents were controlled by one side while also ostensibly spying for the other side. But in his case, neither side knew he was also working for the other. At least he'd managed to avoid the Soviets, otherwise his life would be unimaginably complicated.

He did recall that there'd been some point during the meal on the Thursday when Percy had asked him if he was happy with 'all of this', as he put it, and Cooper had only hesitated very briefly before saying he was happy, because he knew by then it was too late.

They wouldn't have approached him like this if they were going to allow him to decline their offer.

It was, he concluded, the most unspeakable dilemma.

And it was one he had no possibility of extricating himself from.

Part 2

Chapter 14

Austin Branstone found it hard to fathom what an extraordinary eighteen months he'd experienced. More often than not he woke up convinced the whole business had been a dream.

Prior to January 1937 he'd become accustomed to the solitary and measured life of an academic specialising in Russian icons, but the approach from Moscow had changed that. The opportunity to study icons normally hidden away in the Kremlin was totally unexpected and seemingly too good to be true.

Austin Branstone may have been unworldly in many respects, but he liked to think he certainly wasn't nearly as naïve as people often took him for: he knew full well he was being asked to be a spy and he appreciated he had little choice but to go along with it. After all, the Provost had promised him that if he did so then the College would grant him a paid sabbatical to complete his PhD.

And Moscow had gone well, despite all his misgivings and his fear of ending up in a prison camp, disowned by a British government that would no doubt deny any knowledge of him.

On his return from the Soviet Union, he'd barely been back in Cambridge for a few hours – he'd not finished unpacking – when he was summoned by Dr Paxton at Gonville and Caius.

Paxton had congratulated him and said he was pleased to see him back in one piece and his friends, as he called them, were especially interested in the man he'd met in the Kremlin and please could he tell him in as much detail as he could manage about what had happened.

Over the next week Branstone visited Paxton on a number of occasions to go through over and over again what had happened in considerable detail.

He told of how he'd seen the man leaving the Council of Ministers building, how his attention had been drawn by the man's attire, which was certainly not Russian and of how Big Boris, who was meant to be following him, wasn't doing so and when the man walked close to him there was something familiar about him...

And even this part of the encounter took hours to go through, as Paxton produced diagrams of the Kremlin and Branstone had to indicate who was where and when and then when he described the man's attire they spent many hours poring over pictures of men's clothing and he had to describe what he was wearing, even down to the shoes, which he couldn't recall exactly other than they appeared to be very well made.

And at one meeting Paxton told him that a woman would be joining them, an artist he said, skilled at producing sketches of people from verbal descriptions, but Branstone was not to give her any details other than what he could recall the man looked like and most certainly wasn't to mention anything about the Soviet Union.

But it turned out to be a futile exercise: the man had been wearing a hat, which had... well, not so much obscured his face, but made it difficult to recall details and when the sketch was shown to him the following day, he said it could look something like the man, but he wasn't sure and Paxton looked annoyed and said frankly it looked like almost any chap in his early thirties.

And then they turned to the encounter in the Taynitskaya Tower.

'I remember asking him if he knew where the Komendant-skaya Tower was. That's the Commandant's Tower, which I knew is on the other side of the Kremlin. I said I was going round in circles, or words to that effect.'

'And this was all in English?'

'Yes.'

'You're sure?'

'Absolutely: I told you, I used it because I thought I recognised him… well recognise may be a bit strong, but he was certainly familiar.'

'And he replied?'

'He said he didn't know and that he was stranger himself but if I kept walking round the wall, I'd come across it.'

'And those were his exact words?'

'More or less, sir, yes. I mean, not verbatim but as close as, dammit.'

Paxton had raised his eyebrows, surprised at Branstone's tone. 'And his accent?'

'Certainly upper class, I'd say.'

And a long discussion had followed on exactly what Branstone meant by that and he said he couldn't put his finger on it but after all Cambridge was full of people who'd been to public schools and who all spoke in a similar manner, as far as he was concerned, and he imagined it was the same at Oxford, even all those years ago.

Paxton paid particular attention to the chess tournament at Merton College in Oxford, which Branstone seemed to think was in 1930. No, he couldn't be sure his opponent whom he'd beaten with the Scholar's Mate was a student of Merton: he was sure there were students from at least two other colleges taking part and, no, he couldn't recall the names of those colleges, though it was possible that at least one of them was a neighbouring college, but he really wasn't sure.

Dr Paxton had become impatient and said everywhere in Oxford was near somewhere else because it was just a market town after all and they'd left the matter for a week or so and when they resumed, Paxton's desk was covered in photographs he'd obtained from Oxford, mostly of students who'd been at Merton College from 1928 to 1932 but study them as he did – with a magnifying glass, for heaven's sake – Branstone could not identify the man.

At one stage Branstone had suggested they check with Merton College and Paxton looked annoyed and said of course they'd done that and it appeared that Merton College had no records relating to its chess team and the same applied to the other colleges they'd enquired of, not least because they were talking eight years previously.

'I have to say, Oxford colleges are most dilatory in their record keeping. Much as one would expect!'

—

The Provost had been as good as his word and Austin Branstone had indeed been granted a paid sabbatical, to cover the whole of the 1937–1938 Academic Year. He was even given better rooms in College, in Bodley's Court.

He continued to meet regularly with Dr Paxton and the conversation would always be the same: yes, he'd been thinking about the Englishman in the Kremlin and, no, he was none the wiser as to his identity, and Paxton would look disappointed and said if you do recall anything you know where I am and Branstone nodded but thought that was highly unlikely, if not impossible.

Until that warm Wednesday morning in July.

—

By July 1938 Austin Branstone was making good progress with his PhD. His thesis was based on the schism in the Russian Orthodox Church in the 1650s and the ensuing effect on icons, with the traditionalists retaining the old style of icons which they believed had its origins in biblical times, whereas the more official church believed icons could reflect more modern Russian and European styles. He doubted he'd have been as advanced in his thesis had he not visited Moscow the previous year.

He was spending the last two weeks of July doing research at the British Library in Bloomsbury and the Provost had generously agreed to fund a stay in a small bed and breakfast hotel on

Brunswick Square, which was a pleasant ten-minute stroll from the library.

It was a Wednesday morning in his second week in London and Branstone left the hotel just after nine and headed to the library. As he approached Russell Square tube station, he saw the same man he'd encountered a year before in the Taynitskaya Tower in the Kremlin and unquestionably the same person he'd faced across the chess board at Merton College some eight years before.

This time he was wearing a dark suit, carrying an umbrella in one hand with his other hand holding a hat and with a raincoat draped over the arm. The man paused outside the station and looked around, though thankfully not in Branstone's direction. He then turned left towards Russell Square.

Branstone hurried across the road to follow the man. He wondered about shouting at him to stop and then thought it may be better to go up and greet him, but by the time the man had reached Russell Square, Branstone resolved he'd follow him as far as he could and if they passed a policeman on the way then he'd alert him.

As the man turned in to Russell Square, he approached a taxi on a stand outside a hotel. Branstone hurried after him, but by the time he reached the stand the man's taxi was heading towards the centre of London and someone else was climbing into the one other taxi waiting there. There was nothing Branstone could do; by the time another taxi appeared it was hopeless. He could hardly tell the driver to follow a taxi which was now out of sight.

He stood disconsolately by the road, before heading to the British Library. It was frustrating to say the very least: the man had been within his grasp.

He was returning to Cambridge on the Friday evening, so on the Thursday and Friday morning he made a point of waiting outside the entrance to Russell Square station on Bernard Street at around the same time as he'd seen the man on the Wednesday. But there was no sign of him, and when he returned to Cambridge he spent the weekend worrying that he should have done something about the matter on the Wednesday, though he wasn't sure what he could have done. He'd go and see Dr Paxton at Gonville and Caius once he was back in Cambridge next week. He'd know what to do.

Chapter 15

'What do we make of Cooper, then?'

The oldest person in the room replied to Percy Burton first. He was a formally dressed man who said in his middle-European accent he thought Cooper was a model student. 'I found him to be an intelligent man: he grasped the rudiments of Marxism surprisingly quickly, as he did the structure and organisation of the Communist Party in the Soviet Union and in this country. He even managed to remain awake throughout my sessions!'

There was a ripple of laughter and then the man next to him spoke. 'Thank you, Alfred. I also found him to be a first-class recruit. He picked up the key principles of how to follow someone in an effective yet inobtrusive manner almost immediately and when we set him off to see how he coped with being followed himself… well, I have to be honest, he shook off a couple of our very experienced chaps without any problem. It was almost as if he…'

'As if he what, Tony?'

'As if he was familiar with the techniques, which I have come across before, recruits who intuitively know what to do. I'm told he was less confident at the farm though: he's not what I'd call a tough character.'

'And the interrogations?'

'Relied a lot on his charm and his verbosity and was good at spinning out his story, but I'm not convinced that if he were really under pressure…'

'Pamela, what do you make of him? You spotted him in the first place.'

'I'm not sure: bright, obviously, and terribly likeable while at the same time being able to remain inconspicuous, which are qualities we really do look for. But I too remain to be convinced how much steel he really has.'

There was silence as Percy Burton closed his eyes in deep thought and then nodded, having made up his mind.

'I think we're agreed we carry on with Cooper.'

–

It was all rather rushed and somewhat confusing, not unlike the first day at school, and it had begun at eight o'clock on the Monday morning when he'd done as instructed and met Pamela on the corner of Chiltern Street and Paddington Street. She'd been more formal and business-like than previously – certainly no peck on the cheek or hand on his arm and as far as he could tell, no perfume. She glanced at her watch as if to check he wasn't late and then apologised for the rain and said they ought to get a move on and to follow her.

They hurried across Baker Street and then down Dorset Street, where she paused outside the Swiss Embassy to ask him if he was all right and for a moment he wondered if they were going into the embassy, but she carried on and were soon outside a six-storey Regency building in need of a lick of paint on the west-side of Bryanston Square, with a brass plaque announcing this was 'The Ministry of Transport'. The entrance hall was divided into two areas: one large and open with people visible through it; the other area smaller, with a guard standing in front of a closed door, who inspected Pamela's pass and nodded when she pointed at Cooper and said he was with her.

The guard pressed a buzzer and almost immediately the door opened and he followed Pamela down a tunnel-like corridor, at the end of which was another guard behind a desk who unlocked a door to let them through.

As far as Cooper could tell, it seemed they'd entered a building behind the first one. He was shown into a small, windowless room and Pamela suggested he hang up his coat and he was to wait there because someone from Personnel would be coming in to see him.

He was left alone for a few minutes before a woman entered and announced herself as being from Personnel and when Cooper said he hadn't caught her name she looked at him in a disapproving manner.

'That is because I didn't give it. You need to understand that in here few people give their names and you most certainly should not ask. Before you are taken to see Mr Burton, I have to go through some matters with you.'

She glared as Cooper took out his notebook and a pen.

'You can put those away for a start. We most certainly do not take notes in here. As far as the world outside is concerned, you are employed by a section of the Ministry of Transport that deals with the regulation of inland waterways. The main part of this building, through which you entered, is indeed part of the Ministry of Transport. You should not volunteer details about your employment, but that is what you tell them if anyone asks. This document is a briefing on the work of the inland waterways section: you should read it so you are familiar with what you are meant to be doing here.'

She then explained that for the purposes of his employment he would receive his salary from the Ministry of Transport and it would be paid into his Martins Bank account, one month in arrears, and that he would not be part of any superannuation scheme. If he was unwell or had any welfare concerns, he was to contact her and she would make what arrangements were necessary because they preferred medical and related matters to be dealt with by approved people, given the highly sensitive nature of the job.

'And now, you need to read this. I will leave you for a while and when I return, you'll sign it.'

The document was the Official Secrets Act, 1920 and reading it made Cooper break into a cold sweat. Each page sounded more portentous than the previous one and when he'd finished reading it his throat was tight and he had a headache and he turned back to Section 2 which described how an offence would be committed under the act if someone was in contact with 'a foreign agent… for a purpose prejudicial to the safety or interests of the State, obtained or attempted to obtain information which is calculated to be or might be or is intended to be directly or indirectly useful to an enemy'.

It rather neatly described what the Soviet Union expected of him.

Cooper realised he'd been a fool: he could have declined Burton's offer the previous week in the restaurant or he could have told Pamela that morning that he'd had second thoughts, that he realised he wasn't up to it and if the truth be told was a bit of a… well, coward, actually, and he really wasn't the right man for the job. But as was his want he'd been agreeable and hadn't wanted to say 'no' and just as he'd allowed himself to be swept along by Eduard and the Maurers in Berlin and tricked into going to Moscow, so the same was happening here in London. Being press-ganged into joining Soviet Intelligence was bad enough. Adding British Intelligence to that doubtful curriculum vitae was deeply regrettable. One of his school reports had described him as being too eager to please. 'Too biddable.'

'Are you all right?'

The woman had returned and was peering at him quizzically and Cooper realised he was perspiring heavily and said it was actually very warm in here and she said not to worry and handed him a pen and explained he was to sign and date every page of the Act as proof that he'd read it and did he have any questions?

Ten minutes later he was in an office on an upper floor of the building, facing Percy Burton across his desk. The blinds were drawn and the main lighting came from a desk lamp, meaning much of Burton's face was in the dark.

'This has all been something of a whirlwind, I imagine?'

'It certainly has.'

'But no second thoughts?'

Cooper didn't reply. He thought about the Maurers and Eduard in Berlin and Nikolai in Moscow and school teacher who'd described him as too eager to please and too biddable and he realised this was his chance to say actually he was having second thoughts, as it happened. Maybe if he said he wanted some more time to think about it then they'd lose interest in him, but he hesitated because he couldn't think of how to say it in a manner that didn't arouse suspicion.

'I asked if you had any second thoughts, Cooper?'

He knew this was the moment to say something, to voice some doubt, express some reservations – but he had an instinctive feeling that to do so could alert Burton to something. Maybe it was best after all to go quietly along with it and not be difficult.

Best to be eager to please. Even biddable.

'Well, not so far...'

'I ask because after this session, there'll certainly be no opportunity for second thoughts. There's no going back once I've briefed you on your mission and explained the role of my organisation. Are you clear?'

Cooper nodded.

'This organisation has no formal name as such, but those aware of its existence know it as The Annexe, which derives from the fact that we're based in a building which is in fact an annexe to the Ministry of Transport. But the name also rather neatly describes our position with the intelligence community in that very few people know of us: we're an adjunct to the intelligence world, an annexe to it, if you like. We were formed in 1931 to act as a point of liaison for the two main intelligence and counter-intelligence bodies – MI5 and MI6 – and the Special Branch. It was originally envisaged that our function would last around one year, at which point it was hoped that the relationship between the other intelligence bodies and their effectiveness would have improved.

'But somehow, we have continued. Our role has evolved and now our purpose is to carry out highly clandestine work on behalf of this country with minimal oversight – tasks which are considered too sensitive for the other agencies. We have the luxury of not having to worry about politicians or the press asking awkward questions about us, because we do not officially exist.

'One of the projects we have at the moment is related to the Communist Party of Great Britain. Technically, Special Branch and MI5 have responsibility for matters of security and counter-espionage within the United Kingdom, but as far as the British communists are concerned, they're all over the place. They waste an inordinate amount of time and resources coming up with what I regard as second- or third-rate intelligence; membership lists, the names of people who sell their newspaper and hand out leaflets and if we want to know who's on their committee in Birmingham or Portsmouth they'll certainly oblige and they get terribly excited at even the hint of a strike. To be frank with you, that's the kind of information which can be gathered through research more than anything else – scrutinising the *Daily Worker* and their other publications, for example. It's clerical work rather than espionage; a competent librarian could compile a list of the members of the Central Committee of the Communist Party of Great Britain.'

Percy Burton leant forward, his arms resting on the desk, which meant that Cooper could now see all of his face.

'The problem with information gathering like this is that it's not really intelligence: it puts undue emphasis on figures who are in fact of minor relevance. Those who make the loudest speeches or are what we'd call agitators are highly unlikely to be persons who are a serious threat to the security of this country, they're more of a nuisance than anything else. Too much attention is paid to the Communist Party itself – they have less than ten thousand members and at the last general election they got around twenty-seven thousand votes. But there is a view in Whitehall that there are very high level and clandestine links between the communists here and the Kremlin, and that is what we should be gathering intelligence on. If we can break into that then not only will we discover what the Soviets are up to over here, but we will also gain a valuable insight into what is going on in the Kremlin itself. To do that, we need to get into King Street.'

'King Street?'

'In Covent Garden: the headquarters of the Communist Party of Great Britain is at number sixteen King Street. We need to infiltrate it, but it's run as a rather tight ship: they're distrusting to the point of paranoia of what they describe as the British state. MI5 claim they have sources inside King Street but I'm most sceptical about how highly placed or reliable they are. And this is where you come in, Cooper.'

Percy was watching Cooper carefully. 'Miss Clarke's job has been to find someone credible we could recruit to join the party and get into King Street. You seem to be an ideal candidate: you're smart, you've travelled, you speak French and German and there's nothing we can discern from your past that you're anything other than trustworthy. Your mission will be to identify any clandestine links which exist between the Party here and Moscow and to find out what Moscow is saying and what they're thinking and planning.'

Burton leant back and folded his arms and adjusted his shirt cuffs, a gold watch glinting in the lamplight.

'You'll spend the next month being trained. In the evenings and weekends, you'll attend Communist Party meetings. Until you've completed your training, you should just be there as a member of the audience – to be seen, so in time you'll become a familiar face. We won't rush you: The Annexe has the luxury of being able to proceed at our own pace, without unhelpful pressure from politicians and Whitehall. This means that you can work your way into King Street without drawing undue attention to yourself.

'Miss Clarke will introduce you to the people responsible for your training. She will of course be the person to whom you report, but I shall be taking a very keen interest in your mission.' He shuffled the papers on his desk and placed the cap on his fountain pen, signalling this meeting had come to an end.

'May I ask you a question?'

Percy Burton leant forward, a look of surprise on his face. 'I'd rather hoped I'd covered everything.'

'You said The Annexe has minimal oversight and that very few people know of its existence. So, I was just wondering, who it actually works for?'

'We work for the British state, Cooper. Welcome to The Annexe.'

–

'I expect this is rather like being back at university? Hope it's not too much of a strain.'

He and Pamela were eating their sandwiches on a bench in Bryanston Square at the start of his second week of his training, a slightly awkward business given the light but persistent rain, but Pamela had insisted they eat outside.

He'd nodded in reply, though in truth, the training was nothing like being back at university: it was more intense and the reason why it wasn't too much of a strain would have shocked Pamela and indeed everyone else in The Annexe.

It was actually very familiar.

He'd been through a process very similar to it not that long ago, when he was being trained to be an OMS agent.

Then the training had been conducted by Nikolai Vasilyevich in a curtained-room on an upper floor of a building around a quarter of an hour's drive from the Lux Hotel.

He'd been trained on the kind of information he should seek out once he'd worked his way into the British system, as he'd been instructed to do. He'd been taught how to identify the most important documents, how to summarise them, how to operate a dead letter box and pass on information, how to cope if he came under suspicion or was questioned, how to avoid being followed and how to befriend contacts and develop a relationship with them.

The training in London was in some ways different. Most of the training in Moscow had been carried out by Nikolai Vasilyevich himself and much of it took the form of the Russian talking, often at length, and in truth it was sometimes hard to concentrate as he had a tendency to go off at a tangent, with what were often quite interesting anecdotes.

But in London the training was far more structured and delivered by different people. Most of the sessions were held in The Annexe in Bryanston Square, two floors of which appeared to have been designed for this purpose, with narrow corridors leading to small, windowless rooms, all of which were sound-proofed. The layout of these floors ensured it was difficult to bump into anyone else on them.

Three or four times a week a man in his sixties with a strong German accent met with Cooper. He was most apologetic that he was not permitted to give his name but he could call him Alfred if he wished, and said he wasn't permitted to say much about himself, other than that he'd had to leave Germany when life became too difficult, but he'd been a Marxist in his youth and had become an academic and an expert on communist parties and since settling in London had studied the Communist Party of Great Britain in some detail and was here to pass on his knowledge of it and also to explain Marxist theory to him.

He tried to make his tutorials as interesting as possible, explaining that the better he understood the more credible he'd be and less likely to arouse suspicion. He explained the structure of the Communist Party in Britain and how it related to the Soviet Union and asked Cooper if he'd ever heard of the Comintern and Cooper was glad Alfred was looking at his notes when he asked that because he'd been shocked.

Alfred talked about dialectical materialism and how it was a way of describing Marxist philosophy, at the core of which was a scientific study of society and its rules, because understanding society – historical materialism as he called it – was the key to Marxism.

There was another session on Marxist economics, which meant studying capitalism so as to understand why it was always in crisis, and when Cooper questioned whether capitalism was really always in crisis Alfred sighed and closed his notebook and said he agreed, but that wasn't the point: the point about being a good communist was not to question Marxist–Leninist orthodoxy.

Alfred was one of half a dozen tutors: there was a woman, who reminded him of one of his English teachers, who taught him about coding and how to pass messages; a man with a Welsh accent called Tony who took him around London and trained him on how to follow people and how to avoid being followed himself; a series of sessions from Percy and Pamela themselves on how to gather information and build relationships with people and earn their trust while at the same time remaining in the background; and then a week spent on a farm, which he was told was in Northamptonshire, where he was trained in physical combat and how to defend himself.

The training was exhausting, but he was constantly aware of his predicament – that somehow he'd ended up working for not one but two intelligence agencies from hostile countries. It was what he thought about until the early hours and was the first thing he thought about when he woke up.

And during this period, he also attended Communist Party meetings, sometimes as many as three nights a week in different parts of London and what were described as education conferences around the country at weekends. He was given a new identity – Frank Reynolds – and a room in a lodging house in Hackney where the other residents were transient – here one day, gone the next – so it would be difficult to check him out should anyone be minded to do so.

And, as instructed by Pamela, he kept his head down and said very little. He began to recognise people and learn their names and what they did and people didn't ask Frank too many questions, though he had no doubt that they were suspicious of him as they were of pretty much everyone else. It was that kind of environment, where it went against the grain to trust people and it was assumed that any meeting had one or two infiltrators in it.

'You don't need to worry,' Pamela assured him. 'They suspect any newcomer, any person they can't account for. You'll be being checked out. We've ensured that your identity as Frank Reynolds is absolutely watertight, so you don't need to worry there, and the bedsit in Hackney helps. Just don't volunteer too much information – sometimes a very plausible and coherent backstory can be suspicious in itself. The main thing is to use this time to be seen around so that people don't think of you as a stranger.'

–

'I think we can consider that you've graduated, though I'm afraid we don't have a certificate for you.'

It was a warm morning in the middle of July and for the past few days there'd been very little in the way of training – other than lots of documents to read – so the news that his training had come to an end came as little surprise.

Cooper found himself shaking hands with the older man, as if he was indeed attending his graduation, and Burton guided him to the door with a friendly hand on his shoulder and said something about what a pleasant change it was to have no rain and then something about his garden and Cooper was already in the corridor when the older man said to hang on.

'I almost forgot: pop back in for a moment.'

And this time Cooper was told to sit in the upright chair in front of the desk and Percy Burton now looked more serious as he opened a dossier in front of him. Cooper began to form the impression that rather than this being something the other man had almost forgotten, it was quite possibly the main purpose of the meeting.

'As you know, one of the roles of The Annexe is to carry out tasks which cannot be attributed to the British government.' He glanced up at Cooper, who nodded. 'Although your main role is to infiltrate the upper echelons of the Communist Party, you will from time to time be asked to assist with some of these other missions. Your French is up to scratch, I understand?'

Cooper nodded.

'Something's cropped up next week in Brussels that we just need a bit of a hand with. Shouldn't take up more than a day or two.'

Chapter 16

London and Brussels
July 1938

Charles Cooper stood alone in the centre of Parc du Cinquantenaire, the city of Brussels stretching below and a strong wind whipping through the Memorial Arcade, tousling his hair.

This felt like a surprisingly exposed place for a clandestine meeting. But he was mindful of Burton's warning before he'd left London: the person he was meeting was not to be questioned.

He moved along the path towards the Tournai Tower and spotted the bench where he was to wait and saw it was shielded by a high hedge on one side and a row of trees on another, but with good views down the sweeping pathways, and realised it was actually quite a cleverly chosen location.

And there he waited; he'd arrived ten minutes early and perhaps shouldn't have approached the rendezvous spot quite so soon, but he always took the view that it was better to be early than late and so he sat on the bench and lit a cigarette and then decided to go for a stroll and when he returned, a tall man was sitting at the bench and Cooper realised this must be the man he'd been told was called Murray, which was somewhat unfortunate as he was meant to be waiting on the bench, not the other way round.

Murray was dressed as he'd been told to expect: a dark brown suit with brown brogues and a red tie with a matching pocket handkerchief and when Cooper asked if the seat was free – which was awkward because the man was meant to ask him that – he nodded and said nothing at first, looking at Cooper in what he took to be a disappointed manner.

'Have you visited the Royal Palace in Brussels?'

'Yes, but I'm afraid it was raining.'

'I recommend Restaurant de la Monnaie, close by on Rue Léopold.'

'Thank you. I found a charming little place on Rue de l'Evêque.'

The man nodded and said nothing as he stared ahead and when he did speak, he sounded angry.

'What on earth where you playing at arriving so early? Didn't Burton tell you to arrive at the bench at exactly eleven fifteen and then sit down? Not lounge around, have a cigarette, then wander off. Jesus… give me a cigarette.'

Cooper's hand was trembling as he handed Murray a cigarette and lit it for him. Murray leant back and said nothing as he concentrated on the cigarette and it was only when he'd finished it that he leant forward and spoke, now sounding more business-like.

'You arrived in Brussels the day before yesterday?'

'Yes, Monday.'

'And you did as instructed?'

'Yes: boat to Ostend, train to the Gare du Nord, overnight at the Palace Hotel by the station and the following morning I checked in to the Hotel Europe on Place Royale.'

'In a different name?'

'Of course.'

'In my job, there's never an "of course": I cannot risk taking anything for granted.'

Cooper said he understood and was sorry and by now he was feeling quite shaken by the whole business because up until a couple of minutes before he'd been hoping this was some kind of elaborate training exercise or a final test organised by Burton, but the man seemed deadly serious and even menacing, which was really quite chilling.

'And tell me what you did yesterday after checking in at the Hotel Europe.'

'I went to the British Embassy on Rue de Spa—'

'How did you get there?'

'I walked.'

'Good, carry on.'

'I asked to see the military attaché and after presenting my letter of introduction was taken to see Brigadier Moult. He told me that the package had arrived in the diplomatic bag over the weekend and he handed it to me.'

'And you've kept it with you the whole time since then?'

'Absolutely, yes.'

'Please...'

The man held his hand out in the direction of Cooper's briefcase, so he opened it and handed the package to the man who smiled and held it gently in an admiring and even loving manner before starting to unwrap it, which shocked Cooper because he thought a park was the last place in the world where you'd open something like this.

'It's a Smith and Wesson Model 27 revolver,' said Murray, slowly running a finger along the barrel. 'Also known as a Magnum. The Americans only began to manufacture it last year and it's an outstanding weapon. A significant improvement on our Webley.'

He stroked the revolver one more time and then wrapped it up, putting the box containing the cartridges in his pocket. He seemed much more relaxed now, even quite jovial.

'Now, I need to tell you what this is all about. Listen carefully.'

Cooper did listen carefully, reacting with a mixture of shock and incredulity.

He was to be a party to murder.

—

It was the seventh time Percy Burton had met the man he knew only as Murray and as on the previous seven occasions, he was astonished how different he looked.

Burton prided himself on having a good memory and an accurate sense of recall, but with Murray it was hopeless: if he was asked to describe Murray he'd come up with some vague description, which he realised, of course, was the point. The last time they'd met – just one month before – Murray had appeared to be over six foot and held himself in an upright, military bearing. He'd been hatless, with his thick fair hair catching in the wind – Murray always insisted on meeting outside – and had spoken with a soft Scottish accent. The time before that Murray looked more well-built, rather too-well-fed, as his mother would have put it, and was wearing a trilby and spoke with a hint of a northern accent.

And now, the man who sidled up to him as he reached the part of Fulham Palace Road where it approaches Putney Bridge, looked quite different: dressed slightly shabbily with a broad-brimmed cloth cap – the type one wears when shooting – and a mud-spattered raincoat.

'We'll turn left here and walk through Bishops Park.' It was unmistakably Murray, but with an accent he'd not heard before – possibly Welsh, and if he was pushed Burton would have said North Wales. They walked towards the park and then alongside the river bank in the direction of Hammersmith and Percy Burton didn't say anything yet because he was only too well aware that the man he knew as Murray would decide when it was safe to speak.

Close to Craven Cottage, the ground of Fulham football club, Murray stopped under the enormous bough of an oak tree and leant against the iron railings and Percy Burton joined him. Both men gazed out over the Thames, staring straight ahead at the opposite bank. This was how Murray liked to conduct business, with minimal eye contact.

'The last job went well, thank you.'

'Really?' Murray sounded annoyed.

'Well, we certainly thought so... yes.'

'This was the fourth job I've done for you and I've told you: I require the information you give me to be unerringly accurate, as was the case with the first three. The information I was given for the last person was inaccurate.'

Percy Burton spread his hands out apologetically and was minded to reply that surely it didn't really matter, did it, because he'd killed the right person, but the last thing he wanted now was to rile Murray, not as he was about to tell him about another important target.

'The information I was given was that the target would be driving a black 1932 Austin 7, registration number BCA 313. In fact, he was driving a dark blue 1934 model Austin 7, registration number BCR 313.'

Percy Burton didn't reply because he knew full well that if he said that surely it was close enough Murray would be furious.

'It meant that when he got out of the car I was in the wrong position. It was fortunate that I was using a Polish Nagant revolver which has seven chambers: I had to use all seven. Normally, I expect to finish someone off with two shots, three at the very most.'

'You haven't used that gun before?'

'Of course not. I've told you this before, I use a different weapon each time. This was the first time I've used a Nagant.'

Murray said nothing as he gazed across the river. The wind was blowing into their faces and Burton was worried his voice may carry in an unwanted direction.

'I take it you have another job for me?'

'I do, actually: all the details are in this envelope.' Percy Burton palmed a brown envelope to Murray who slipped it straight into his inside jacket pocket.

'And the money?'

'There's eighty pounds in there, with a further eighty to follow in the usual manner upon completion – as per usual.'

'As per usual indeed – and, as per usual, the name and address are in the envelope?'

'Of course, along with details of their routine and photographs.'

'And I presume this is to be carried out as soon as possible, as per usual?'

He'd said 'as per usual' with more than a hint of sarcasm so Percy Burton nodded and then said there was something else.

'I ought to point out that this job is to be carried out overseas.' He spoke tentatively, nervous of the man's reaction.

'Where?'

'Brussels.'

Murray nodded and didn't appear to be concerned but said perhaps Mr Burton could go over the job because if it was to be in Belgium then he may need some extra help.

Percy Burton explained that the target this time was an anarchist, an Englishman who was linked with Irish Republicans and was believed to be behind recent bombings at British army barracks in the Midlands.

'He's very, very clever — we cannot pin any evidence on him — but we know what he's been up to and we know he's planning more attacks. We have to stop him. We'd lost track of him, but he emerged in Brussels last week.

'If we build a case against him and tell the Belgian authorities then by the time he was arrested and extradited it could well be too late...'

'I don't need to know all this: as long as it's been decided then that's fine. But I will need someone from London to go over to help me — a French speaker. Someone good and certainly not a local. And I'll want to collect my weapon in Brussels, I don't fancy taking it over with me. I'll want the new Smith and Wesson for this: get it to the embassy and the person you'll send over to help me can collect it. I don't want to go anywhere near there myself.'

It was only just after ten o'clock but was already a warm July morning when Cooper carefully parked the dark red Renault Celtaquatre on Chaussée de Vleurgat and remained in it for a few moments in an effort to regain his composure. He still couldn't believe what he was being asked to do and part of him hoped this was still something devised by Burton to test his mettle.

Murray had been very clear with his instructions.

'We will meet at nine fifteen tomorrow morning – Thursday – in Square Ambiorix and you'll drive me to Ixelles, which is about two miles south of here. You're to drop me on Place Flagey and then drive up Chaussée de Vleurgat and park close to the junction with Avenue Louise. Have you got all that?'

Cooper said he had.

'Make sure the car's facing away from Place Flagey. Leave the door unlocked and the key under the driver's seat.

'You're to leave the car by a quarter to ten and enter Rue de la Vallée from Rue Vilain, which is very important because I'll be entering it from the opposite direction. Still with me?'

Cooper nodded.

'Wait diagonally opposite the house: when you see me you're to go to the house and down to the basement flat and ring the bell. If the man in this photograph answers you should ask him – in French – if a Monsieur Lambert lives there. You should then apologise and leave: at that point I'll know the man is there. You're to wait further up the road. I'll then go in and when I leave, I'll hand the gun to you and you're to go straight to Place Flagey and from there take a tram to Gare du Midi and then the train to Calais and back to London. You change at Tournai. Got that?'

Cooper nodded. He'd not eaten and had hardly slept since he'd received his instructions in the park the previous day and was feeling light-headed. He was still in shock.

'And, of course, you'll have taken your case to the left luggage at Midi that morning. Meanwhile I'll leave through Rue Vilain and pick up the car where you've left it on Chaussée de Vleurgat.'

It was the most terrifying morning of Cooper's life.

He'd parked the car as instructed and walked slowly towards Rue de la Vallée because Murray had impressed on him not to get there too early as he didn't want to draw attention to himself by hanging around. And all the more so because this was a very smart area – 'quiet and affluent' was how Murray had described it – and when he reconnoitred the area that Wednesday afternoon, as instructed by Murray, he'd been most impressed. The streets of handsome Art Nouveau houses were set around two small lakes – the Étangs d'Ixelles – and he noticed two pairs of police officers patrolling the area, which seemed ominous, but he thought better than to mention it to Murray when he met with him the next morning on Square Ambiorix.

The Renault Celtaquatre had been a tricky car to drive – it seemed to be reluctant to leave first gear – and he noticed another pair of policemen on Avenue Louise, but carried on nevertheless and found himself trembling despite the heat. It was just before five to ten when he entered Rue de la Vallée, so he dropped his pace and when he was diagonally opposite the house he paused and took his time lighting a cigarette.

When he saw Murray enter the street from the other direction he crossed the street and went down the small flight of steps to the basement. He rang the bell and it was a good minute before the door opened, though only partially, as the unshaven face of a man peered out from behind the narrow gap.

'*Monsieur Lambert, il est ici s'il vous plaît?*'

The man paused for a moment and then shook his head and closed the door.

Cooper crossed the road and watched as Murray waited for a couple of minutes and then approached the basement. He'd told Cooper that he'd be able to break the lock in a matter of seconds and sure enough he was quickly inside the flat.

But he'd also told Cooper he'd be in and out inside a minute, two at the very most, and as Cooper nervously glanced at his wristwatch it was apparent that something wasn't right.

Murray had said that if he didn't come out after four minutes Cooper was to investigate, and it was now five minutes.

The door of the basement flat was ajar and in the tiny hallway lay the lifeless body of a man, a small pool of dark blood surrounding him. Behind the body, Cooper saw through the open door of a bedroom, a woman was on the bed, frozen in absolute fear, clutching a sheet to her neck. At the foot of the bed, Murray was pointing his revolver at her, holding it with two hands, but he too was frozen, with an unmistakable look of fear on his face.

He seemed unaware of Cooper's presence and when Cooper said 'it's me' he didn't react at first and only did so when Cooper gently tapped him on the arm and then he looked shocked, and began to tremble and Cooper noticed his wide-open eyes fill with tears.

'I can't do it,' he whispered.

'Do what?'

Murray gestured with his head at the woman. 'You'll have to.' He handed the revolver to Cooper.

'No, I simply can't, I—'

'Do it!' Murray hissed. 'The police will be here any moment – get on with it!'

Cooper took the revolver from Murray and pointed it at the maid, who now began to cry. Without hesitating any further, Cooper shot her, in the chest, from close range. The white sheet turned bright red as it fell away to expose her naked body.

Murray looked as if he'd emerged from a trance. He told Cooper to put the gun in his briefcase and get a move on. 'Not a word to Burton, understand? Not a bloody word!'

–

It took all the restraint he could muster to avoid running to Place Flagey, where there appeared to be policemen wherever he looked, and he began to panic because he now couldn't remember which tram to catch and he thought about taking a taxi to the station but Murray had been absolutely insistent that whatever he did he wasn't to do that because the first people the police would question would be the taxi drivers.

And then he remembered his training and what the Welshman – Tom or Tony or whatever his name was – had told him about needing to escape from an area.

Get out as soon as you can. Don't hesitate, you'll only draw attention to yourself. Don't wait for a particular bus or train: take the first one you can get on. And get on it at the last possible moment, just in case anyone's following you.

Cooper pulled himself together and did just that. He spotted a tram with 'St Gilles' on the front and hopped on it just as it was about to leave. The tram was crowded and stifling hot and as he clutched the briefcase, he worried that there could be some terrible mishap and the gun could go off. He left the tram at Boulevard de Waterloo, walked for a few blocks to ensure he wasn't being followed and then took another tram to Midi.

–

'What in heaven's name is that, Cooper!'

'Murray called it a revolver, sir.'

'And what is it doing here?'

'I brought it back from Brussels, sir.'

'Is it loaded?' Percy Burton looked furious. It was the Friday morning, the day after his return from Belgium, and they were in Burton's office in The Annexe in Bryanston Square.

'I think there are two or three bullets still in the cylinder, sir, and I didn't want to fiddle around with getting them out.'

'And you didn't think to get rid of this damn thing?'

'Murray said it was a brand-new model and one of the best and I—'

'And surely he instructed you to get rid of it?'

'He did mention it, sir, but I seem to recall he said only to do so safely and I'm afraid that opportunity didn't arise. I thought about throwing it overboard when we crossed the Channel but when I went up on deck it was very crowded, so I thought it best not to do so then.'

'Thank heavens the safety catch was on!' Percy Burton shook his head and then removed a crisp white handkerchief from his top pocket and used it to gingerly pick up the revolver and moved it to a side table.

'I understand all went to plan in Brussels?'

Cooper hesitated only very slightly before nodding in agreement.

'You sure, Cooper?'

'More or less, sir, yes.'

'More or less?'

Cooper hesitated. This was the moment to tell Burton that actually it had been a disaster and every time he closed his eyes, he saw the face of a terrified woman in the bed in the basement in Brussels who he'd killed, which he still found hard to believe, and he doubted that memory would ever leave him.

'Cooper?'

'Yes, sir, I mean, it wasn't pleasant but—'

'This is not a pleasant job, I'm afraid. And did Murray say anything to you afterwards?'

'Only to get a move on.'

'Murray tells me there was a woman in the flat who he had to dispose of too. You do realise, Cooper, that had you been caught you'd have been charged with murder as well as Murray? Travelling back here with this gun was reckless and irresponsible. Let that be a lesson.'

'Presumably I'd have had some kind of diplomatic immunity, sir?'

'I don't follow you, Cooper.'

'Immunity from prosecution had I been arrested – the embassy would have sorted me out, surely?'

Burton smiled broadly and shook his head. 'I'm afraid that's not how it works, Cooper. If you're caught, you'll find you're very much on your own. Murray tells me you were very helpful and it's good that you've been on your first mission for us, but if it's taught you just one lesson, Cooper, it's that you must not get caught. The Annexe, you'll recall, does not officially exist. You don't need to know who was killed or why. It should suffice that everything done by The Annexe is done in the interests of this country, however unconventional and even irregular our methods may seem to be.'

Cooper was shocked and must have showed it because Percy Burton said not to worry and he should look upon Brussels as very valuable experience.

'Before Brussels you were a new recruit to The Annexe, Cooper. Now, you're very much one of us.'

–

Murray found him on the Sunday afternoon as he was strolling through Regent's Park. He didn't say anything for a while, but led him to a quieter area.

'What happened in Brussels – it's never happened to me before. I wasn't expecting to see the woman there and she looked so young and pretty and… look, my hesitating like that… it was unforgiveable and will never happen again and… you got me out of a hole there and I'm terribly grateful. You did very well, and I'm indebted to you and I'm most grateful you didn't tell Burton.'

Cooper said not at all, and he was glad to help, and Murray held up his hand again.

'I owe you: you'll never know when you need me, but the line of work you're in, odds are you will one day. There's a pub in Holborn – The Seven Stars on Carey Street, just south of Lincoln's Inn Fields. It's been around forever, rumoured to be the oldest pub in London. There's an elderly barman there called Bernard who works every evening apart from Wednesday. If you ever need me, find Bernard and ask him if they have any Islands malts. He'll ask which one you prefer and you're to say a Talisker.'

'And then?'

'Leave it to Bernard.'

Chapter 17

'May you never be noticed!'

He was thirteen when his grandfather pronounced this in his usual solemn manner as they were walking along a country lane. At first, he'd dismissed it as one more of the old man's often obscure Ukrainian proverbs, which he was so fond of. In fact, he'd said it twice, once in Ukrainian and then in Russian, as if nervous that the crows looking down on them would disapprove of him having spoken Ukrainian.

It was around the time Sergei Grigoryevich Volkov had become active in the Komsomol, the youth league of the Soviet Communist Party and of course he'd nodded and thanked his grandfather and thought no more of it until the following week when he was deep in a game of chess with his grandfather and they were alone in the house and the old man had picked up a bishop and held it in front of his grandson's face and once again said 'may you never be noticed' and this time Sergei Grigoryevich noticed that there were tears in his grandfather's eyes and he asked him if he was all right and he'd replied that he was worried about him.

'But why are you worried about me? I'm doing well at school, I can sometimes beat you at chess and I'm about to be elected to the neighbourhood committee of the Komsomol!'

'Exactly – you are a very bright boy and you've entered the ranks of the Communist Party. You will have the opportunity to enjoy a privileged life but it'll also be a very...' He'd paused, searching for the right word. 'Exposed one. It will bring you many advantages in life, but you'll risk danger. That is why I say may you never be noticed: it is safer to be anonymous, for people not to notice you.'

His grandfather had died two years later and the next time Sergei Grigoryevich heard that phrase was when he was sixteen and about to leave his hometown of Yefremov in Tula Oblast to go to technical college in Moscow.

It was quite an achievement – there'd even been a paragraph about him in the local newspaper. This was one of the best technical colleges in Moscow and not only did you have to be very bright to pass the tests, but you needed to be loyal, too. His membership of the Komsomol had served him well.

A week before his departure he bumped into one of his former schoolmasters. The man had left the school somewhat hurriedly about four years before and the rumour was that he'd been sacked because he wasn't a Party member and as far as he was aware, the distinguished-looking and cultured man whose voice would choke with emotion when he was reading particular passages of literature was now a labourer in the iron foundry.

He certainly looked about ten years older when he stopped Sergei Grigoryevich in the street. His face was grimy and his clothes filthy and he asked him how he was and Sergei replied he was well and was about to go to Moscow and the old man – to his shame, he couldn't remember his name – said he knew, he'd read it in the paper.

'And I read too that you're an important member of the Komsomol?'

'Maybe in Yefremov, but in Moscow... I'll be no one!'

The former teacher nodded and appeared lost in thought. 'Maybe that is for the best, Sergei Grigoryevich.'

'Pardon, comrade?'

The older man fleetingly flinched at the word 'comrade'. 'The only advice I would presume to give you is that if you do stand out, then in the long run no good will come of it. There's an old Ukrainian saying: "may you never be noticed".'

–

Sergei Grigoryevich Volkov arrived in Moscow in the summer of 1924 and for the next twelve years at least he never looked back and rarely returned to Yefremov.

He graduated from the technical college in 1927 and was then sent to an institute in the south of Moscow which specialised in the intensive teaching of foreign languages. He spent the next two years immersed in French and English and was told that the languages would be useful in his 'next job', though it was never explained what that job would be.

That only became apparent in 1929 on his graduation. He would be joining the Comintern, he was told – the international communist organisation based in Moscow. He was informed that extensive checks had been carried out and his loyalty was not in doubt.

He was now twenty-one and rather pleased with himself. He had a good job which came with the privileges one would expect of that position, not least of which was his own room in an apartment he shared with three other Comintern employees in the Danilovsky district, close to where the Garden Ring crossed the Moscow River. The apartment even had its own bathroom and kitchen, no sharing with other apartments. And he had access to the shops for Party members with more plentiful supplies and an exemption from military service as long as he completed a set number of civil guard training days each quarter.

It took him until 1937 to gain a serious promotion: until then he'd been rather stuck in the Archives and Records Department and although he was forever being told by his supervisors that this was an important role, he did get the impression he could remain there forever and occasionally thought of his grandfather and former teacher's saying – may you never be noticed – and decided that was a curse as much as anything else because he certainly wasn't being noticed and that was doing him no good whatsoever.

And then he did get noticed.

The Archives and Records Department was in the basement of the Comintern headquarters, so the other departments were invariably referred to as 'upstairs'. And though it was not very noticeable at first, from sometime in 1936 onwards, people began to disappear from departments upstairs. Not in large numbers and not that people discussed such matters, but he'd notice that someone he saw regularly in the canteen or when he visited their office was no longer there.

And of course, it was hard to escape what was going on throughout Moscow: people arrested late at night or in the early hours of the morning, often loyal Party members, many in senior positions – and never seen again. Sent to the camps in the east, the rumours went. Or killed within hours of their arrest. It was best not to think about it, it was nothing to do with him.

And just as Sergei Grigoryevich Volkov was thinking that maybe never being noticed was not such a bad thing after all, he was approached by Nadezhda Nikolaeva Kuznetsova, an impressive lady who ran the department that liaised with the French, Swiss and Belgian communist parties. She explained that 'due to circumstances', there was a shortage of French speakers. Was he perhaps interested in an attachment to her department?

Naturally, it was a rhetorical question because this was how the Comintern worked: employees had no say in what part of the organisation they worked in. She was just being polite.

It was the end of 1937 when he began work in that department, which involved a good deal of translation and clerical work at first but over the weeks more people disappeared and one morning Nadezhda Nikolaeva informed him he was being sent to Paris for a conference.

The conference took place in the middle of May 1938, his first ever visit outside the Soviet Union. The venue was in La Villette in the north-east of the city. The delegates were mostly from the

French communist party, along with representatives of the Belgian and Swiss parties and to Nadezhda Nikolaeva's surprise, from the British Communist Party. She wasn't expecting them to attend and was thrown by this because there were no English speakers on her delegation – until Sergei Grigoryevich reminded her that he spoke English.

This was how he came to be the principal liaison with the small British delegation, a position that would normally have been occupied by someone more senior.

The British delegation were a poor bunch, intellectually out of their depth and notably lacking in their grasp of Marxist–Leninist ideology. They were all men in their fifties or sixties. But there was one woman, a teacher called Margaret, with extraordinary blue eyes and long blonde hair who told Sergei he could call her Maggie and she was in her early thirties and by far the brightest of the British delegates.

Over the course of the first two days, he and Maggie got on very well: she complimented him on his English and he was fascinated by her beauty and her sophistication and by everything she had to tell him about Great Britain. He realised he was falling in love with her, which was typical – he only ever fell for women who were unattainable.

On the third night she appeared in his hotel room at two in the morning. He had no idea how she'd got in – after all, there were NKVD guards on the corridor where the Soviet delegates were staying – but never got round to asking. The curtain was open just enough to flood the small room with moonlight and he watched as she undressed and slipped into bed beside him and when she left it was past four o'clock and the last two hours felt like twenty minutes and she returned the following night and the one after that, which was his last night in Paris, and this time she arrived earlier and stayed for longer and in between the first and second time they made love, they talked.

She said he was the most wonderful man she'd ever met and the age difference was immaterial and if he ever came to visit England he was to be her guest and he could stay for as long as he liked and he found himself agreeing, though he did wonder whether she had any idea of what the Soviet Union was like, because the notion that he could just go and visit England was about as far-fetched as him being co-opted onto the Central Committee, but he was so captivated by her he decided he really must try in any way he could to get to England.

That was not all that happened on his penultimate day in Paris. They'd been joined the day before by another Comintern official, a nervous-looking man who avoided the conference but remained in the hotel and spent much of his time in conversation with Nadezhda Nikolaeva and that morning she'd told him that he was to accompany the man into the centre of Paris because he had to meet someone but spoke no French and Sergei Grigoryevich's job was to guide him to his destination and translate if there was a problem and he was to do exactly as the man said.

When they left the hotel in La Villette he did suspect the man had been drinking, which was not in itself unusual for a Comintern official, but he insisted they stop at the bar by the metro station where he told Sergei Grigoryevich to order him a Cognac and after three of these, they made their way to centre of Paris. It was a tortuous journey. Every so often the man would lean into Sergei, his breath heavy with alcohol and say they should change at the next stop and after more than an hour of this they reached Boissière metro station and the man said they should exit there and when they came to the street level, they were on Avenue Kléber.

'We need to get to Avenue d'Eylau, do you know it?'

Sergei shook his head.

'It's meant to be nearby.'

'I don't know Paris. I could ask someone – or we could get a map?'

'A map? Don't be ridiculous! Where do they find people like you! I'll wait here, you go to that stall on the other side of the road and ask where Avenue d'Eylau is.'

When they reached Avenue d'Eylau the man looked round and seemed to have an idea of where he was going. He looked at his watch.

'It's only noon; I'm early. We'll go into this bar.'

They remained there for another half hour, during which time the man drank two more large Cognacs and by the time he was ready to leave, Sergei noticed he was unsteady on his feet and he thought that whatever he was doing, he was in no fit state to do it.

'Wait here,' he said, his words slurring, 'and I'll return in around forty minutes.' He looked at his watch, his hands shaking slightly. 'It's twelve thirty now: if I'm not back by a quarter-to-two, you are return to the hotel and tell Nadezhda Nikolaeva what has happened. Whatever you do, make sure you're not being followed. And you'd better drink while you're here. It'll look suspicious if you don't.'

The man returned just before one thirty. He looked exhausted, his face flushed, and he was clearly out of breath and he told Sergei he needed another drink and they found a table on its own at the rear of the bar and there was no one close to them and the man moved closer and spoke with a strong northern accent, which if Sergei had to guess he'd say was from somewhere like Volgoda.

'Do you know Zaslavsky?'

Sergei Grigoryevich shook his head.

'Nikolai Vasilyevich Zaslavsky, he's my boss in the International Liaison Department: a very important man.'

Sergei Grigoryevich felt a cold shudder run down his spine. The OMS was the most clandestine and feared section of the Comintern.

'He was meant to do this job today but he's ill so I've been sent and...' He gripped Sergei's forearm with his hand, not letting go. 'It's very dangerous... they should have called it off rather than sending me. Just because I speak English!'

'What were you doing, can I ask?'

'Seeing as you ask, no, you shouldn't ask, but all you need to know is that Nikolai Vasilyevich was meant to meet with a very important Englishman, one of our top contacts. They call him Archie, Agent Archie. Apparently, he's very highly placed in London and the intelligence we get from him is top secret – the best – and he's visiting Paris and it was felt this would be a good opportunity to pass on a new camera and instructions to him and money too and in return he has documents and film for us.'

The man patted his chest, indicating that was where the material was being kept.

'Should you be telling me all this?'

'Of course not, but these days, the pressure is so great that sometimes you need to unburden yourself by sharing what you know. But not a word of it, right? In return I'll tell Nadezhda Nikolaeva how good you were and I'll not whisper a word to her about the Englishwoman you've been spending the nights with: that's a deal, eh?'

–

During the long rail journeys back to Moscow Sergei Grigoryevich developed a plan. He couldn't stop thinking about the Englishwoman who said he could call her Maggie and who wanted him to be her guest and now he had a way of getting to England.

He knew what he was planning carried an enormous risk. It could easily prove to be his death warrant, so he didn't rush.

He waited until the beginning of August to make his first move. It was a warm Sunday, a day when more people than usual were out and about and he took two trams until he came to the banks of the Moscow River, opposite the Kremlin, and walked along until the British Embassy on Sofiyskaya Naberezhnaya came into sight.

He found a bench overlooking a path leading from the embassy and after an hour watched as a tall man wearing a dark suit left a side gate and walked towards him. Sergei waited until he'd walked past and then followed the man for about ten minutes as he headed south across the bridge into Zamoskvorechye and when the man was close to the Church of the Resurrection he caught up with him.

'Please keep walking and please listen carefully. I have important information for the British authorities. If you're interested, I will be here this time next week. Tell whoever comes to carry a pair of gloves in their right hand and an umbrella in their left and when I approach, I will ask for a light. Do you understand.'

Sergei had spoken in English and to his credit the other man stayed impressively calm, nodding his head and replied 'of course' and walked on, without turning round.

–

There'd been much discussion in the embassy about what to do.

The man Sergei Grigoryevich approached was one of the commercial attachés at the embassy and of course he'd reported the encounter immediately to his superior and George Banks had been informed and it was agreed he'd be the man who'd meet the Russian.

'It's not unknown for the Soviets to use a trap like this but if it was a trap, I'd have expected them to ask us for something in return first, like bringing money.'

'So do we go ahead with it, George?'

'Do you mean, do I go ahead with it, Ambassador? Yes, I think so. It's one way of spending a Sunday, after all!'

A week later and George Banks followed the man's instructions, appearing outside the Church of the Resurrection with a pair of gloves in his right hand and an umbrella in his left. Those stipulations felt to him too much like the way an amateur would imagine spies to behave, rather than something decided by the NKVD.

The man who came up to him was clearly nervous and Banks suggested they walk on towards the Church of the Oppressed and was going to make a joke but decided against it and once they were in a side road, in the shadow of the church he shook the man's hand and noticed it was clammy and he said he'd better make it snappy.

'I have some information for you but in return I want a guarantee that I will be able to live in England and you will help me reach there.'

The man spoke fast, peering over Banks's shoulder towards the road. Banks took a step to his left and they both moved deeper into the shadow of the church.

'What information?'

'Important information about an Englishman who is a Soviet spy. He was in Paris in May as was I and he met with a Comintern agent while he was there.'

'I need to know more.'

'I understand he is very highly placed and the Soviet Union gets excellent intelligence from him. The Comintern agent who met him in Paris handed a camera over to him and got some documents in return.'

'What is this man's name, please?'

'His codename is Agent Archie but I don't know his real name, though I can endeavour to find out. However, first I need a guarantee that I will be granted sanctuary in England.'

George Banks nodded and said 'of course' and then asked the man how he could be sure he was genuine.

'You will have to trust me, but I work for the Comintern. This is my identity card. You speak Russian?'

Banks said 'of course' and looked at the man's card. It was certainly a Comintern card and the photograph was of the same man, though he'd covered up his name.

'I will get to Warsaw: I need papers and assistance to enable me to get from there to England. If you can provide that by this time next week then I will have more details of this man who is spying against you.'

'How can you be so sure you'll be able to get his name?'

'I have some clues already. And I will have enough to help you find him even if I don't get the exact name. You call this a traitor, don't you?'

George Banks nodded. 'Meet me at Mayakovski metro station this time next week. Wear a different coat, as will I. I will carry a copy of that day's *Izvestia*. If I see any sign of danger, I will remove my hat. I would suggest you travel to Belorussia station and then walk to Mayakovski.'

—

It all came together for Sergei Grigoryevich Volkov on the Tuesday. He'd waited until then for an excuse to visit the Archives and Records Department and waited until late in the afternoon to do so when he knew it would be quieter, and when no one was watching he was able to take the key for the Registry, where the International Liaison Department files were kept, and then sat in a corner waiting for everyone to leave, until just he remained.

He'd already established that the Nikolai Vasilyevich the agent had referred to in Paris was Nikolai Vasilyevich Zaslavsky, a senior OMS officer. He knew the files in the International Liaison Department registry were organised under the names of the case officers and it took him half an hour to find the correct file, a sense of utter fear combined with mounting excitement. It was more than he could have hoped for: the man's full name, his codename and details of how much he'd been paid and where and when he'd met his Comintern contacts.

He was surprised the much-feared OMS could be so incautious, it had been something of a long shot expecting the file to be kept in the Registry. The British would not fail to be delighted; with intelligence like this they'd probably fly him to London!

He wrote all the information down and took it home that evening.

That night, he memorised what he'd written down because he knew better than to risk taking the piece of paper to the meeting at Mayakovski metro station. He waited until he was alone in the apartment and then burnt the piece of paper and flushed the ashes down the toilet.

In the unlikely event of him ever being questioned they'd find nothing incriminating on him.

–

It unravelled for Sergei Grigoryevich Volkov in the most dramatic fashion on the Friday morning.

No sooner had he arrived at work than he was marched into the security office and asked what he'd been doing in the International Liaison Department Registry on the Tuesday evening and he replied he didn't think he had been there: he'd been in the Archives and Records Department, and he supposed it was possible he could have passed by the Registry if the door was open and at that point the man who was questioning him started shouting and told him if he was going to lie then at least he ought to make a better fist of it, rather than treating him like a bloody idiot.

At first Sergei Grigoryevich was relatively calm: he knew there was nothing incriminating against him and so did his best to appear confident and said he really didn't know what the problem was and then another man came up to him – just an inch or two from his face, so close he could smell the garlic on his breath – and he grabbed Sergei Grigoryevich roughly by the lapels and asked what he made of this and held up a photograph, which was unmistakably of him and the Englishman outside the Church of the Resurrection the previous Sunday, followed by more photographs, including one of them in the narrow street by the side of the Church of the Oppressed and he had no idea whatsoever how they'd managed to get that one.

'Do you know who that is, Volkov?'

'Which one?'

Sergei Grigoryevich became aware of the silence which greeted his reply and three pairs of eyes staring at him, unblinking and all unsure as to whether this man was possibly mad to have responded in such an impudent manner.

'The man you're talking to, you fool.'

'I've no idea. It could be a man who stopped me for directions, I seem to recall that.'

There was another bout of silence then the third person, who'd not spoken yet, said to listen very carefully. He had a Georgian accent and spoke in a typically slow and deliberate manner.

'You were spotted outside the British Embassy on Sofiyskaya Naberezhnaya the previous Sunday: it's a place we monitor extremely closely – I'm surprised that didn't occur to you. We followed you, established who you are and where you work and continued to keep an eye on you. We were watching you when you met this man last Sunday: he is a British diplomat called Mr George Banks who we assume is a British spy. We've been watching you even more closely since then. You were seen in the International Liaison Department Registry on Tuesday evening but unaccountably the officer who was monitoring you simply put it in his written report, which we only saw late last night.

'We want to know everything: the nature of your contact with the British, what information you were seeking in the Registry and what you were going to do with it.'

He folded his arms and the other two did so at the same time and the three men watched him and Sergei Grigoryevich weighed up the situation in his mind. All things considered, it was bad, but possibly not nearly as bad as it could be. There was nothing incriminating against him other than a couple of blurred photographs: no doubt they'd be turning his apartment upside down, but they'd find nothing.

On the other hand, he had been spotted with the two Englishmen and in the Registry. He couldn't deny that and nor could he think what to say so he told them he was very sorry, he'd been foolish – out of curiosity he'd gone to see the British Embassy and had been intrigued to meet a diplomat and one thing had led to another and the crucial point was they had asked him to get any intelligence he could lay his hands on but once he was in the Registry he'd realised what a fool he'd been and so had left it and to prove that was true, they could search everywhere but would see he'd taken nothing.

'I may be guilty of poor judgement and letting curiosity get the better of me, but I'm no spy!'

'Who said anything about you being a spy?'

Up to that point Sergei Grigoryevich was reconciled to losing his job. Now he realised he was likely to spend some time in prison, possibly at one of the dreaded prison camps. He'd have plenty of time to reflect on his foolishness.

He stood up meekly when told to do so and was handcuffed and was told he'd be taken to prison and dealt with in due course.

When he was out of the room the three men who'd been questioning him agreed that it was all most unsatisfactory.

'He was certainly up to something, but without any evidence...'

'Are we sure there's no evidence?'

'I'm assured there was nothing in his apartment or at his desk or on him. Of course, we do have the evidence that he met with that man Banks, but... that's all.'

The most senior of the men repeated how unsatisfactory this was.

'And the last thing we need is involving the NKVD: we don't want them poking about in our affairs.'

'Absolutely, definitely not!'

'So, all in all... would it be best to...?'

The senior of the men said it would be best and ideally before the end of the day, before the NKVD got wind of it.

–

George Banks turned up at Mayakovski metro station on the Sunday, though not without taking the usual precautions. There was something very credible about the Russian he'd met the previous Sunday. He'd spoken with London and had details of where to tell the man he should go to in Warsaw. But he wasn't terribly surprised when he didn't show up. After waiting for an hour, he slipped into the station, out of another exit and into a van waiting to return him to the embassy.

He was left to ponder what may have been and wonder who the traitor was, if he really did exist. He was weary and supposed to attend the church service in the ambassador's residence but decided to write his report to London instead.

At least he could tell them about Agent Archie.

–

The man who'd been told to see to it was a Belorussian from Minsk called Ivan who lived in constant fear of an early morning knock on his door and so was only too happy to oblige his masters.

He arrived at the prison and demanded to be taken to the prisoner Volkov's cell and told the guard accompanying him to make sure the prisoner was shackled before he went in.

Sergei Grigoryevich Volkov looked terrified, as if he had an inkling of what was about to happen. He tried to explain everything and started to talk about an Englishwoman and a traitor and a spy in Moscow and he gave names, but it was such an incoherent babble the man ignored him.

When Sergei Grigoryevich saw the man take out his pistol he began to weep.

If only he'd listened, he thought. If only he'd listened to his grandfather and his former teacher.

May you never be noticed.

Chapter 18

The meeting took place in a sweltering and dingy basement in the War Office, the brown wallpaper stained with damp and a large, noisy ceiling fan doing little more than circulating hot air around the room.

It was in almost every respect an inappropriate venue for such an important meeting, other than the fact it was one on which all four parties could agree.

The meeting had been called by MI6, but at least one of the participants had declined to go to their headquarters at 54 Broadway and when it was suggested that they meet at St Ermin's Hotel, just round the corner, another participant had an issue with that, which was something to do with a disputed invoice. It had been proposed they hold the meeting at The Annexe's offices in Bryanston Square, but Percy Burton said that was completely out of the question. How could you hold a meeting at a place which doesn't officially exist?

The War Office, then, was the neutral venue for this intelligence community skirmish. Along with MI6, MI5 was there, as was a senior officer from the Special Branch of the Metropolitan Police and Percy Burton of The Annexe.

They gathered in silence, like estranged family members at a funeral — reluctant attendees only present out of a sense of obligation and not a little curiosity.

The meeting was being run by a severe-looking MI6 man called Phillips — with two 'l's, as he never failed to point out

– who Percy Burton knew little about other than he'd been a Royal Navy officer until the late 1920s and very much had the ear of Sir Hugh Sinclair, the head of MI6.

'We have reason to believe that we may have a traitor.' Philips looked around the table with an awkward smile on his face.

'Are you not able to be more specific, Phillips?' It was the man from MI5, a waspish type with the hint of a lisp. Simpkin, or something like that, Percy Burton seemed to recall.

'I was about to say... In June, one of our diplomats in Moscow was approached in the street by a Russian gentleman in his late twenties or early thirties who spoke good English. He said he had some important information for the British authorities and he wanted to meet someone to discuss it. He asked to meet in the same place and at the same time the following week and said the person he met should carry a pair of gloves in his right hand and an umbrella in the left – or possibly the other way round.'

'Sounds like he was playing at being a spy!'

'Good procedure actually, Percy.'

'Not in June: no one wears gloves in Moscow in June.'

Phillips looked furious, but continued. 'There was some discussion between us and Moscow station and it was agreed that George Banks would meet the man. George is one of our more experienced and level-headed officers and although we were quite aware that this could be a trap, we felt it was nonetheless worth the risk.'

He paused to sip from a glass of water.

Simpkin from MI5 asked why it was worth the risk. 'Sounds rather like a set-up to me, Phillips.'

'Well, that's the whole point of espionage, Simpkin: finding foreign spies in one's own country as you do is all well and good but relatively risk-free. However, spying in a foreign country – as is our job – is by its very nature a risky and invariably dangerous business. If our agents were to sit in an office and read newspapers then they wouldn't get very far. Often an approach to us from a foreign national proves to be very fruitful in terms of intelligence gathering. People have all kinds of motives for offering us inform-ation – be it financial, or personal, or a political disagreement – and an experienced agent like George Banks knows how to handle and assess the situation.'

'And he was sure this wasn't a set-up by the Soviets?'

'No, he wasn't sure – which is why I said there's always an element of risk. But Moscow Station was of the view that this approach lacked some of the typical characteristics of a Soviet trap: such as us being asked for something in return first, or even provided with some information at the first encounter to draw us in.

'Banks met with the chap the following week. He says that had the man been a Soviet stooge then he'd have expected him to be more confident – polished, was the word he used – but apparently this chap was polite, but clearly nervous and noticeably inexperienced in what he was doing. He told George that he had important information about an Englishman who's a Soviet spy, codename of Archie. He said this man is "very highly placed" and the Soviet Union gets "excellent intelligence from him" – I'm quoting there from George's report.

'He told George he works for Comintern – he showed him his card – and that he was in Paris in May when this Archie met a Comintern agent there, who gave him a camera and received documents in return. He wanted a guarantee from George that in return for giving him the spy's name he'd be provided with papers which would get him from Warsaw to England.'

'Warsaw?'

'Clearly, he wasn't expecting us to provide papers from Moscow. I imagine he was planning to make his own way to Warsaw. Fairly easy from Moscow.'

'And no clues as to the identity of this mysterious Englishman?'

'I'm coming to that, Simpkin. George asked him how he was sure he could get the man's name and he said – again, I'm quoting – "I have some clues already. And I will have enough to help you find him even if I don't get the exact name." He also referred to him as a traitor.

'George arranged to meet at the same time the following week at Mayakovski metro station, but he never turned up.'

The man from the Special Branch – who Percy Burton thought looked to be too short to be a policeman – spoke next. 'If this Englishman – this traitor, as he so rightly called him – is so important, how would this man be in a position to find out his name? Can we even be sure he works for Comintern?'

'When he showed George his Comintern identity card he covered up his name with his thumb, so that George could see the words "Communist International" at the top, the correct address on Gorky Street and the man's photograph with the official stamp. But he made a mistake. On the bottom right of the card was his signature, which George is certain was SG Volkov – or SN Volkov, apparently the "G" and the "N" look similar in Cyrillic script.

'In the week after the chap didn't show up, George was able to establish that many Comintern employees live in a series of apartment blocks in the Danilovsky district, which is in the city centre and south of the Kremlin. Apparently, it's not unusual for organisations like the Comintern to provide accommodation like this, not least because it helps them to monitor their workers. George found a "Sergei Grigoryevich Volkov" listed as a resident in one of those blocks. The directory he saw was a year old, but we believe this is the man – and he was sharing the apartment with three other men.

'He waited another week and then sent in one of our agents in Moscow, an electrician who works for the city council. He visited the block and found the apartment. Next to the door were the names of the occupants: the name of one of them had been removed.

'So, there we are, gentlemen. We have reason to believe we have a traitor in our midst and that the person in Moscow who was going to give us his identity has disappeared. We know next to nothing about this traitor other than he was in Paris in May, has the codename Archie, is highly placed and is providing "excellent intelligence". It should go without saying that finding the identity of this traitor is a matter of the utmost priority. The only way we're going to find him is by co-operating with each other, which I will be the first to acknowledge is not always the case between our organisations. This country's national security should transcend such relatively petty internecine issues as exist between us.'

'One can see that, of course, Phillips,' said Simpkin from MI5, 'but this is all rather tenuous, isn't it? And you say this happened back in June – if it's so important, why have you waited until now to tell us?'

'Because there's been a recent development we believe corroborates the story about the traitor. At the beginning of last year, an academic from Cambridge was invited by Soviet authorities to visit Moscow to conduct an evaluation of icons stored in the Kremlin. We understand this is almost certainly connected with the Soviets selling some icons on the black market, especially in France where there's quite a market for them. The academic's name is Austin Branstone and when we found out about the visit, we asked the Provost of King's to make co-operation with us a condition of his being permitted to go to Moscow.

'We never expected an awful lot of him, to be honest, because he came across as a rather meek and ineffectual type; nevertheless, because he was going to be operating inside the Kremlin itself, we felt we had to ask him to keep an eye out for us and let us know of names and places he came across.

'But something very interesting did happen. The Kremlin is a very secure area: it is extremely difficult to get into, not least for foreigners, and it's simply not the kind of place where one can just wander around. Branstone said that he always had someone with him and he was also invariably followed by one or two men. However, one day early in May – this is last year, remember – he went for a lunchtime walk and noticed after a while that the man who'd been following him was nowhere to be seen so he decided to head towards the Council of Ministers building, where he spotted a man leaving the building. Branstone said that when the man walked past him there was something familiar about him and he also noticed that he was wearing what he described as British clothing.

'He followed the man through the Kremlin and towards what is called the Taynitskaya Tower and he went in there after the man and spoke to him in English.'

'Really, just out of the blue like that?'

'Indeed so. Branstone says he asked the man – in English – if he knew where one of the other towers was and the man replied – in English – that he didn't and that he was a stranger there himself. And then he hurried off.'

Phillips continued with the story of how the man seemed so familiar to Austin Branstone – how he recalled having played him at chess at Merton College in Oxford in what he thought was 1930 and how he'd beaten the man with the Scholar's Mate and the man had reacted very badly and Branstone remembered him as being upper class and slightly older than him and it was possible the man was at another Oxford college.

'And you say there's no trace of that event?'

'None whatsoever, Percy. One can only assume it was an informal tournament, and remember: it was something like eight years ago. Of course, if we had an idea of which other colleges may have been involved, but nothing… we were left with Branstone encountering an Englishman in the Kremlin, which is highly significant.'

'Which may well be the case, but it doesn't follow that this Englishman in the Kremlin is therefore this Archie character, does it?'

'There's been another development, which I need to tell you about.' Phillips shuffled awkwardly in his chair and fiddled with his fountain pen. Never a man who looked comfortable, now he looked distinctly ill at ease.

'Last month, Austin Branstone was in London for a fortnight's research at the British Library in Bloomsbury. He was staying nearby in Brunswick Square and on the twenty-seventh of July, he was passing Russell Square underground station as a crowd of people were exiting the station. According to Branstone, he's absolutely certain he recognised the man he encountered in the Kremlin. He also says he was even more convinced that it was indeed the same person he'd played chess against in Oxford in 1930. He followed the man into Russell Square but unfortunately, he got into a taxi, which headed south.'

'In this direction?'

'I suppose so, yes.'

'Let's hope he wasn't headed here – the last thing we need is a traitor in the War Office!'

There was nervous laughter around the room but Phillips from MI6 wasn't laughing.

'Unaccountably, Mr Branstone waited until the following week to contact our man in Cambridge, Paxton at Gonville and Caius.'

'Why on earth did he leave it so long, did the fool not realise the urgency?'

'Apparently not, though one should remember the chap's an academic – he probably did think he was getting on with it. The Monday was a Bank Holiday so he didn't actually tell Paxton – and therefore, us – until the Tuesday. Paxton contacted us immediately and we instructed Branstone to come down to London the following day.'

'The Wednesday?'

'Yes, the third of August. And indeed, we'd recently managed to get our hands on photographs from every college in Oxford for the three years, from 1929 until 1931, and needed to show them to Branstone. The man he saw in Moscow – and outside the station – was almost certainly bound to be amongst them: there was a very good chance he'd finally be able to identify him.'

'That's an awful lot of photographs, Phillips!'

'Over one hundred and twenty.'

'One hopes it proved fruitful?'

The others noticed Phillips' head was slightly bowed and his hands clasped on the table as if in prayer and when he spoke it was quieter than before and he was looking down.

208

'That's the awful thing, you see – poor chap never got the chance!'

–

Of course Archie had recognised that wretched man when he'd accosted him in the tower in the Kremlin the previous May.

He'd been a damn fool that day and he was furious with himself not only for how he'd reacted but also how he'd behaved prior to it. There he was in the Kremlin, of all places, one of the most guarded and secretive places in the world. He should have taken a good deal more care: replying in English, for a start – such a schoolboy error.

In fact, the idea of leaving the Council of Ministers and wandering off like that was rash in the extreme. He ought to have remained where he was inside the building, but no... he had to stroll off without an apparent care in the world as if he was going for a lunchtime walk around St James's Park when he was likely a good deal more cautious than he was on that fateful day.

After all, in St James's Park there were always people one wanted to avoid – disagreeable colleagues, of whom there were plenty, bores from university or, his pet hate, former schoolmates, who seemed to flock around the park as if they were on Lower Field at school.

But there in the Kremlin he couldn't have behaved more irresponsibly, oblivious to any danger, apparently confident no one could possibly recognise him, so much so that he didn't even take the simplest of precautions, such as wearing a Russian coat and hat, which would at the very least have enabled him to blend in.

As he walked through the Kremlin, he'd ignored all the basic techniques he'd been taught about being followed. They'd impressed on him that rule number one was to check for a tail. And rule number two? Check for a tail. Only then could you start employing the evasion techniques. He'd never bothered to check even once that day, but at least it had proved to be an important lesson. He was meticulous about it now.

He only spotted the man when he was already in the Taynit-skaya Tower and that was only because he could hardly miss him. He thought he recognised him even before he spoke and asked whether he knew where one of the other towers was, and like the bloody fool he was he'd replied in English — in English! — that he was afraid he didn't know because he was a stranger here himself.

The depths of his stupidity were hard to fathom. He'd even said he was 'afraid', as if he owed the damned man an apology. Speaking English and admitting he was a stranger here... why didn't he just go and tell him he was a Soviet spy and would he like his card?

Once he'd got away from the man, he remembered exactly who he was. A chess tournament in Oxford years ago — possibly in his third year, so 1930, and possibly at Merton — and it involved two other colleges plus King's from Cambridge and he'd been prevailed upon to take part even though he really wasn't in the mood because he'd been away for a golf weekend, which had rather got out of hand at the nineteenth hole, and he had to get an essay in, which was long overdue, and he was still hungover from the weekend, so he was roped into it if against his will, if the truth be told.

His first game was against a young chap from King's who he'd taken an instant dislike too, not least because he was clearly what they called a 'squib' at school, which described the scholarship boys, usually very clever, but with no interest in sport or much else beyond their books.

This squib had wanted to chat and was trying to be friendly and he really wasn't in the mood and then the next thing he knew he'd walked into a Scholar's Mate, which was, of course, quite humiliating and that was exacerbated by the squib sitting there with a broad grin on his spotty face and then he chuckled and said something about 'bad luck' and frankly he could have landed him one there and then, but instead just stormed out, which did cause a bit of a scene later because that meant Oriel was a player down.

He rarely forgot a face, particularly that of someone who'd rubbed him up the wrong way.

He had wondered whether he should report the encounter to Nikolai, but very quickly thought better of it. He wasn't naïve about his Soviet masters: if they found out he'd been seen in the Kremlin by someone who knew him from England then they'd no longer see him as an asset.

And in their eyes, if you weren't an asset, you were a liability, and he was in little doubt as to what they did to liabilities. He'd decided to do nothing, not least because he doubted the other man would remember who he was.

And for the next fourteen months that's how it remained. His career was going very well indeed, giving him access to excellent intelligence, and the Soviets were clearly very pleased with him. He was considerably more alert and constantly checked whether he was being followed and over that time developed the skill of checking he wasn't being tailed or observed without it being at all obvious that he was checking.

And that Wednesday morning in July was a case in point. He'd travelled to Russell Square station because he was due to meet his Soviet contact, which was always a protracted business – changing underground lines, walking, different buses – and he'd told work he was going to be late because he had a dental appointment, but as he left the station he did his first check, surreptitiously scanning the street and that was when he spotted him, unquestionably the same man, and it was obvious he'd seen him because he looked startled. He'd hurried off into Russell Square and took a taxi to work, where he announced his dental appointment had been cancelled.

The next day he'd anticipated the man would be there waiting for him, so he wore a different coat and hat and waited further down the street and sure enough spotted him and it was evident he was only watching people leaving the station, so he didn't notice him when he followed the man to the British Library and it was the same the following day – the Friday – and this time he watched as the man went to the Readers Desk and signed in.

He waited for half an hour and went up to the Readers Desk and told the man there that a letter should be waiting giving him permission to register as a Reader and the man seemed rather put-upon and said to please give him a moment because such letters were not kept there and that gave him the opportunity to look at that morning's list and just eight people had signed in so far and he'd been observing it all from across the hall and so could work out which one was the man he'd been watching.

Austin Branstone

King's College, Cambridge

–

That Friday evening he'd met Osip, his Soviet contact, who was furious that his agent had aborted two meetings and there'd been an argument when he'd told him that's how it was, not everything could go to plan, and there's been some urgent issues at work and did he really want him to draw attention to himself by being absent?

Osip said probably not, and then he'd handed Osip a film and said that ought to keep Moscow satisfied and Osip told him to keep his voice down and it wasn't for him to decide what satisfied Moscow and what were these issues at work, because he didn't seem to be his normal self?

'What do you mean?'

'You appear to be agitated.'

'I'm fine: sometimes the pressure... you know, doing two jobs... But I'll be fine, there's really nothing to worry about. It's the Bank Holiday weekend so we're in the country and I'll go for a couple of long walks with the dogs and I'll be as right as rain next week.'

As right as rain was one way of describing it. He managed to drive to Cambridge on the Sunday, which was a more rushed visit than he'd hoped for, and did necessitate a bit of explanation as his wife had 'plans', but it did mean he was well prepared. Branstone was back at the College and he found out where his rooms were.

He left work early on the Tuesday and took the four-thirty from Liverpool Street and was in Cambridge by six thirty and hoped he wasn't cutting things too fine but nevertheless decided against taking a taxi, so he walked up to King's College, skirting round the college to the lawns at the rear and then through the Back Gate, the gown he'd brought with him enabling him to enter and move around the place with the confidence of someone who felt he owned the place, which a distant branch of his wife's family did.

Austin Branstone's rooms were in Bodley's Court. It was a quarter past seven when he arrived at the foot of his stairwell and he knew he needed to move fast. From now on people would notice him.

–

Austin Branstone couldn't decide whether to go to Hall for dinner or to stay in his room and work. The meeting with Paxton at Gonville and Caius that day had rather thrown him: Paxton had torn him off a strip or two and said waiting so long to tell him about seeing the man outside the station was 'inexplicable' and now he had to travel to London the next day to explain himself and his carefully made plans had been thrown into disarray.

There was a knock on the door and he sighed because he really wasn't in a mood to be disturbed and this was probably Babcock wondering if he was ready to go down to Hall and he'd have to make his excuses.

He called out 'hang on' and opened the door and for a moment he assumed it was Babcock because he was wearing a gown and was a similar height and build to his colleague.

But that was Branstone's last ever rational thought. The figure barged into the room, clasping a gloved hand over his mouth, and with his body weight propelled him across the room and bundled him onto the bed, pinning him to it.

Branstone could barely breathe and it felt as if the man was crushing him and in his terrified state he wondered if this was one of these awful sexual assaults of which there'd been a spate involving undergraduates the previous year. Then the scarf the man had round his face slipped and the face appeared in front of him and Branstone was gripped by a fear so powerful he lost the ability to move.

It was the same man he'd seen in the Kremlin and outside the station last week and the very same man he'd beaten at chess in 1930.

The man said nothing. He was much stronger than Branstone and had his hand over his mouth, but Branstone wouldn't stop squirming, even when he felt the sharp pain in his side and, at first, he was unsure what caused it but then he saw the knife, a surprisingly short blade, and the man appeared to be smiling as if he was enjoying this. Branstone's last thought was that with some luck Babcock would hear all the commotion and knock on his door any minute and it would all be over.

–

When it was over, Archie sat on the bed for a while to catch his breath. A look of sheer horror was frozen on Branstone's face and that was quite disconcerting so he hauled him under the covers and then tidied things up, though in fact it wasn't too bad. It had been quick and efficient, thirty seconds at the very most from entering the room to Branstone dead. He had wondered about the knife, but the Soviets had impressed on him how reliable they were.

And silent.

He removed the gloves, washed his hands and face in the small sink and checked there were no visible signs of blood anywhere on his clothing.

He'd slip out through the Queen's Lane exit and hopefully be in good time for the last train to London.

All things considered, he thought he'd handled the whole business quite well.

It hadn't been pleasant but nor was it quite as awful as he'd feared.

And it was one less thing to worry about.

—

'And they found Branstone's body the next morning, you say?'

A sense of deep shock now mixed with the oppressive heat in the basement of the War Office. 'Around mid-morning: no one missed him that evening because it's the holidays and dinners are less formal and it was only when he didn't turn up in London that we alerted Paxton and he went over to King's. Apparently, the door was locked. Messy business.' Phillips shook his head. He still couldn't quite believe it.

'And no sign of who killed him?'

'Very few people around. The porter seems to recall a man in a gown walking through Back Gate but that hardly narrows it down; it would have been suspicious had he not been wearing a gown. But nothing more than that.'

'Fingerprints?'

Phillips shook his head.

'Sounds as if it was a professional job.'

No one else said a word for a while. They'd turned the ceiling fan off because it was so noisy and now the room was deathly silent and the atmosphere sombre and unbearably hot. Eventually Simpkin from MI5 spoke.

'Are you suggesting that the traitor, the man in Moscow Banks was told about, is the same as the man in the Kremlin who

Branstone also saw outside the station – and who possibly killed him or caused him to be killed?'

'I'm not certain,' said Phillips, 'but my gut feeling is that they're one and the same. I hope so.'

'Really? Why on earth do you *hope so*?' It was the man from Special Branch, sounding incredulous.

'If I may presume to answer on your behalf, Phillips?' Percy Burton looked worried. 'Because if it's not the same person then the likelihood is we have two traitors, do we not? And for what it's worth, I agree with Phillips – my instinct, too, is that it is the same person. I believe that the case of Branstone most probably corroborates what Banks was told in Moscow. We have a high-level traitor operating in London and we need to make it our priority to find him.'

'I would ask that we all put aside whatever rivalries we have and commit to finding this man. We need to make him our top priority.'

'And this codename, Phillips: Archie. I trust there's no clue there?'

Phillips assured them this was the first thing they'd checked out and no one in the Service with the name Archie or Archibald was a suspect.

Chapter 19

The Hague, Holland
November 1938

As soon as Andriy Oleksandrvych Kovalenko heard he was to be posted to The Hague he did his best to find out what he could about the place that would be his home for the next three years.

There were plenty of foreign ministry briefings to read prior to his posting: lengthy papers which no one had bothered to edit about Dutch politics and foreign affairs and the state of the Dutch economy, along with interminable screeds about the Dutch Communist Party and the prospects for proletariat revolution in Holland and the continuing and regrettable presence of Trotskyites and Social Democrats.

He found a guidebook in the library at work and The Hague sounded a pleasant enough if rather small place. It was on the North Sea coast, with little industry but plenty of artists and craftsmen, lots of woods and pleasant squares and was a controversial seat of government given that the place was known as 'the largest village in Europe'. It had originally been, he read, a hunting resort for Dutch nobility.

He hoped its hunting days were over.

The subject of hunting was a sensitive one for Andriy Oleksandrvych Kovalenko. He'd been sent back to Moscow in February 1937, under something of a cloud. Until then he'd been a third secretary at the Soviet Embassy in Vienna and was on track for promotion to second secretary and there'd even been talk of a posting to Paris, which made sense as he spoke good French.

Being a third secretary meant his wife, Tatyana, wasn't permitted to join him, so she remained in Moscow with their children, Maksym and Larysa. His life in Vienna was a lonely one. The restrictions imposed on a Soviet diplomat in a city like Vienna and his paltry salary and allowances meant there was precious little to do outside work.

He hoped that if he became a second secretary it might be possible for Tatyana to join him and this was a cause of some optimism.

His career was going well. Everything was fine.

Until one night in Vienna when he went out for dinner.

–

It had seemed innocent enough at first: an elderly Austrian couple – the Doblers – lived on the floor below and he was on friendly terms with them; he would hold the door open for them and nod and smile and wish them a good morning or similar.

However, one day he caught the woman struggling up the stairs with her shopping and insisted on carrying it to her apartment and when they reached the entrance was shocked to hear the woman address him in broken Ukrainian.

Her mother, God rest her soul, had grown up in Lvov and Andriy told her that his own mother was also born and raised in Lvov, and who would believe it!

'And where are you from?'

He was already saying far more than he ought to because diplomats weren't supposed to share personal information, but he didn't see what harm a little old lady could do so he told her he was born and raised in Kharkiv.

A week later he was invited to the Doblers' for tea on a Sunday afternoon. Naturally, Andriy Oleksandrvych reported this contact to Yegorov, the NKVD *rezident* at the embassy. Yegorov was of course a complete bastard, but that was understood: he would not have reached his position in the NKVD without being a complete bastard. But as complete bastards and

NKVD *residents* went, Yegorov wasn't too bad. He'd even been known to smile on occasion and when Kovalenko went in to see him to get clearance for tea at the Doblers he seemed relaxed enough, so much so that he told Kovalenko that there were circumstances when even a third secretary could use his judgement and this would be one of them and he really didn't need clearance every time he took a shit.

They'd had a good laugh about that and then Kovalenko realised he'd omitted mentioning that Frau Dobler spoke some Ukrainian because Yegorov would certainly have wanted to know about that, but by then he was halfway out of the office and he took the view that it was probably best not to mention it now.

The tea had been pleasant enough: very formal in the Austrian way of things and their apartment was far too warm and he spoke a little with Frau Dobler in Ukrainian and he and Herr Dobler made polite conversation in German about nothing in particular.

Two weeks later the Doblers invited him for dinner and he wasn't sure whether to report it to Yegorov but decided this was one of those cases where he could use his judgement and, after all, what harm could there be in having dinner with elderly neighbours?

Quite a lot, as it happened.

When he entered the Doblers' apartment, Andriy Oleksandrvych noticed that the dining table was set for four and at that moment a tall man in a well-cut brown suit appeared and introduced himself in rather poor German as 'Michael' and Michael said little during the meal and it was never explained who he was or why he was there and Andriy Oleksandrvych spent most of the evening unsettled because really he ought to report this to Yegorov, but then he'd have to explain why he'd not told him about the dinner in the first place and it would all feel rather awkward.

But by the end of the evening, no harm appeared to have been done. Michael came across as being disinterested in him, he was more interested in Frau Dobler's food.

Two days later Andriy Oleksandrvych was walking through the Naschmarkt after work to buy vegetables when he found himself walking alongside Michael, the man who'd been at the Doblers' but now instead of speaking in poor German he spoke good Russian, though with a foreign accent.

'It was a pleasure to meet you at our friends'.' He walked with Andriy Oleksandrvych as he headed towards a stall which heavily discounted some produce at the end of the day and waited patiently as the Russian diplomat made his purchases and then continued alongside him.

'If ever we can be of mutual assistance to each other then I'm sure we could have a very' – he'd hesitated, searching for the right words – 'Positive relationship.' Andriy Oleksandrvych was in no doubt this was a clandestine approach of some kind or the other so he said he had no idea what he was talking about and that he could conceive of no circumstances in which he could be of assistance, or vice versa.

The man nodded and said of course but perhaps he'd want to think about it and if he was interested in having a further chat – with no commitment, of course, just a chat – then all he needed to do was leave this postcard – he handed him one with a view of the Danube on the front – in the Doblers' letterbox and then meet him at eight o'clock the following morning in the Schwarzenberg Park in the 4th district.

And just as Andriy Oleksandrvych was about to tell Michael to get lost, the man grasped his forearm and leant close to him.

'If we agree to work together, we will open an account in a Swiss bank for you with a considerable amount of money in it. We'd just want some information, that's all.'

Andriy Oleksandrvych pushed the man's arm away and hurried off, but not before the man called after him.

'We do hope Tatyana, Maksym and Larysa are safe: Moscow is such a dangerous place these days!'

–

There was no question whatsoever that Andriy Oleksandrvych ought to have reported the encounter to Yegorov immediately, preferably that evening. But he needed to get his story straight; he needed a good explanation for why he'd not reported meeting the man called Michael at the dinner.

But as he walked back slowly to the apartment just off Kärntner Ring he started to think. The situation in Moscow *was* dreadful these days: so many people – including friends and colleagues – were being arrested and then disappearing and it was clear that no one was safe. Being a loyal Party member was no guarantee of anything, in fact, it could count against you.

And the man had mentioned a considerable amount of money and at the very least he could find out what the man wanted, so when he entered the apartment block, he slipped the postcard with the Danube on the front into the Doblers' letterbox.

By the time he entered the tiny apartment he regretted what he'd done. What on earth had got into his mind – was he completely mad? During the course of a sleepless night, he resolved to go to the Schwarzenberg Park where he'd tell the man he wasn't interested, that there'd been a misunderstanding and he was never to contact him again.

He left the apartment just after half past seven and took a circuitous route to the Schwarzenberg Park. He was less than five minutes from it and waiting to cross Favoriten Strasse when a lorry paused in front of him, with large panels of glass strapped to the side.

The lorry stopped long enough for him to see himself reflected very clearly in the glass. And not just himself: behind him he spotted two of Yegorov's NKVD officers.

They'd been following him.

He must assume he had been spotted with the man the previous evening at the Naschmarkt.

He had seconds to compose himself and decide what to do. The lorry pulled away and he crossed the road, turning left towards a kiosk selling newspapers and cigarettes, where he bought a packet and then headed towards the embassy, not once turning round.

As soon as he entered the embassy, he headed straight for Yegorov's office. He was still wearing his coat and holding his hat as he breathlessly explained what happened. When he finished, still breathing hard, Yegorov indicated he should sit down.

'If I understand you correctly, Comrade Kovalenko, you met a foreigner at dinner in your neighbours' apartment, which you failed to report to us, and then last night this man approached you in the Naschmarkt and asked if you were interested in talking further and you told him to get lost. Is that correct?'

'Yes, comrade. You'll recall I'd already cleared with you visiting my neighbours' apartment. When I was invited for dinner, I had no idea this man or indeed anyone else would be there, but his presence seemed to be inconsequential. I realise now I ought to have reported it. I was shocked when he approached me in the Naschmarkt last night. I decided to report it to you, hence my presence in your office now.'

'Tell me the route you took to the embassy this morning?'

Andriy Oleksandrvych was certain that Yegorov didn't know that he knew he was being followed, so he described the route in detail.

'I realise that may seem a somewhat roundabout route to the embassy, but I sometimes like to leave early and have a good walk. I often visit the kiosk on Favoriten Strasse to buy cigarettes.'

Yegorov said nothing as he watched him very carefully, his eyes narrowing as if he was concentrating.

'Let's go through once more what happened at the Naschmarkt.'

A series of questions followed, many of which were repetitive but phrased slightly differently, a standard NKVD tactic to catch someone out.

What exactly did he say to you?

How was he dressed?

What language did he speak?

Did he offer you money?

Did he threaten you?

And Andriy Oleksandrvych stuck to a simple and only partially true account. He assumed he'd been followed to the Naschmarkt so he kept that in mind. He said the man spoke in German and asked him – repeatedly – whether he was interested in talking further and he'd made it very clear to him that he wasn't.

'And did he give you anything, Comrade Kovalenko?'

'No, comrade.'

'You're sure? You hesitated then.'

'I'm sure.'

Appear confident. Stick to your story.

This went on for another two hours and he got the impression that Yegorov wasn't sure whether to believe him or not. He told him to wait in his outer office. He needed to speak with the ambassador.

–

Which was how Andriy Oleksandrvych Kovalenko ended up back at the Foreign Ministry in February 1937.

It had been made very clear he'd shown a serious lack of judgement, but to his immense relief that was as far as they went. He attributed this to the fact they had no real evidence against him, just a rather weak set of circumstances in which he'd failed to report a dinner invitation and had encountered a foreigner in the market. Against that – and very much in his favour – was the fact that he had reported the initial invitation from the Doblers and had gone straight to Yegorov when he realised he was being followed.

He shuddered when he thought of the extraordinary stroke of luck that had enabled him to spot he'd been followed, but then there was a Ukrainian saying about a wise man being the creator of his luck. He'd not panicked when he spotted the NKVD men in the reflected glass. He was impressed with how calm he'd been.

That's not to say all was well back in Moscow. The arrests he'd heard about now appeared to be on the increase. Hardly a day went by when one didn't hear of someone – a neighbour, an acquaintance, a colleague or an acquaintance of a neighbour or a colleague – being arrested and after that one rarely heard anything about them, other than whispered gossip about their wife being arrested too or having to leave Moscow and even of children being sent to an orphanage and given new names.

So Andriy Oleksandrvych learnt to keep his head down. He learnt to be guarded in his conversations, even with Tatyana. The chaos and fear around him meant that he could afford to be philosophical about being effectively demoted: he was now based in the department that handled consular matters throughout Europe. For the first few months his work was little more than clerical, certainly not fitting for someone who'd already served as a diplomat, albeit a fairly junior one.

But suspicion was never far around the corner. In the August he'd been shocked when Makarov, who sat opposite him and with whom he got on well, disappeared. He was fine on the Wednesday as he talked about taking the family to his in-laws' dacha for a few days. On the Thursday morning he wasn't there. No one said a word about him. Later that morning two men from the security department came to clear out Makarov's desk.

Makarov no longer existed.

The following week every member of his department was called in individually to see one of the security officers. The man who Andriy Oleksandrvych found himself facing in a stifling room was a short, red-faced man called Tarasov.

Through the fug of cigarette smoke, he glanced up, shaking his head.

'I see you left Vienna in disgrace, Kovalenko.'

He didn't reply at first because he took an exception at the man's tone.

'There was a misunderstanding over how soon I reported a foreign contact. There was never any question as to my loyalty and my—'

'There is ALWAYS a question as to your loyalty, Kovalenko! There is always a question as to everyone's loyalty these days! The achievements and policies of Comrade Stalin are constantly undermined by oppositional forces and disrupters, many of them at the heart of government.'

Andriy Oleksandrvych nodded and said 'of course'.

'One way in which comrades can assure us of their loyalty is to bring to our attention anyone they know of who acts against the interests of the Soviet Union.'

He stared at him through the smoke and raised his eyebrows to show that this was actually a question.

'Fortunately, I have not come across such disgraceful actions, comrade.'

'There is an expectation of someone in your position that encountering such treason is inevitable. A failure to inform us of this will inevitably bring into question your own loyalty. I hope you understand, Kovalenko.'

–

Andriy Oleksandrvych understood perfectly well. He was expected to inform on someone, to give the NKVD another victim. If he didn't do that, he would be that victim. It was like a plot from one of the novels he used to read before reading novels became an act of suspicion.

The victim presented himself just a week later, when they were spending a weekend at Tatyana's grandparents' dacha. It was a large family gathering and included a number of her cousins, one of whom was married to a man called Belov, a disobliging drunk with a grossly inflated opinion of his importance. Belov worked as a manager for a group of state farms and as far as Andriy Oleksandrvych could gather, this involved being driven around the farms to check they were keeping up with their quotas.

On the second evening he found himself sitting outside with Belov and a couple of other family members and Belov was already drunk on homemade brandy that Andriy Oleksandrvych thought was strong enough to fuel a car.

'I hear you were demoted, Andriy?'

One of Belov's many dislikes were Ukrainians and so he made a point of exaggerating Ukrainian names, over-pronouncing them to emphasise their difference from Russian. Andriy was pronounced 'Andree', as opposed to the Russian version Andrei.

'What makes you think that?'

The farm manager shrugged and said something about him being well informed and Kovalenko said not in this case and decided it was best to switch topics and asked Belov how his job was going.

'I hear you have your own driver?'

A self-satisfied grin lit up Belov's face. He drank another glass of fuel and said indeed.

'You must be doing very well.'

Belov shifted his chair closer and slapped Kovalenko's thigh and said he was and, in confidence, you understand, there's talk of a further promotion.

He noticed that Belov was slurring his words now and his eyes were bloodshot and when he gazed into his empty glass Kovalenko reached over and filled it.

'Some of the state farms fail to reach their quotas and it needs someone like me to sort them out!'

'I thought all state farms were exceeding their targets?'

'Ha! If only that were the case. The attitude of some of these fools...' He waved his hand as a way of illustrating how poor their attitude was.

'Let me tell you something, the People's Commissar for Agriculture visited one of these farms and asked the manager how their turnip production was going and the man replied, "Commissar, we have produced so many turnips that if they were piled on top of each other, they'd reach all the way to God!" And do you know what the Commissar said?'

Kovalenko shook his head. Belov was speaking loudly and a few others had joined them.

'He said, "God does not exist!" And do you know what the manager said?'

No one was looking directly at Belov.

'He replied, "I know — and neither do the turnips!"'

There was a marked silence before Belov laughed uproariously at his own joke and pushed Kovalenko's shoulder and told him to laugh too.

—

On his first day back at work he asked to see Tarasov and repeated what Belov had told him, adding in some extra material to show just how disloyal and indeed dangerous this man was.

'Can you imagine, Comrade Tarasov, being driven around and sowing who knows what kind of dissatisfaction?'

Tarasov nodded in an appreciative manner, busily writing down everything he'd been told.

'And you say he criticised Comrade Stalin?'

'Indeed, comrade, in quite despicable terms.'

Tarasov thanked him and said he had done well to demonstrate his loyalty. It would not go unnoticed.

Later that week Tatyana waited until they were in bed before she whispered what her mother had told her: Belov had been arrested the previous day and no one knew where he was. His wife had been arrested that evening and no one had any idea what had happened to their daughters.

Kovalenko had every reason to believe his informing on Belov put him in line for promotion. When a fellow Ukrainian called Lysenko was appointed head of the Consular Desk looking after Belgium and Holland, he soon became his right-hand man. Lysenko trusted him and valued his work and at his suggestion Andriy Oleksandrvych began to study Dutch.

In October 1938 Lysenko called him into his office and told him how impressed he was with his work and how much he'd come to rely upon him. He'd been appointed to the embassy in The Hague, he said. And he'd like Kovalenko to come with him.

'You'd still only be a third secretary, but I would hope you'd take the view that after your difficulties in Vienna... it would be an opportunity to rehabilitate yourself.'

–

Andriy Oleksandrvych Kovalenko arrived in The Hague in early November and soon appreciated he'd struck lucky with his new posting. Despite the near-constant presence of a North Sea squall he found the Dutch capital a relaxed and charming place, nothing like the intrigue and formality which so characterised Vienna.

The work at the embassy was straightforward and Lysenko was clearly delighted to have him there. The only worry, if that was the right word, was that the NKVD *rezident* was none other than Yegorov, his nemesis from Vienna.

But even that didn't appear to be a problem. Yegorov told him that he'd personally vetted him when his name came up for the posting and he was prepared to put his error in Vienna in the past. He was especially pleased with what Comrade Tarasov had described as his co-operation.

'I'd like to think that you'd continue this co-operation here in The Hague. Should you come across anyone at the embassy whose loyalty you have cause to doubt, be sure to let me know.'

'Of course, comrade!'

'And, likewise, should anyone approach you... this time, don't leave it until the next day, eh?'

He shared a house with other junior diplomats on Nassau Plein, close to Alexanders Veld, and assumed he was being closely monitored and occasionally followed, but he didn't regard this as a problem.

On his third Sunday in The Hague, he'd been the early duty officer in the embassy, meaning a six o'clock start and a mid-afternoon finish and rather than return to Nassau Plein he decided to head to the centre and get to know the city and find somewhere cheap to have a drink.

He took a tram to the station and from there headed west, across the canal and through Nieuwe Markt and he'd just entered Turfmarkt when he became aware of someone behind him, which he assumed was one of Yegorov's men and he was calm about that because he was doing nothing wrong. He made sure he walked at the same pace, but was surprised as the footsteps closed in on him.

'Fancy meeting you here! Who'd have thought it?'

The man to whom the voice belonged moved alongside him and, being taller, lowered his head and briefly raised his hat so that he'd recognise him but Andriy Oleksandrvych had already realised it was Michael, the man from Vienna, the man who'd suggested they could be of mutual assistance to each other and the man who promised him a considerable amount of money.

The man who'd very nearly cost him his life.

They were alongside a set of narrow steps leading down to a bar and Michael guided him by the elbow down the steps. Although Andriy Oleksandrvych did wonder about leaving there and then, he'd been caught by surprise and before he knew it, he was in the bar and allowing Michael to lead him to a room at the rear, which he then locked.

'Before you say anything, you're not to worry. This place is perfectly safe and I can assure you that you were not being followed – I wouldn't have come within a mile of you if you had been. Not like in Vienna, eh?'

Kovalenko was too shocked to reply. The man removed his hat and coat and his jacket too and loosened his tie and told him to make himself at home because they had plenty to chat about and would he like something to drink, or to eat, perhaps?

Kovalenko said he was fine, thank you, which could not have been further from the truth.

'I am sorry we didn't get to meet as arranged in Vienna, but I'm quite aware of what happened. It was very clever of you to spot you were being followed and to get away with it: if I'm honest with you, I feared the worst. When we heard you'd been sent back to Moscow, well… with all that's going on there… and yet, here you are, what a marvellous turn up for the books. I could hardly believe it when I was told you'd arrived in The Hague! We can now resume our relationship!'

'Who are you?'

'Do you mean in the way that those psychiatrists in Vienna ask the question?'

'You know what I mean.'

'I work for British Intelligence. We had our eyes on you in Vienna and believed we could form a relationship, hence my approach to you there. The offer I made then still stands: the equivalent of one thousand pounds in whichever currency you wish in a Swiss bank. We would require you to provide us with top-quality intelligence for at least two years, after which we'd undertake to provide you with a new identity and a home in England. And—'

Kovalenko shook his head.

'… and we also undertake to bring Tatyana, Maksym and Larysa out to join you.'

'You're assuming I'm interested.'

'I know you're interested because you put that postcard through the Doblers' letterbox. Interested is possibly overstating it, but curious at the very least and that's enough of a basis for us to commence a relationship. And remember, Kovalenko, this will be of at least as much benefit to you as it is to us.'

'You're asking me to be a traitor.'

'I'm asking you to help us and in return we'll help you.'

'Thank you very much, but I can assure you I don't need any help.'

'Do you know how many people we estimate have disappeared and then been executed in the Soviet Union over the past two years?'

Kovalenko shrugged and said he wasn't sure what he was talking about.

'Half a million – and that's a conservative estimate. Our American colleagues are convinced the number is higher. I find it impossible to believe you're unaware of the scale of what's going on, Mr Kovalenko. A professional diplomat like you — a decent, intelligent man, a family man — surely you must be worried about what fate awaits you. And what will happen then to your wife and your children? We hear the most dreadful things.'

The silence that followed was longer than Kovalenko would have liked, but he was using the time to concoct a plan. Although there was a degree of truth in what the Englishman said, he was certain that the risks involved were too great. And, in any case, he had no desire to be a traitor. The tensions in Moscow would soon pass. This time he'd more cunning. Not only would he avoid walking into any trap himself, he set one up for the Englishman.

He'd hand him on a plate for Yegorov and, as with Belov, it would count in his favour.

'I need to think about it.'

The man called Michael smiled. 'When is your next day off?'

'Wednesday.'

'Go to the art gallery in Mauritahuis by the Plein between ten thirty and eleven that morning. On the first floor — in room 8 — is a marvellous painting by Rembrandt called the "School of Anatomy". I'll be waiting in that room. Will you remember all that?'

Kovalenko said of course and he'd see him on Wednesday, and he hoped matters would work out, though when he said that he wasn't sure it sounded right: too ambiguous, maybe.

—

'Yes, it's definitely him — no question about it. Look, here — compare the two photographs.' Yegorov placed them alongside each other and angled a lamp over them.

'This one taken of the Englishman in Vienna last February and the one taken today on Turfmarkt. And this is a better one, taken as he leaves the bar.'

'With Kovalenko following him!'

The four NKVD officers laughed and one of them commented that it was such a basic mistake – the two men leaving together. The Englishman looked like an amateur.

'And Kovalenko too.'

'Kovalenko's a traitor.'

'Of course, comrade, I wasn't suggesting that...'

They were in a NKVD safe house on Prinse Straat, close to the Fish Market because what they were discussing was far too serious and sensitive to risk meeting at the embassy. The other three men were Yegorov's trusted NKVD officers and they had been following Kovalenko since he'd left the embassy that afternoon.

'What do we do, sir, bring him here and then get him to Moscow?'

Yegorov leant back in his chair and studied the unlit cigarette he'd been holding for a while.

'That's too risky... there's a Swedish Airlines flight from Amsterdam, but it has too many stops before Moscow. The train journey is too long, and crosses too many borders. The safest way would be to get him out by sea through Rotterdam but you say none of our ships are sailing from there for a few days?'

'Correct, sir: there's a sailing to Leningrad on Thursday.'

'We can't wait that long. We'll deal with Kovalenko here.'

Another long silence and the other three men nodded. They appreciated that Yegorov was always clear in his instructions.

'And do we interrogate him, sir, or just... deal with him?'

'Just deal with Kovalenko, I've had enough of the bastard!

-

They found Andriy Oleksandrvych Kovalenko's naked body floating in the Hofvijver – the large lake in the centre of The Hague – soon after first light on an unseasonably calm and bright Monday morning, the weak sun picking out the blotchy, pink body bobbing in the choppy grey water.

The police surgeon who examined the body estimated it had been in the water for between eight and sixteen hours and apologised for not being more precise. But he was able to be precise about the cause of death, but then even the young police officer who'd pulled the body out of the water could tell that: the man's head was only just attached to the rest of the body.

'And there is no other way of identifying the body, doctor?' The surgeon shook his head and the police officer did likewise. He could do without this and would probably write it off as a drunk who fell into the Hofvijver, though why he'd be wearing no clothes in November was beyond him.

Chapter 20

London
November 1938

There were far more people present than was normally the case for meetings at 54 Broadway. The way business was conducted at MI6 tended to be very much in keeping with the nature of the organisation: highly secretive – even clandestine – and with a presumption of mistrust. Meetings were held with the minimum number of people necessary and behind closed doors with the blinds drawn. Whispered conversations in corridors would pause suddenly when anyone else approached, the participants and the passers-by doing their best to avoid eye contact.

Occasionally Sir Hugh Sinclair as chief of MI6 would call a meeting of all officers based in London, but these were very rare occasions and tended to be social rather than a place where anything secret was discussed.

So, the presence of more than two dozen officers in the large room on the third floor was most unusual, so much so that many of those present were suspicious and awkward as they waited for it to begin. More than one person muttered to the person next to them that maybe the rumours about the organisation being disbanded were true.

And then the door swung open and Phillips – the man with two 'l's – entered, followed by the chief who told everyone not to get up and he wanted to let everyone present know that what Phillips was about to tell them was most important and had his full backing and then Phillips said something about the entire ship's crew being assembled and suggested they pay attention because what he had to say was, as Sir Hugh had indicated, really most important.

'Indeed, I'd go as far as to say that it is the most serious challenge facing the Service.'

He paused, gathering his thoughts. Following the meeting in August at the War Office with representatives of The Annexe, MI5 and Special Branch Phillips had hoped it would be a matter of weeks before he managed to discover the identity of the traitor. But by late September he realised he was no closer.

He had to admit defeat and realised he'd been foolish expecting to discover the identity of the traitor quite so easily so he went to see Sir Hugh who was most decent in the circumstances and said of course he was aware of this traitor and absolutely it should be a priority for the Service and really Phillips should feel no shame whatsoever in asking for help and, after all, when they were at sea and there was a storm, it needed the whole crew to get through it, did it not?

So now Phillips looked at the officers gathered around the table. They were from the parts of the Service looking after Europe, divided between a dozen senior officers who looked after specific country desks and some fifteen or so younger officers, some with only a couple of years' service but who'd already been marked out for preferment.

They were what the chief liked to call his high flyers and Phillips was not alone among the senior officers in sometimes feeling intimidated by their relative youth and their blatant ambition, all so bright and sharp and terribly confident, with enormous energy and drive. They made him feel terribly old.

He was quite nervous as he began, concentrating on his notes as he told the meeting how Moscow Station had been informed in June by a local contact that a 'highly placed' Englishman – codename Archie, apparently – had been recruited as a Soviet spy and was providing what was described as 'excellent intelligence' and had met a Comintern contact in Paris in May. He paused and carefully turned the page of his notebook before continuing: in return for certain assurances this contact would endeavour to pass on the name of this person when they met the following week but he failed to make that meeting and Moscow station had good reason to believe he may have been caught.

'If I may interrupt. Phillips?'

'I had hoped to—'

'Who was handling this for Moscow Station?'

'George Banks.'

The man who'd asked the question was called Williamson, who'd been Banks's predecessor. 'Naturally, one trusts George's judgement, but what makes him believe this contact has been caught?'

'He managed to identify him and discovered he had vanished from where he lived.'

'Or he could have been stringing us along, of course.' It was Coombe who looked after the Balkans.

'He could, but Moscow believed he was credible. I need to continue: last year a Cambridge academic was invited to Moscow to study icons in the Kremlin and it was made clear to him that there was an expectation he was to co-operate with us.'

And Phillips proceeded to tell the story at some length about Branstone, who he only referred to as 'the academic', and how they'd had very limited expectations of him but that in May – this was last year, 1937, he reminded them – this chap was in the Kremlin when he spotted a man leaving the Council of Ministers who he says was dressed like an Englishman. Furthermore, he thought he recognised him, so he followed him and caught up with him in one of the Kremlin's towers, where they had a brief conversation in English, after which he was more convinced than ever that he'd encountered him before.

'And do we have a name, or at least a description, perhaps?'

Phillips wasn't sure who'd asked the question and nor was he sure how far he was to go in answering it. He said there was no name and admitted the description was so bland as to be useless, but the academic did recall he'd met the man and it was at a chess match at Oxford most probably in 1930 but despite that they'd drawn a blank in identifying the man.

Phillips paused and looked up and around the table, where the faces peering at him were mostly indifferent. A friend of his from school had gone on the stage and told him an actor's enduring fear was of losing one's audience. As Phillips looked around, it seemed he was losing his audience.

But one of those round the table was listening with rapt attention. He was one of the high flyers, one of the fifteen or so bright and ambitious young officers, destined for an assured career in the Service and he was making a supreme effort to retain his composure and show no reaction. But he'd become accustomed to thinking quickly and controlling his emotions, so he did his best to look slightly bored while at the same time every one of his senses was heightened: it felt as if the room had become unaccountably loud and Phillips was speaking at the top of his voice.

Phillips proceeded to tell them how in August the academic had spotted the man he'd last seen in the Kremlin leaving a tube station and to cut a long story short, well... he'd delayed reporting this, would you believe, and the day before he was due to come down to London to discuss it and hopefully help identify the man, he was found dead in his room, in Cambridge.

This had the desired effect because he now had the attention of everyone in the room: there was a good deal of muttering around the table and people looked up, now interested.

There was a long discussion about whether the man who'd met a Comintern agent in Paris in May was indeed the same man who'd been seen in the Kremlin the previous year and again in London in August, but the clear consensus was that the most sensible course of action – 'sensible' was a very MI6 word – was to proceed on the basis that they were one and the same man and therefore there was a traitor at the heart of the British establishment.

The most persuasive intervention was from Williamson, who said that in his experience it was hard enough for a Russian to get into the Kremlin, let alone a foreigner, but to get into the Council of Ministers building – which the traitor had been seen leaving – well this was most significant because the Council of Minsters was very much the inner sanctum of the Kremlin – the Holy of Holies, he added, to nervous laughter.

And Phillips then came to the point: the view of all branches of British intelligence and counter-intelligence and one strongly endorsed by the chief was that the search for this traitor was a priority.

'An absolute priority, if I may so. Such unanimity is, you will appreciate, unprecedented. Whatever cases you're working on at the moment, whatever agents you're running – this goes to the top of your list. I hope that is clearly understood.'

And then one of the younger officers said that of course he understood the need to prioritise this case but didn't it rather conflict with their being told in recent weeks that there should be increased focus on the threat of Nazi Germany rather than the Communists?

There was some muttering of agreement and Phillips thought that he'd never have dreamt of questioning a superior officer, but then this was the world they lived in.

'One understands that, but treason is treason and needs to be dealt with.'

The man who'd asked the question had made a calculated decision. Of course, there was a risk in sticking his head above the parapet, so to speak. But he felt that by articulating what many round the table felt, it could actually draw attention away from him.

Coombe from the Balkans asked if there was really nothing further Phillips could share regarding the traitor's identity and Phillips said a file would be circulated following the meeting summarising everything which was known.

'Which is, I'm afraid, very little. We are dealing with a profes-sional here, a person who would appear to be able to move around the Kremlin and then go into someone's rooms at Cambridge without leaving a clue.

'There is a possibly very significant development though, one which gives us some considerable hope of being able to identify the traitor. We've identified a person we're confident may be able to help us. It's someone we've had our eyes on a for a while: he's a Soviet diplomat with whom we've had contact in the past and who we were confident of turning last February when he was based in Central Europe. He's a very bright chap, resourceful and almost certainly a professional diplomat rather than a committed Marxist. He disappeared back to Moscow rather suddenly and we feared he'd suffered the fate accorded to so many of his comrades. But in the past week he's emerged at a new posting in Northern Europe. We're making contact with him now and we're confident that once he joins us, he'll be able to point us in the direction of this traitor.'

He left work at the normal time that day and took his usual route home, all the while checking he wasn't being followed. It had crossed his mind after Phillips' meeting that this could be some elaborate kind of trap, that maybe he was under suspicion all along, but they were being clever by calling such a large meeting and imparting just enough information to see what he did next.

But he was satisfied that he'd not been followed. Once home he went up to the attic and watched the street from behind a drawn curtain, carefully scanning every direction.

He acted normally enough after that, perhaps not as attentive to his wife during dinner and he apologised saying he had a bad headache and she suggested he go out for a walk to shake it off and he gave every impression of reluctantly agreeing to do so.

Ten minutes later he was in the telephone box behind the church, a place few people passed by in the dark, but he unscrewed the light bulb anyway and dialled HAC5453 and waited for it to ring four times before replacing the receiver and then counted slowly to twenty, his long breaths noisy and visible like cigarette smoke in the cramped telephone box, the only sounds that of his breathing and his foot tapping nervously on the concrete floor. Then he dialled the other Hackney number, HAC9792, and this time let it ring twice before replacing the dial and then another wait, this time for thirty seconds, and the telephone box felt as if it was deprived of oxygen and the small glass panels were steaming up.

The final number now, this one on the Stepney Green exchange, STE7312, and three rings before he replaced the receiver and when he did so he realised how fast his heart was beating and his throat felt tight, as if someone had their fingers round it and he leant against the side and lit a cigarette and thought it was a ridiculous way of letting them know he needed to meet urgently.

It was far too convoluted. He must tell Osip that.

After work the following day he travelled to the safe house on Stannary Street in Kennington, not far from the cricket ground and close to the park. Although in normal circumstances it was a straightforward enough journey from St James, his roundabout route had taken him close to an hour and a half and he was exhausted when he arrived.

The woman who opened the door said nothing by way of a greeting, telling him to go to the first floor where 'the gentleman' was waiting.

He found Osip in a bedroom, sitting on a chair with his back to a window with the curtains drawn, a single bed in front of him and a chair on the other side of the bed for him to sit in, his back to the door, which he was told to close.

'So, who is trying to kill you, Archie?'

'I beg your pardon?'

The Russian shifted his considerable frame in the small chair and he wondered whether it was going to hold his weight. The room was warm but the Russian was still wearing his large overcoat and a scarf. His trilby and gloves were on the bed between them, and he couldn't help noticing it had a floral pattern embossed on it.

'You used the "most urgent" code. Here we are. I hope this is not to ask for more money.'

'You know I rarely ask for money and I thought this code was urgent rather than most urgent. And, if I may say, it's a complicated way of contacting you, don't you think? Ring one number, four rings or is it three and then wait and then another number and then... What if someone was on to me?'

'Then you have another number to call: you know that. Is someone on to you?'

He knew it was by and large pointless to argue with a Russian, they always knew best and wouldn't concede an inch, so he decided to leave it for now and removed his own coat and unbuttoned his jacket and frankly would have given anything for a whisky. He looked around the room and his eye caught on an embroidered quote in a frame above the bed:

God bless this house and all who sleep in it

He'd thought carefully about how much he was going to tell Osip. If he told him how British Intelligence was convinced there was a traitor somewhere at the heart of the establishment and seemed to have evidence pointing to him, then he feared that the OMS would feel he was no longer worth the trouble, that he'd served his purpose and was now disposable.

So, he didn't mention what Phillips said about the contact in Moscow who knew he'd met a Comintern contact in Paris, and the encounter with that wretched man in the Kremlin and how he saw him outside Russell Square station and then killed him in Cambridge... not even a hint of all that. But he did tell him about the diplomat. That was enough.

'I am told that there's a Soviet diplomat who the Service has had its eyes on for a while: he's described as being a professional diplomat and very bright and resourceful. They hoped they were going to turn him last February when he was based somewhere in

Central Europe but he returned suddenly to Moscow. Last week he emerged at a new posting in Northern Europe. He's about to be approached, if he's not been already.'

'No name?'

He shook his head. 'You ought to be able to work it out from that, surely?'

—

When Phillips' group reconvened the following Wednesday, there was a markedly sombre atmosphere in the room. The purpose of the meeting, Phillips said, was to inform them that there'd been a very serious setback in the hunt for the traitor: a most upsetting and frankly worrying development.

'At our last meeting I said we were hopeful that a Soviet diplomat we were in the process of recruiting would lead us to the traitor. Gentlemen, I regret to inform you that on Monday morning the naked body of a man was found in a lake in the centre of The Hague. His throat had been cut and it appears his body had been placed there sometime on the Sunday.

'The Hague Station has excellent contacts with the local police who're convinced the body is that of a recently arrived third secretary, a man called Andriy Oleksandrvych Kovalenko. I'm afraid that Kovalenko is – was – the man we were in the process of recruiting.'

Phillips spread out his hands to indicate the hopelessness of the situation.

'And you think a third secretary would have been able to identify a traitor here in London?'

'Possibly not immediately, Williamson, no. But the reason we've been keen on Kovalenko for so long is that we thought he was the kind of person who's smart and inobtrusive and would be able to dig around for information. After all, we only needed one decent clue.'

There was a consensus that this was bad luck and, indeed, most unfortunate and then the discussion opened out as to how everyone was getting on with their hunt for the traitor and no one had anything of any consequence to report and Phillips said he'd call another meeting in a week or so, unless they caught the man before then, and no one could work out whether that was an attempt at humour or misguided optimism.

Chapter 21

Charles Cooper had become a fully fledged Annexe agent in the July, after acting as an accomplice for the assassination carried out by the man called Murray in Brussels.

At the beginning of August, he'd met Pamela for one of their weekly catch-up sessions and she said there could be a problem.

'One of our informers told us about a man called Frank Reynolds who they'd spotted at a lot of Communist Party meetings recently and—'

'You mean me!'

'Yes, but let me finish, please. This informer knows nothing about you, of course, he was simply passing on what he had heard and seen. When he asked a Party official about you there was some remark along the lines of "we'd like to know ourselves".'

'Oh Christ.'

'That's not necessarily a bad thing, our informer took it that they're interested in you in a positive way. But nonetheless, perhaps you've been seen around too frequently. We think it would be a good idea if you weren't seen at any meetings for the rest of August. Your cover story is that you're a door-to-door salesman—'

'Of kitchenware...'

'Let people know you're moving on. And then we'll see.'

Which is how Charles Cooper came to spend August back living as Christopher Shaw at his apartment on Dorset Square, a preferable existence to that of Frank Reynolds in an unpleasant and noisy lodging house in Hackney.

And he used his time wisely, starting a complete re-write of his novel, and he went back to the idea of it being about the diamond thief called Louise moving elegantly but furtively around Europe and now he was free from the shackles of his erstwhile Soviet masters the story no longer needed to be encumbered by political rhetoric.

By the end of August, he was up to sixty-five thousand words and pleased with how it was coming together. He was unsure as to how the story was going to end, but excited to see how it developed: the plot felt as if it had a life of its own. It was just a shame that at the end of the month he needed to return to work.

–

They were sitting around a table in a darkened room in The Annexe and it was as if Percy Burton and Pamela were a married couple proudly showing their holiday snaps and Cooper a polite guest. On the table a noisy slide projector was throwing a bright light onto the wall opposite and Percy Burton was in a bit of a flap as he tried to sort a box of slides into the correct order and eventually Pamela Clarke took over.

As the image of a station appeared on the wall, Percy began his commentary. 'This is the nearest station... Covent Garden on the Piccadilly line. This shows the main entrance on Long Acre and here... next slide, please, Pamela... is the side entrance on James Street and if one heads south down James Street and across Floral Street... thank you, Pamela... then one ends up on King Street by the side of St Paul's Church... there we are... which was, I believe, designed by Inigo Jones, of whom I'm afraid we have no photograph! Next slide please, Pamela.

'And then as we walk down King Street towards Bedford Street one moves from the holy to the profane because this building – number sixteen – is the headquarters of the British Communist

Party and has been since 1921, I'm told. The next few slides show the building from different angles.'

Percy Burton sat back and they watched in silence as a dozen or more photographs of the exterior of the four-storey building appeared.

'Nothing of the interior, sir?'

'No,' said Pamela, 'but we do have one or two old diagrams, architectural drawings really. However, what really matters is how you get into the building and what you do when you're there. Mr Burton, sir?'

Percy Burton had lit a cigarette and in the darkened room it was only possible to make him out by the red glow of the tip.

'The Communist Party relies for the most part on volunteers, unpaid labour: that's your best way in.'

'Rather exploitative for communists, wouldn't you say, sir?'

'Indeed! But you'll need to be very careful, Cooper. MI5 and the Special Branch claim to have agents inside King Street and that may well be true, though going by the quality of their intelligence they're not very good ones.'

'In what sense, sir?'

'In the sense that they seem to be incapable of discriminating between political agitation and espionage and other activities carried out by and on behalf of a foreign power, namely the Soviet Union. But the communists know full well that the British state, as they call it – the Establishment, if you like – are spying on them, so they're alert to the point of paranoia as to who may be a spy. Certainly, anyone volunteering to work at their headquarters will be looked at very carefully.'

'And my cover story?'

'Pamela, perhaps you could explain…'

'You'll move into a house in Willesden where your cover is that you're looking after an infirm elderly gentleman at night. There will be a nurse caring for him during the day and you take over in the evening, meaning you're free during the day. The elderly gentleman who's lived there for a number of years is a retired army officer and very much one of us. Another agent will be there during the day so the whole story checks out.'

'You'll need to be aware of who's who at King Street and what they do and who they associate with and where their offices are. Pamela, please?'

The first slide came into view: a large, thickset man with what his mother would call an interesting face and a trace of a smile.

'That's Harry Pollitt, general secretary of the Communist Party, a post he's held since 1929. Very much Stalin's man in London. Uncompromising and blunt, we're told. I doubt you'll get too close to him as a volunteer, but you never know, and we do need to know who appears to be close to him. Next slide, please, Pamela.'

Their faces appeared on the wall, accompanied by Burton's commentary: *Willie Gallacher, Communist Member of Parliament for West Fife since 1935... JR Campbell, editor of the* Daily Worker *and also a member of the Politburo... Rajani Palme Dutt, Balliol College Oxford and very close links indeed to Moscow, highly placed in the Comintern.*

He asked Cooper if he'd heard of the Comintern and he replied, asking if it was something to do with communist parties outside of the Soviet Union.

'I'm glad you've been paying attention! Palme Dutt is an intellectual, something the Party was very suspicious of until recently. Another intellectual is this chap... James Klugman: he's a Jew, born in this country, Trinity College Cambridge, and also very strong links to Moscow, quite possibly even to the NKVD, though that's based on a single unsubstantiated line in an MI5 report. We do know though that Klugman has a habit of disappearing onto the Continent for months at a time. Can we have the next slide, please, Pamela?'

Bill Rust... former editor of the Daily Worker, *always in and out of Moscow... as is this man, Dave Springhall: former head of the Young Communist League and involved with Comintern... possible links with Soviet Intelligence.*

More faces appeared on the wall, people who they couldn't put a name to, and part of Cooper's job would be to assist with that and not to worry, he'd be given copies of all these photographs. One of these nameless men did catch Cooper's eye, a very thin man with a large moustache, ears which stuck out and thinning hair. There was a startled expression on his face. He looked familiar: Cooper was convinced he'd seen him before, but for the life of him couldn't place him and he could hardly ask Pamela to go back on that one slide.

A photograph of a man possibly in his mid- to late thirties appeared on the screen, a thin face, tilting upwards in an almost arrogant manner, his fair hair carefully brushed back.

'Cliff Milne: we know little about him other than he has an office on the top floor of King Street which is always locked, even when he's in it. He's meant to be close to Springhall and we've seen reports that even Politburo members have been seen deferring to him. We think – though we have nothing in the way of evidence – that he has particularly strong links to Moscow: quite possibly to Soviet Intelligence.'

'Your job,' said Pamela, 'will be to get as close to him as possible.'

'Once you get into King Street, of course.'

'And any thoughts as to how I'm to do this?'

'That, my dear chap, is up to you to work out!'

–

It took Charles Cooper two months to get a job at the headquarters of the Communist Party.

He'd resumed going to meetings at the start of September and in the middle of the month moved into the house in Willesden where the owner, a retired army officer in his seventies called Meldrake, duly played the part of an invalid gentleman.

As Frank Reynolds, Cooper attended no more than three Communist Party events a week, including educational ones at a weekend. Whenever the opportunity arose, he volunteered to sell copies of the *Daily Worker* on street corners or outside stations and at least twice a week he'd be up before dawn to help leaflet workers outside a factory.

And it was early one morning in the first week of October that he finally got to talk to a man he'd had his eyes on for a couple of weeks. He was with three others at an aircraft factory in Acton handing out leaflets promising peace and better wages and so far none of those going in for the early shift had shown the slightest bit of interest. The man turned up half an hour after the rest of them. Cooper knew he was called Wright and he'd seen him at meetings and knew he was an organiser for the Communist Party and although he wasn't sure what it was he organised he also knew he worked full-time at King Street and so was clearly of some importance.

He stood next to Wright and got talking and hoped he came across as committed and intelligent and absolutely dedicated to the Party. He could tell that Wright was interested, so after they'd finished leafletting, he asked him if he fancied some breakfast, which is how they ended up in a steamy cafe on the corner of Du Cane Road and Common Lane.

Cooper was pleased with how well he handled it. He spoke of how he despised Left Oppositionists – the Party's code for Trotskyists – and how they were the enemy of the working class and of how the only hope for the future was the Communist Party and he was determined to devote himself as much as possible to the cause now that he had some time on his hands.

Wright asked how come he had so much time on his hands and Cooper explained he'd been a travelling salesman but had come to resent his employers, especially after he read Tressell's *The Ragged-Trousered Philanthropists*, and although his circumstances weren't identical he felt he identified in some ways with the characters in the book and certainly with its central theme of poverty and exploitation being an inevitable consequence of capitalism.

Wright nodded approvingly, and Cooper continued. Through a friend of a friend of the family he heard of a retired gentleman living not too far from where they were sitting who needed a male companion to live in and take care of him at night, which meant his days were his own and so if he could do anything to help the Party, well it would be an honour and at this point Cooper worried he may have rather over-egged the pudding, but Wright said he was sure he could arrange something and to meet him here at the same time the next week.

Wright was waiting for him when Cooper arrived at the cafe as arranged. He watched as Wright spooned half a dozen sugars into his mug of milky tea and noisily sipped from it before rolling a cigarette and beckoning Cooper to come closer.

He could smell the milk and the cheap tobacco and traces of the previous night's dinner on Wright's breath.

'We can take you on at King Street, but you won't get paid: it will be routine work, clerical more than anything else, and sometimes taking stuff around London and acting as a messenger.'

He paused and slurped his tea and looked at Cooper in a quizzical manner and Cooper said thank you, yes… he was fine with all that.

'I'll need your address.' Wright had produced a small notebook and pushed it and a much-chewed pencil towards Cooper. 'Write down your address and your full name and your date and place of birth and where else you've lived and worked.'

–

The previous week Percy Burton called him in to The Annexe on the Thursday for a briefing and Cooper could tell it was important because the older man had locked the door of his office and led him over to the two small armchairs and indicated they should be pulled as closely together as possible because he needed to talk in absolute confidence.

Percy Burton went over his mission once more: to spend the first few weeks working in King Street and being as helpful and hard-working as possible and not doing anything that may arouse suspicion. He was to gather as much information as possible on the people working there and what they do… and, well, you know the score and Cooper said yes, we've been through it many times.

'And in particular I'm to try and find out what I can about this Cliff Milne and see if I can get to work in his office.'

And there was a long silence after this, the only sound coming from a carriage clock behind Burton's desk and Cooper wondered what he was going to say because so far he'd only been repeating what had been covered countless times over recent weeks.

'There is something else.' Burton's voice was so quiet now Cooper had to lean even closer.

'We have a traitor.'

Just those four words and then silence.

'Where?'

And Burton told him everything he knew about Archie, telling him that despite the hunt for this traitor being a top priority not just for The Annexe but also for MI6 and MI5 and the Special Branch they'd drawn a complete blank and whoever Archie was, he was very clever and so well concealed that it may well take a stroke of luck or a slip-up by someone for his identity to be revealed.

'And there's nothing on him other than this?'

'As I say, Cooper, we know very little about him, other than he's English, is very highly placed and works as a Soviet spy, providing them with what is described as "excellent intelligence" and his codename is Archie and he was in Paris in May this year.'

Percy Burton held open his hands as if to emphasise the paucity of the information he was providing. Charles Cooper could feel his body tense. Could it be that this 'highly placed' agent was actually him? Of course, he wasn't in Paris in May and he'd never heard that codename before, but this could be Percy Burton's subtle way of raising the subject of his loyalty.

'And this—'

'Hang on, Cooper, I've not finished: in May 1937 – a year before Archie was in Paris – an Englishman was spotted in the Kremlin where he had a short encounter with someone working for us. We believe this Englishman had a connection with Oxford University in or around 1930. I'm afraid the description of him is so bland as to be useless. But we have reason to think this person spotted in the Kremlin in May 1937 is the same person who was in Paris a year later.'

He dropped his head and exhaled deeply. 'We therefore have a traitor in our midst. Finding him is an absolute priority. We know that he was spotted in London in August this year by the same person who saw him in the Kremlin. Suffice it to say that this Archie is very dangerous indeed. It's a long shot, I admit, but it may well be that as you hopefully infiltrate your way into the deeper recesses of the Communist Party, you may pick up some hint or clue about Archie.'

Cooper was relieved that Burton was clearly not linking him with being Archie. But as he was talking, he recalled the dacha outside Moscow in September 1937, the atmosphere as relaxed and calm as it could be in the circumstances and Nikolai telling him they had another agent in London.

...someone in a similar position to you, though he has been with us longer. We cannot tell you much about him, other than that he is already very highly placed, and we believe he is on course to go to the top of his organisation. In time your role will be to support him.

This person sounded very much like Archie.

'And there's no other clue as to who he is?'

'I'm afraid not, Cooper.'

'And this codename, could that mean anything?'

'I think not. Of course, we do look most carefully at these codenames but these days the Soviets choose random ones for their agents. There was a time when they tried to be clever, but it rather backfired a few years ago. They were running an agent in Lisbon, a well-connected British businessman called Walker, links with the embassy and pretty much anyone who mattered in Portugal. All we knew about him was his codename: Agent Peshekhod. One of our Russian speakers pointed out that Peshekhod translates literally as a 'pedestrian' and it didn't take terribly long to get from 'pedestrian' to 'walker' and consequently poor old Mr Walker is currently a guest of His Majesty. The Soviets no longer use cryptic codenames.'

–

What Cooper wasn't to know was that the day before Percy Burton had told him about Archie another meeting had taken place, although it was one of those meetings which officially – and even to an extent, unofficially – did not happen, so much so that the two participants met in a deserted lane off a small road between Marlow and Henley as dusk fell over the Berkshire countryside.

Phillips was already waiting when Burton arrived and suggested they walk for a while and Burton followed him along the slippery edge of a field towards a small wooded area, where they stood and lit their cigarettes and looked out over the fields, listened to the rustle of the wind and bird noises in the far distance.

'This meeting isn't happening, Burton.'

'As you said, Phillips: understood as always.'

'This hunt for Archie… he's going to be the death of me. I'm beginning to doubt we'll ever find the bastard. We know he's out there but…' His voice tailed away in the wind and he was staring dead ahead.

'It's certainly looking like it's going to be a long haul and of course until we know what intelligence he's actually passing on we—'

'No, it's more than that Burton. Very confidentially, I'm beginning to wonder whether he could be in 54 Broadway.'

'Really – you mean working for MI6?'

Phillips was standing a full yard ahead of Burton but he nodded and said why not and then he turned round and told him how the previous week he'd set a trap.

'I have a large team of two dozen working on the hunt for Archie: half of them senior officers from the European desks, the other half the younger officers, the ones the chief thinks so highly of. I've wondered if one of this team could be Archie, so two days ago – on Monday – I told them we had an informer linked to the Soviet embassy who was going to be passing on intelligence to us regarding Archie that evening in the foyer of the Phoenix Theatre on Charing Cross Road. I've used this place before: there's a secret mirror behind the main ticket desk that gives a good view of the foyer.

'All part of the trap, of course, but I had the place very carefully watched and I was behind the mirror and I'm as certain as I can be that someone did indeed turn up – we had a couple waiting on the corner of Charing Crossing Road and Flitcroft Street and they spotted a man acting suspiciously but before they could do anything about it he hurried away. I think it could well have been Archie and he smelled a rat and scarpered.'

'Which means…'

'Which means Archie could well be inside 54 Broadway.'

'You could continue with this deception: feed false leads to smaller groups until you find Archie through a process of elimination?'

'I could, but I fear I've shot my bolt on this one. He's smarter than us. I trust you, Burton, so not a word of this, eh? Even the chief doesn't know about this. Sinclair would never believe that one of his chaps could be a traitor. But there's a reason I've called you here.'

He took a while to light another cigarette in the wind and looked over the fields before beginning to slowly walk back to the cars now that darkness was taking hold.

'I know little about The Annexe, Burton, and I'm one of the few who know you even exist. But I'm pretty sure you've got your best sorts on this. If I was a betting man, I'd say you were the odds-on favourites to find Archie. I just ask you to keep me in the loop.'

Chapter 22

Once Archie had calmed down — which wasn't for a few days —
he was able to reflect in a more measured manner on the events
of that Monday.

He realised it could have been a good deal worse. For a start,
his wife hadn't been in town. Recently, she'd been in the habit of
accompanying him when he drove back on Sunday night: she'd
spend Monday and much of Tuesday there, catching up with
friends and shopping, before returning to the country on Tuesday
afternoon.

But that week she'd remained in the country because new
curtains were arriving or something tedious like that and as a
consequence wasn't there to observe the mood he was in when
he arrived home.

He was furious when he flung open the front door and waited
for a minute or two in the dark hallway to check there were no
other sounds before locking the front door and bolting it twice.
He closed the second door leading through to the rest of the
house and kicked the door into the lounge, slamming it against
the sideboard, grabbed a bottle of whisky from the drinks cabinet
and drank straight from the bottle and this only seemed to make
him more angry, because in his fury he flung the bottle against
the fireplace, the contents spraying everywhere and shards of glass
spreading over the ridiculously expensive rug, which his wife
assured him was worth it because it had been hand-sewn over

a period of God-knows-how-many months in a part of Persia he'd never heard of.

He slumped into an armchair and remained there until the clock on the mantelpiece chimed eleven o'clock and as if on cue but quite unexpectedly, he felt tears well in his eyes and thank heavens he was on his own because this had happened before at times of extreme tension – there'd been enough of those – and he knew better than to suppress them, so he allowed the tears to flow down his face and although he wiped them away at first with the back of his hand, he soon gave up because the more he cried the less angry he felt.

–

He'd been caught completely off-guard by Phillips at the meeting that morning, although it had started promisingly enough with Phillips announcing in his usual tedious tone that the search for the traitor had made no progress and things were really most disappointing.

And then he announced there was a very important development, pausing and looking around the room as if to make sure he looked at every person in it.

'The Service has an informer, a person linked to the Soviet Embassy, who is somewhat elusive and can be hard to make contact with but they have been in touch to tell us they have information that will lead to us identifying Archie... He is prepared to pass on this information in return for a large sum of money. I will be meeting our informer in the foyer of the Phoenix Theatre on Charing Cross Road this evening in the half hour prior to the performance of *The White Guard*, which ironically is based on a novel by Bulgakov and is set in Kiev during the civil war. Obviously, the theatre will be busy then so one hopes the chances of them being spotted are less than they could be, and I imagine the subject matter of the play will mean there's a more cosmopolitan audience.'

Phillips paused once more, and Archie glanced up to observe that one or two of the senior officers looked surprised and he did have to admit that this all sounded a bit odd, not least the fact that Phillips was sharing it with so many people, but of course he just concentrated on remaining as impassive as possible, not displaying any sign of his utter shock.

'Hopefully, by this time tomorrow we'll know just who Archie is!'

It made little sense that Phillips had said there'd been no progress and then went on to announce what appeared to be a significant development. He knew this could be a trap, but he knew he simply couldn't take the risk.

Nor could he take the risk of telling Osip: as far as Osip was concerned, the British knew nothing of Archie.

He left Broadway just before five thirty that afternoon, walking towards Victoria and then taking a taxi to Kentish Town, getting it to drop him five minutes' walk from the small lock-up he rented in a quiet alley behind a parade of shops.

It looked like a garage from the outside but was too small for a car and the owner had been more than happy to take two years' rent in advance, cash no questions asked. Archie waited after he'd turned in to the alley and when he was sure no one else was around he retrieved the key from its hiding place between the gutter and the roof. At the rear of the small room were three suitcases and he opened one and selected a set of clothes – a pair of shabby trousers, a pullover, a pair of scruffy shoes, but with good quality soles in case he needed to run, a large raincoat and a cloth cap. In the unlikely event of someone affording him a second glance he looked every bit the labourer on his way home from a tiring day.

And those few looking so closely at him would see a man with dark hair, perhaps a bit too long at the collar and with a moustache and a goatee beard, which along with a heavy pair of cheap-looking spectacles ensured he was quite unrecognisable. The wig, moustache and the beard had been very expensive, but worth every penny.

He left the alley through the other end to the one he'd entered from and walked to Kentish Town underground station. By ten to seven he was leaving Charing Cross station and heading towards the Phoenix Theatre.

It took him five minutes to spot the trap. In Moscow, he'd been trained to look out for people who may be following or watching him: people hanging around with no apparent purpose, constantly looking in different directions, good quality footwear, possibly with or very close to another person but having little direct contact with them... and the couple on the corner with Flitcroft Street looked like typical followers, standing close to each other but apart, looking around much in the manner that a dog does when trying to catch a scent, standing close to the edge of the pavement so as to get the optimum view.

Archie moved to the other side of the road and into the shadow of a doorway of an umbrella shop, with a clear view of the Phoenix Theatre.

But it seemed the woman may have spotted him because he saw her beckon the man over and as she spoke with him, she gestured in his direction.

He hurried up Charing Cross Road, north towards Tottenham Court Road, left into Oxford Street and then down a side street and into the rear entrance of a pub, which was thankfully quiet, and in a cubicle of the filthy toilet he removed the wig and the false beard and put them along with the raincoat in a shopping bag he kept in the pocket and hoped he looked different enough from the man who'd hurried away.

He remained in the pub for an hour and a half, sitting in an unlit corner of the bar with a good view of the entrance. When he was satisfied all was clear he picked up a bus on Tottenham Court Road.

He left the lock-up in Kentish Town just after nine and decided to walk home to Hampstead: it was safer that way and, in any case, it was an opportunity to clear his head.

But that didn't work, all he could think was how foolish he'd been to fall into Phillips' trap – or if not actually fall into it, get perilously close to its edge. It was the same as in the Kremlin the previous May with that damned Branstone chap: he'd rushed into things, hadn't bothered to stop and think because if he had, he'd have realised that Phillips announcing this to all and sundry was utterly implausible.

–

And it was a few days later when he was able to consider the saving graces: his wife not being at home, of course; the fact that he'd not told Osip, because that would have been a disaster in more ways than one; the incompetence of the couple, making it obvious they were watching him; and then his coming to his senses so quickly and getting out of the predicament.

But they were small consolations.

The fact of the matter was that if Phillips had set a trap – in however heavy-handed a manner – then that was because he suspected someone in MI6 of being the traitor.

Until then they could quite reasonably assume Archie worked at one of any number of organisations – MI6 or MI5, the Foreign Office, the Colonial Office, the War Office and even Downing Street or one of the armed forces, meaning he could be one of many thousands of people.

Now they may well have narrowed it down to one or two hundred at the very most.

The odds were dangerously short.

There was no room for any more mistakes.

Part 3

Chapter 23

London
November 1938–January 1939

Charles Cooper started work at the headquarters of the British Communist Party on a damp Monday morning, the last day of October.

It had rained all weekend and on the Sunday night he'd been kept awake by the rain driving against the window in the house in Willesden where he was now living. It showed no sign of abating on the Monday morning and he was drenched when he arrived at 16 King Street, waiting forlornly and shifting uncomfortably as a puddle of water formed under him in the surprisingly small reception area as someone went to find Comrade Wright, all the while being watched suspiciously.

It had been quite a miserable first week: he was treated very much as the newcomer and there were a lot of questions and he was given precious little to do other than carry packages from one floor to another and he began to worry that maybe he was suspected of being an infiltrator, but Burton told him not to worry. Everyone, he said, is suspected of being an infiltrator.

'That building thrives on suspicion, the whole Communist Party does: it's how it works – different factions, different centres of power, almost imperceptible differences in ideology. Frankly, I'd worry if they appeared to trust you from the outset.'

And at the start of his second week there'd been what turned out to be a positive development. A woman had turned up at the house in Willesden one morning while he was out and had met the old man and the woman who was there during the day and she'd said she was from a local church and left a list of services. And two evenings later, after Cooper had arrived home, the doorbell rang and it was a man offering his services as a gardener and was this his house and Cooper patiently explained that it belonged to an elderly gentleman and he looked after him and, no, there was already a gardener, thank you.

Evidently, he'd been checked out and had passed the test and after that, Cooper began to be entrusted with more work: taking messages across London and around the building, helping in the library and a range of other clerical tasks, all of which were rather mundane, but he did notice that as each week went by, he was given more interesting work.

He was particularly keen to volunteer for what they called – half-jokingly – the porters office. It was not the most popular place in the building as it was mostly manual work and there was a general aversion to that, with little appreciation of the irony.

But it did give him something of a *carte blanche* to wander around the building at will: the set of overalls he wore seemed to afford him a degree of invisibility and he found that if he carried a small ladder with him and a tool kit and made a point of checking light bulbs and fixing door handles then he could go wherever he wanted.

Which was how, towards the end of November, he came to meet Cliff Milne.

–

He finished his novel at the end of October.

He gave it a title – *The Jewels of Europe* – which he wasn't sure about but assumed publishers were bound to come up with a better one. And he was pleased with how the story developed: plenty of intrigue and action as Louise stole diamonds across Europe, all the time pursued by an enigmatic private detective of uncertain nationality.

He hoped the ending worked – it could be considered perhaps too violent – but this was something else the publishers would no doubt have a view on.

Thanks to judicious use of carbon copies, he had five copies of the book. He sent four of them out to publishers in the first week of November and felt full of optimism.

One of them, surely, was bound to be interested.

–

It was rare for him to be called to the top floor at King Street, where Harry Pollitt, the general secretary, had his offices along with members of the Politburo and other important people, though there were no names on the doors, which were always locked.

But at the end of November the main handyman – a cantankerous type who had little time for Cooper – was off work for a couple of weeks and another handyman had broken his wrist. Although Cooper was a porter rather than a handyman he quickly volunteered when there was a call to fix a lock in an office on the fourth floor.

Office belonging to a Mr Milne, he was told: Cliff Milne.

The man who let him in introduced himself as Sidney Dunn and said to call him Sidney, if he wished, and explained that the lock to the inner office where Comrade Milne himself sat was quite stiff and if he could sort it, he'd be very grateful.

Sidney Dunn was a slightly dishevelled type, probably in his fifties and wearing a thick, knitted scarlet pullover, a check shirt with frayed collar and cuffs and a tightly knotted red tie. He was chatty, fussing around Cooper as he checked the lock to Milne's inner office. He was a clerk, he explained, looking after Comrade Milne's office.

'You're a volunteer, are you, Frank?'

Cooper said he was.

'And a Party member?'

'Of course.'

Sidney moved closer, bending down, his hands on his knees and his mouth close to Cooper's ear.

'Thought so: not many people are aware of Comrade Milne, but what he does...' He paused and looked round. 'It's some of the most important work in this building. Even I only know half of it, if that. But he trusts me, I keep my mouth shut.'

He leant back, his arms folded across his chest and a knowing grin revealing a set of stained teeth. He clearly wasn't very good at keeping his mouth shut.

Cooper unscrewed the lock and applied plenty of lubricant and thankfully it didn't need changing because he wasn't sure he was up to that and as he was tidying up, the door to the outer office swung open and Cliff Milne hurried in, his arms full of papers and a briefcase tucked under his arm, which Cooper noticed was attached to his wrist with a chain.

Sidney deferentially explained that Comrade Cooper was from the porter's office and had come to sort out the lock and Cooper said it was all fixed and was there anything else that needed sorted while he was up here with all his tools?

He expected to be sent away, but Cliff Milne was standing behind his desk, his briefcase on the chair and still attached to his wrist and looking up and down at his bookcase. He looked older than in the photograph he'd seen of him at The Annexe; more like mid-forties, and his fair hair was now greying and thinning.

'Is there anything you can do about this?' He was pointing at a bookcase that took up the whole of one wall. Half of the shelves were stuffed with box files, their contents overflowing, and the other shelves were filled with books and piles of magazines and newspapers.

'Every morning when I come in, I'm surprised it's still standing, but it's only a matter of time. All those files... It would be a disaster if the whole thing collapsed. It would take Sidney and I months to get it all back into some kind of order.'

Cooper walked up to the bookcase and moved one or two items to the side. It was obvious that the brackets that attached the shelves to the wall were coming loose. It was the kind of job which would normally be handled by one of the more senior handymen, but this was too good an opportunity to miss.

As he moved along the bookcase, he noticed that behind Milne's chair was a low cupboard, which was now open, exposing a heavy iron safe. Milne was bending down, putting some items from the briefcase into the safe, trying to shield what he was doing with his body.

'I'm sure I can fix this: it will take a few days though.'

–

The week leading up to Christmas was a distinctly miserable one for Charles Cooper. On one of his infrequent visits to his mother and step-father he'd allowed himself to be talked into spending Christmas Day with them – a prospect that filled him with dread, but that was the least of his problems.

In the middle of the month, he received his first rejection for *The Jewels of Europe*. It was from Holborn Books, one of the larger publishers, and he'd been surprised to hear back from them so quickly. He'd hoped that in the event of a publisher turning down the book at least they'd provide helpful feedback he could use for an improved version. But this was barely a letter – the date filled in by hand above what was clearly a pro-forma rejection slip: the book was not one they'd consider publishing but they were very grateful for the submission.

No name, no helpful comments.

Two days later two rejections arrived on the same day, which felt particularly cruel. Corton and Wild – who had quite an extensive crime list – did provide a couple of sentences, which in the right light could be construed as feedback of sorts: *a slightly uncertain and, if I may say, meandering plot… is the character Louise meant to be a villain or a heroine?* And from New End Publishing another pro-form letter informing him this was not the type of story they were looking to publish.

The last post before Christmas dashed his hopes that he may enjoy some kind of stay of execution over what passed for the festive season, but Passport Books – who had both crime and travel lists – said they wondered whether he ought to consider tackling a different genre altogether.

He took a week off over Christmas and apart from the day with his mother and step-father, he spent it back at Dorset Square. He had a list of publishers, which he'd copied out from a book in the Reference Library, and he went through them carefully to decide who to send the book to next.

Which was how, on the day following Boxing Day, he was scanning the list when he came across Francis Randall Books, the company which Misha at the State Publishing House of Fiction in Moscow had mentioned nearly a year and a half ago: he'd described them as their English partners and said Cooper's novel was the kind this company liked.

Early on, Cooper had decided not to risk an approach to this company: the very last thing he was going to do was to take the chance of alerting them to the fact that he was alive and well. But since he'd been back in London – well over a year – Charles Cooper had to all intents and purposes disappeared and now he was happily living as Christopher Shaw and that was the name he used as the author of the book.

The risk, he now decided, was therefore minimal.

-

He returned to work at King Street on 2 January, the first Monday of the new year, feeling decidedly more upbeat than before Christmas. He'd prepared what he thought was a well-written synopsis of *The Jewels of Europe* and had decided to deliver it in person along with a hand-written covering letter to Francis Randall Books during his lunch break. A small touch like that could make all the difference, putting a face to a name and all that.

And the second reason was that in the course of his long walks in Regent's Park over Christmas he'd devised what he regarded as a very clever plan, one he hoped Burton would approve of.

He'd spent much of December in Cliff Milne's office in King Street as he laboriously repaired the bookshelves. He was, he told them, a perfectionist, which hopefully accounted for the job taking so long. At first Cliff Milne appeared too busy and distracted to talk with him, but in time he did begin to engage in occasional conversation and was evidently impressed with the handyman who was clearly a dedicated Party member and a committed Marxist Leninist, who was educated and well-read and obviously had some experience of life, despite his relatively young age.

They began to have conversations. Cooper was careful to avoid coming across as scheming or ambitious. He found himself in the position of almost being Milne's confidante.

'Sidney's a decent type,' he explained one day when the other man left the office. 'A good comrade, of course, and very trust-worthy, but he… he lacks energy and initiative. He's not interested in ideology: maybe that's not such a bad thing.'

Other times, Milne alluded to the pressures of the job and the responsibilities that fell on his shoulders, which were perhaps greater than those for anyone else in the building, including the general secretary.

He was careful not to spell out what he meant and Cooper never pushed it, but Milne was constantly weary: he often remarked he operated on no more than four or five hours' sleep a night and often had people to meet late at night or early in the morning and there was the constant strain of always having to be careful and Cooper had asked him what he meant by that because not to do so could have appeared too innocent. Milne shrugged and leant back in his chair and said that was a good question, but avoided answering it, which was typical of Milne – enigmatic, appearing to be open and even frank, but as closed as the books now neatly arranged on the nearly repaired bookcase.

'The point about being a Marxist revolutionary is that you need to be more committed and work twice as hard as anyone else. You never have a day off. Everything else – and I mean everything – takes second place.'

Cooper said he sympathised and if there was anything he could do to help and Milne was on his knees at this point retrieving something from his safe but he did mumble something about being grateful and you never know.

When he stood up, he looked in pain.

'Doc says I need an operation on my knee, but the idea of that... being in hospital and the recuperation... it's out of the question.'

During his period in Milne's office, he carefully observed his use of the safe. The cupboard it was in was locked, but Cooper spotted him fumbling under the desk to retrieve the key. Milne then reached behind the safe and produced another key, for the safe. But clearly two keys were required to open it – and the second one was kept on a chain round his neck.

Milne hadn't realised that Cooper was watching him, but that didn't seem to matter: with access to just one key the safe would remain locked.

–

It was a pleasant fifteen-minute walk through Seven Dials and Bloomsbury to Store Street, the home of Francis Randall Books.

It was a four-storey building close to Gower Street, the ground floor occupied by a firm of solicitors, the entrance to Francis Randall Books through a door to the side and up a flight of narrow steps to the third floor. The reception was on a landing at the top of the stairs, a formally dressed woman sitting behind a desk, with piles of books stacked up on every available inch of floor space.

She took a while to glance up at him and then only responded with the briefest of smiles when he wished her a good afternoon and said he was sorry to bother her but he'd... well, written a novel, actually, and he'd brought it along because he'd like to submit it to Francis Randall Books to be considered for publication and it's, here…

He opened his briefcase and took out *The Jewels of Europe* by Christopher Shaw.

'I'm Christopher Shaw, you see. And here – in this envelope – is my manuscript along with a synopsis of the novel and also a covering letter with all my details. I wasn't sure whether to put them both in the same envelope but—'

'That is fine like that, thank you,' she said, reaching out for the envelope. 'Mr Randall himself endeavours to read all submissions, therefore it will be a matter of months before you hear from us. By post.'

'I understand and I—'

'We do not appreciate enquiries before you hear back from us.' She said this as she placed the envelope on a large pile to one side of the desk.

At that moment he heard footsteps behind him and turned round to see an older man watching him from a doorway: he was tall, with a full beard and wearing a tweed jacket and a bowtie and holding a pipe.

The woman thanked him and said 'good afternoon' in a manner which indicated it was time for him to go.

As he descended the stairs, he heard snatches of a conversation behind him. '…he brought this manuscript in Mr Randall, sir: name of… here we are, Shaw, Christopher Shaw.'

And as he crossed Store Street he turned round and looked up at the building he'd just left. The bearded man was now watching him from the window and as far as he could tell, continued to do so until he was out of sight.

Chapter 24

London
January 1939

When he finished speaking, it was a good minute before Percy Burton spoke, leaning back as he did so and looking in the direction of the ceiling, his head tilted back.

'So, as I understand it, Cooper, you believe you've gained Cliff Milne's trust and are proposing a scheme which would see you replacing this Sidney Dunn chap in Milne's office.'

Cooper nodded.

'By framing him.'

'Yes, sir – I'm aware you may consider my plan too outrageous but I was thinking that—'

'No, Cooper! Not at all – it's a damned clever plan.' Burton rocked forward now, a broad smile on his face and his arms resting on his thighs and looking directly at Cooper. 'If I may say so, and if you'll excuse me, Miss Clarke, it's a bloody ingenious plan.'

'I would like to hear it once more, sir.' Pamela Clarke had been taking notes as Cooper had been talking.

'My proposal is that we frame Sidney Dunn by planting incriminating evidence on him so that he's dismissed by the Communist Party, thus causing a vacancy in Cliff Milne's office. I believe that I could be in a position to fill that vacancy as during the time I worked there I built up some kind of a relationship with him and hopefully he trusts me.'

'You were working there as a handyman, though.'

'I do realise that, Pamela, but although he's a very suspicious type, he didn't give the impression of distrusting me.'

'And let's assume that we pull this off – that Sidney Dunn is framed and sacked and you replace him: what then?' Pamela pointed at him with the pencil she'd been using to take notes.

'Then I see what I can get my hands on in his office, don't I?'

'You mentioned his safe?'

'Yes, he's forever putting things in it and taking stuff out of it. I think that—'

'Hang on, hang on...' Percy Burton held up a hand. 'First things first, eh? We'll turn our attention to the safe once you're working in his office. We need to deal with this Sidney Dunn first. What's he like, Cooper?'

'Quite likeable, somewhat pedestrian in his ways.'

'Trusting?'

'Yes, sir.'

They then went on to discuss the plan and at the end of the discussion Burton looked closely at Cooper.

'You seem to rather like Sidney Dunn?'

'Yes, sir, I suppose I do.'

'You do realise that what we're proposing will ruin him, don't you?'

–

Charles Cooper was in the habit of stopping by his apartment in Dorset Square two or three afternoons a week on his way back from work, which he did the day after he'd met with Percy Burton and Pamela Clarke at The Annexe to plan Sidney Dunn's fate. He was there to pick up any post and collect a clean shirt.

On the carpet in the hall was a telegram.

DELIGHTED WITH SUBMISSION STOP WISH TO DISCUSS OFFER SOONEST STOP PLEASE CALL TO ARRANGE MEETING AT STORE STREET URGENT STOP KIND REGARDS FRANCIS RANDALL

He was so overwhelmed and excited that he stood for a moment in the hall to re-read the telegram and then went into the lounge where he sat in his armchair and poured himself a whisky, clutching the telegram in his hand. There was no ambiguity in the message, little room for doubt.

He must have been sitting there for close to an hour because when he realised the time he hurried. He was already late for Willesden.

The following morning, he stopped at a telephone box on his way into King Street. The woman who answered seemed to be expecting his call. She said she'd hoped he would have been in touch sooner, but could he come in after work that evening, any time after six o'clock?

—

The door to the offices of Francis Randall Books was locked when he arrived just after six. He rang the bell and soon after heard footsteps and when the door opened it was the tall man with the full beard he'd seen the other day – the one who'd watched him from the window. He proffered his hand and said 'Francis Randall' and Cooper – who introduced himself as Christopher Shaw – did think he could have been a bit more effusive seeing as he'd been so enthusiastic about the book, but then that was probably how it was in the world of publishing: he imagined they made offers on books all the time and didn't want authors to get above themselves.

He waited for Cooper to go up the stairs first and Cooper heard the street door being locked behind him. Randall indicated they should go to the top floor, the one above reception, and when they got there, he closed the door to the stairs and although he couldn't be certain, he thought he'd heard the lock click there.

He followed Francis Randall into a chaotic office, books piled high on every surface, the few areas of the wall not covered by a bookcase displaying framed covers of books. He sat down in the chair by the window and noticed that Francis Randall seemed nervous and wasn't saying anything, so Cooper felt it was up to him to break the ice.

'I must say I was thrilled to hear from you so soon: when I dropped the manuscript off last week, I was told it would be a good while before I was to expect to hear from you. I'm so pleased you're delighted with the book!'

Francis Randall smiled weakly and nodded and then coughed and cleared his throat.

'May I ask, Mr Shaw, is this your real name or is it perhaps a *nom de plume*?'

It was the 'perhaps' that Cooper didn't like: a slight pause before it and a hint of menace in the delivery. He had a creeping sense of unease: he wasn't too sure what he'd been expecting but it was certainly something a bit more positive than this.

'No, that's who I am – Christopher Shaw.' And he chuckled hoping that Francis Randall may do likewise and they could get onto business but the publisher shifted uncomfortably and fidgeted with his bowtie. Randall looked flushed and wiped his brow and then Cooper heard footsteps in the corridor and the door swung open. A heavily built man entered, and Cooper wondered where he'd seen him before. As soon as the man came in, Francis Randall stood up and hurried out of the room. The man settled into his chair and removed his trilby and placed it on the desk. He looked even more familiar.

'Mr Cooper, Mr Cooper...' He shook his head like a school master disappointed in a pupil, his Russian accent was obvious and of course Cooper now knew where he'd seen him before and he felt tears well in his eyes because more than anything else he couldn't believe he'd been so stupid and frankly naïve to imagine approaching Francis Randall Books was anything other than suicidal.

'Mr Cooper, you returned to London fifteen months ago and then you disappeared. We were most disappointed, but I had a gut feeling you'd turn up and, of course, Mr Randall had been alerted to let us know if you approached him and we gave him a photograph of you and fortunately he recognised you when you came here last week and well... here I am! And as you say in English, better late than never!'

Cooper felt his body tense up, as if he was going to make a dash for the door or something like that, but he knew the doors were locked and the Russian was almost certainly armed.

He was trapped. In more ways than one.

He thought he was free of the Soviet Union's embrace. Now, nothing could be further from the truth.

The Russian stood up and Cooper instinctively did the same and when the Russian held out his hand to shake Cooper's, he did likewise.

'I'm prepared to let what happened – the delay, if you like – be put down to nerves: a misunderstanding. From today, we can start afresh, do you not agree?'

Cooper said he supposed so.

'I really ought to introduce myself properly. My name is Osip.'

–

Poor old Sidney Dunn never stood a chance.

Pamela Clarke had organised it all and Cooper had to say he was almost unnerved – if that was the right word – at how hard they went for him. Indeed, he had mentioned this to her at one stage and she told him there was only one way to go about something like this.

'To go for the kill.'

It turned out Special Branch had been watching a reporter on the *Daily Sketch* called Marsden who they suspected was a closet communist with close links to the Party hierarchy. His beat was crime and one Thursday evening in late January he was taken out for a drink – quite a few of them actually – by a detective he knew well and they ended up in a pub behind Fleet Street where they were joined by another policeman and late in the evening Marsden found himself alone with this other policeman, who made a good show of being drunk to the point of indiscretion and confided that he was working on a big case, running an agent inside the Communist Party headquarters in King Street – had he heard of it?

'The Communist Party?'

'King Street – it's where their headquarters are.'

Marsden said he had but managed to appear not too interested and the policeman said this agent was so important that if he pulled it off then he'd be in for promotion and Marsden said this sounded quite big and by now the policeman was slurring his words and had an arm round Marsden's shoulder and his head close to his and he told him – in complete confidence mind you – that it was a chap called Sidney Dunn – D U N N – who worked on the fourth floor of the headquarters and had access to top-secret information, which he'd begun to pass on to Special Branch in return for money, and it just went to show that everyone had their price.

'It's very straightforward, actually: every Monday after work I meet him at the end of Carting Lane, just by Victoria Gardens, and he hands over some files and I give him an envelope with five one-pound notes in it. And from there it's a short walk along Victoria Embankment to my office in Scotland Yard and the files go in my safe and we start work on them the next day!'

When Sidney Dunn left King Street on the following Monday evening, he was followed by two people from inside King Street as he took his normal route south, crossing The Strand, down Carting Lane and then along the Embankment to Temple station and home to Stepney.

He was also being followed by a team of highly experienced Annexe and Special Branch officers. Just before he crossed The Strand came the riskiest part of the operation: as he passed Maiden Lane, a woman called him over to a shop doorway.

'You look terribly kind and obliging,' Pamela Clarke told him. 'You're not going anywhere near Carting Lane, are you, by any chance?'

'Well, as it happens, yes, I am!'

'You're so kind!' Her hand was on his arm and he couldn't help but smell the expensive perfume and notice the quality of her clothes and her smile.

'I was on my way to meet my solicitor at the end of Carting Lane to hand over some important papers, but I've just telephoned my sister and apparently my mother's been taken terribly ill and I really must go to her. Would you mind handing this envelope to him? His name is Desmond, Desmond Stuart. That would be so kind!'

Sidney Dunn said not at all and if he thought it an odd request, he didn't say anything, and he wished her mother well and she said once again how kind he was and then hurried off.

The two people from inside King Street spotted him again as he crossed The Strand and did wonder how they'd lost him, but no harm done and they followed him as he entered Carting Lane, down the side of The Savoy, would you believe, and sure enough at the end of the street he was approached by a man who exactly matched the description they'd been given of the policeman and they watched as he handed over a bulky envelope and the policeman handed him a smaller envelope in return and they shook hands and went their separate ways: Dunn towards Temple station and the policeman towards Scotland Yard.

–

The following morning was brutal. Sidney Dunn was grabbed as soon as he entered King Street and marched down to the basement where he was very roughly pushed into a chair and told the game was up and did he care to confess?

Dunn said he didn't have the faintest idea what they were talking about and a man with a Scottish accent whose name he didn't know but who he'd seen around the building said in that case he'd spell it out.

'We know that you're an informer for Special Branch. We know that you're stealing documents from this building and handing them over to your contact in return for money. We know you meet him every Monday evening in Carting Lane to give him the documents, as you did last night when we watched you hand over an envelope and take money in return. We actually followed the policeman and watched him enter Scotland Yard. He was saluted as he went in!'

Sidney Dunn was so shocked he was unable to reply for quite a while, but the others in the basement room – there must have been half a dozen in there – were patient because they were anxious to hear his confession.

But when he pulled himself together, he said nothing could be further from the truth because a lady had asked him if he could pass on an envelope to her solicitor because she had to visit her sick mother and the solicitor had been so grateful, he'd insisted on giving him something for his troubles.

They all laughed, and he was asked if that was really the best he could do and Sidney Dunn found himself weeping and insisting he wasn't an informer, there wasn't a more loyal Party member than him, and Comrade Milne will attest to that and then someone said Comrade Milne was disgusted with him and wanted nothing more to do with him.

'We know full well the British state is spying on us. It's no surprise there's a traitor in our midst. I suspect you're not the last one.'

And then they spelt out Sidney Dunn's punishment: he was never to enter King Street or any other Communist Party premises again; he was expelled from the Communist Party and was banned from attending any meetings; his local branch would be informed accordingly.

As he was taken out through the rear entrance the man with the Scottish accent leant close to him. 'You're lucky you're not in the Soviet Union, Dunn: they know how to do things properly there. You wouldn't have left the basement, not alive, at any rate.'

Charles Cooper made sure he was around Cliff Milne's office that Tuesday afternoon and again on the Wednesday. Milne was clearly distracted and when Cooper asked if there was anything he could do to help he explained that Dunn had left suddenly and he was left high and dry and didn't know which way to turn and Cooper said he'd be more than happy to help and he'd be honoured to apply for the job if there was a vacancy.

'There's no need for that kind of nonsense, comrade: what I say goes. You'll start tomorrow morning.'

—

Charles Cooper – Frank Reynolds to the comrades – wasn't rushing into anything. Percy Burton had been quite clear about that.

'Give yourself a few weeks before you so much as glance at a document!'

Around noon on the following Tuesday Milne was called to an urgent meeting and when he returned, he looked grey and asked Cooper to come through to his office and said perhaps he'd better sit down and his voice was uneven as he explained that they'd been told that Sidney Dunn had killed himself the previous evening.

'Hung himself: a neighbour found him. He'd lived on his own since his wife died. He had no one else: the Party was his life...'

And his death, thought Cooper.

'Out of all the people here, Sidney was the last person I'd have thought would betray us.'

Cooper nodded and said it was sad and then added that betrayal of the Party was unforgiveable and Milne nodded.

'Another victim of the class war.'

Chapter 25

'You need to leave the city now.'

It was the middle of the afternoon on Monday, 23 January and Douglas Marsh was in the gloomy basement of a barber's shop on Avenida de la República Argentina just behind Plaça de Lesseps and the man who'd just given him this order was sitting directly in front of him in a broken barber's chair, so close that their knees were touching. Marsh only knew him as Comrade Ivan, a senior officer in the GRU, the military intelligence arm of the Soviet Red Army.

That morning he'd been at a hardware store called Rafols on Ronda de Sant Pere. The basement was a secret Republican headquarters and there he'd bumped into another Russian he vaguely remembered had spotted him and ordered him to come here.

He'd not seen Comrade Ivan for the best part of a year and was now in a state of shock because he'd been told by someone who swore he'd seen it with his own eyes that Ivan had been killed in the fighting at Ebro a few months earlier.

But Ivan was still very much alive: his enormous frame slightly reduced, maybe, but the way the tiny blue eyes trained on him, and his pungent odour – a combination of garlic and strong tobacco – were unchanged, along with his insistence on speaking in heavily accented English and when he didn't refer to him by his nickname – Sova – he called him 'Doug', pronounced

'Duck', even though Marsh preferred Douglas and also thought his Russian was better than Comrade Ivan's English, which was saying something.

But Comrade Ivan was one of the few people Marsh didn't argue with. He'd first met him when he joined the Sixteenth Battalion of the Fifteenth International Brigade – known as the British Battalion – in early 1938, just after the Battle of Teruel, and he'd been singled out because he spoke Russian and had recently been in Moscow.

Comrade Ivan announced he'd been selected to assist the GRU – it was as unclear as that – and they'd be keeping an eye on him and at first that hadn't been as menacing as it sounded. He was taken to a training camp near the French border and treated very well and over the next year or so received what he had to acknowledge was preferential treatment, not least at the Battle of Ebro, when the company he commanded was pulled out of a suicidal attack minutes before it began.

The International Brigade had been dismantled in September 1938 and the members of the British Battalion were ordered to return home, but Douglas Marsh didn't march with the Brigade on its final parade through Barcelona in October and nor was he among the three hundred or so British volunteers who were treated like heroes when they arrived at Victoria station at the beginning of December.

Instead, he'd slipped away and found an abandoned house in the Sarrià–Sant Gervasi quarter of Barcelona, and a unit of the Republican Army only too willing to recruit him. They weren't minded to ask him too many questions and that was how Marsh found himself running a small unit of a dozen other foreigners.

Now there were just five of them left and Barcelona was about to fall. Franco's Nationalists had crossed the Ebro in early January, ten days earlier they'd captured Tarragona to the south and were now approaching the city from the north-west: Manresa and Tibidabo had fallen and Comrade Ivan had just told him they were on the banks of the Llobregat.

Marsh didn't need a map of the city to know how close they were: he could see the smoke and smell it too, and for the past week they'd heard far more incoming artillery than outgoing. The Catalan sky was heavy with Heinkel bombers attacking the city.

'The fascists will have captured the city by the end of the week at the latest,' said the Russian, his normally expressionless face now looking worried. As ever, his head was very still. 'What will you do?'

'I'll fight to defend the city. Maybe General Rojo—'

'Forget General Rojo – the battle is lost.'

'Then we'll head for Figueres: I hear the Republicans still hold the city.'

'I mean, when all of Spain is lost, what will you do then, Doug?'

Marsh hesitated because he knew Comrade Ivan and the GRU better than this: they didn't allow discussion or the expression of an opinion and this felt like a test.

'I'll go back to the Soviet Union: I'll continue the fight against fascism from there. I'm not returning to Britain.' That felt like the right answer.

Comrade Ivan shook his head and Marsh worried he'd failed the test but then, quite unexpectedly, the Russian smiled and said to listen carefully.

'Your orders are to return to Britain. The Communist Party there is a useful vehicle for Soviet Intelligence agencies. The Comintern's OMS has people there and so does the NKVD. We want you to be the GRU's eyes and ears inside the Communist Party. Europe is in turmoil and we need to have influence in London. You look disappointed, Doug?'

Douglas Marsh said, no, not at all… if that was how he could best serve the Soviet Union and the cause of peace and socialism then, of course, he would do whatever was required. He'd travel to France and—

Ivan shook his head again. 'Too dangerous. Go to the British Consulate on Diagonal; there's a Royal Navy ship called the HMS

Greyhound currently off the coast waiting to evacuate British citizens. They won't take combatants, certainly not from the Republican side, but we've prepared paperwork to show you've been working with orphans in Aragon. You have the identity of Oliver Lord: only use that name until you get back to Britain. Tell them you're religious. They'll like that.'

'Like what?'

'The British will like that you're religious. They'll trust you then and won't suspect you of being a Republican or a communist. But you need to get a haircut and shave off that beard.'

Ivan looked at Marsh: he had a wild appearance, hair everywhere and his skin tanned and leathered and stained with filth. When he had first met him, he had a pale complexion, like someone who spent most of his time in a library.

'Go upstairs and get a haircut. Then take a shower. There's a change of clothing in the bathroom and a few things in a small case, including a Bible. Tell me, who are the other guys you're with?'

'They're my comrades, Ivan: we've been together for months.'

'Who are they?'

'Otto's a German Jew, Jens is Danish, and Jack and George are brothers from London.'

'And do they know you're Douglas Marsh?'

Marsh said yes, but there was really no need to worry: he trusted them implicitly and they were all good socialists and he was sure he could persuade the British consulate to allow them onto the boat too. Ivan said he'd better get a move on.

'Where are the comrades waiting for you?'

'A bar round the corner on Pàdua – the one with green shutters.'

–

Douglas Marsh felt much better after his haircut, shave and shower and with the clean set of clothes he felt totally refreshed. The barber had given him a large shot of strong Spanish brandy in a cup of equally strong coffee with no milk and when Marsh looked in the case Ivan had left for him there was an envelope full of cash and he decided that once he'd collected Otto, Jens, Jack and George from the bar where he'd told them to wait, he'd be able to buy them all a decent meal before they headed off to the British Consulate.

But when he got to the bar on Carrer de Pàdua the door was locked and the street silent as startled eyes stared at him through shuttered windows.

He stood there trying to decide what to do and almost immediately heard small arms fire just ahead of him and he had enough experience by now to know it was from a semi-automatic: six quick shots, a pause, and a shout and six more. He ran in the direction of the gunshots: on the other side of Avenida de la República Argentina. He saw some movement on Carrer de Velázquez and by the time he got there two figures were hurrying away.

On the ground were the bodies of his four comrades, Otto's face turned towards him and one other body – possibly that of Jack, still moving.

He only hesitated for a moment or two, his head dropping and then he wiped his forehead with his handkerchief and his eyes too as he pulled himself together.

He'd had just over a year of this: getting as close as it was possible to a comrade and then losing them.

The only way to cope was to move on.

To the north, a flight of Heinkels banked over the city.

Douglas Marsh headed to the British Consulate.

Behind him, Ivan watched from the shadow of a deep doorway and nodded to himself.

As long as Marsh remained alive and got to London, he was safe too.

Chapter 26

London
February–March 1939

The situation he found himself in was so complicated and so… well, crazy was the only word for it… that Cooper caught himself thinking of those plays he'd been dragged along to by his mother which were meant to be comedies, where one person was romantically involved with another who in turn was interested in someone else, who also…

Suffice to say that they involved much heavy-handed innuendo, with members of the cast running around the stage and into the wings shrieking, and badly constructed doors slamming and risqué suggestions of 'activities', as his mother called them, offstage.

They were called farces and that neatly summed up Cooper's current predicament. He'd been a Soviet spy and then he'd rather cleverly – or so he'd thought – wriggled himself out of that, only to then become a British spy, which was awkward, certainly, but not nearly as awkward as being a Soviet spy because at least he was no longer a traitor. But now, so it seemed, he was a Soviet spy once more while at the same time as being a British spy.

Neither side knew he was spying for the other, so in that sense, he wasn't a double agent.

Indeed, if only he were something as straightforward as that.

–

Much to Randall's discomfort – he said he really did need to lock up and it was getting terribly late – Osip insisted they'd remain in his office in Store Street because he and Mr Cooper had much to talk about.

'It's nice and warm here and this is a most comfortable chair and I see you have a drinks cabinet, Mr Randall, so I suggest you open it and then go and wait in another room, ideally on the floor below.'

Randall made a fuss about unlocking the drinks cabinet and took out a quarter-full bottle of Scotch and a couple of not exactly shiny glasses and said they really couldn't leave it too late and Osip dismissed him with a wave of the hand and said to make sure he shut the door behind him.

The Russian waited until Randall's footsteps had disappeared down the stairs before removing his large overcoat and then poured them each a generous measure of whisky and from a box on the desk found a cigar, which he lit with some difficulty. Each time he put the cigar to his lips he licked them.

He leant back in Randall's chair, all the while looking terribly pleased with himself, as well he might. Cooper imagined that if you were a Russian spy master who'd been careless enough to lose an agent even before he'd started, it probably didn't go down awfully well in Moscow.

He did ask Cooper if he had an explanation for all this and Cooper said he wasn't sure what he meant, and Osip said he meant disappearing and now calling himself Christopher Shaw.

Cooper shrugged and said that when he returned from Moscow the pressure of things had got on top of him and he needed a break before he got in touch and Osip looked at him as if he didn't believe a word but to his surprise he shrugged and said that was in the past and the main thing was that he was here now and how was he getting on?

'Getting on with what?'

'Getting on with your original mission, which was to join the Foreign Office or the War Office.'

Cooper felt sick and very hot. 'These things take time, you don't just *join*, you know.'

'So, you've applied?'

'After a fashion, yes.'

'What does "after a fashion" mean?'

'It means I'm making enquiries about applying – I'm in the process of it. It wouldn't have been any good if I'd applied straight after I returned from Moscow, because of the state I was in. I worried I could give the game away at an interview and you wouldn't have wanted that, would you?'

'Maybe not straight after, but almost eighteen months? To me that sounds like a poor excuse. I could be forgiven for suspecting that you have had second thoughts and no longer wish to work for the Comintern!'

Cooper was glad a screen of dirty cigar smoke had formed between him and Osip because he worried his reaction would somehow betray him, but then the Russian swept the smoke away with a chubby hand, revealing an innocent smile.

'But you are a very lucky comrade, Mr Cooper! Moscow has decided on a different mission for you.'

Osip paused and glanced towards the door, eyeing it suspiciously, and then shifted his bulky frame so that he was leaning forward, pushing aside a tall pile of papers on Randall's desk. He gestured towards Cooper.

'Come forward, you'll hear me better. From now on, I'm going to use your codename: Bertie. I'll be honest with you, there are tensions within Moscow – there always are – but these days they have become quite marked, not least in the area of intelligence. As well as the Comintern, for whom we work, there are other bodies involved in intelligence-gathering: the NKVD and the GRU both work in a clandestine manner and, of course, there's the Soviet Foreign Ministry, which operates through the Soviet Embassy here in London. There is a degree of co-operation between the different organisations, but, if I'm honest, there's an even higher degree of competition and even hostility. Comintern is very concerned that we need to be better informed about what our comrades are up to and in particular we wish to be better informed on what is happening within the British Communist Party. Do you know much about it, Bertie?'

Cooper replied that of course he'd heard of the British Communist Party and had even bought their newspaper – the *Daily Worker*, wasn't it? – on occasion and he understood that it had a Member of Parliament and was quite influential in certain trade unions and Osip looked impressed.

'That's a good start. You are to get involved in the Communist Party of Great Britain: we want regular reports on its activities and the names of people who are influential within it. We are also particularly interested in anyone who could be suspected of representing these other Soviet organisations, namely the NKVD, the GRU and the Foreign Ministry. It's not an easy task, but it's a most important one.'

Now, not only was he spying for two countries simultaneously, but he was also being asked to do so on the same subject.

–

For a few days Cooper toyed with the idea of disappearing altogether – he still had the funds, after all. But he knew that with both the British and the Soviets looking for him the odds on surviving very long were slim.

Spying for both on the British Communist Party was just about feasible because, after all, it was what he did anyway.

In the weeks after meeting Osip in Store Street he developed a *modus operandi* which was more or less manageable.

In the evenings in Willesden, he would take to his room after dinner and type out his reports for The Annexe: he'd deliver two or three of them a week – running to as much as half a dozen closely typed pages, cramming in as much detail as possible. The Annexe lapped up dates and names and even the gossip and rumour which King Street seemed to thrive on. On other evenings or at weekends, Cooper still attended meetings of the

Communist Party or educational events put on by it and its various front organisations.

He'd post the reports through the letterbox of a nearby Annexe safe house on his way into King Street. Once he'd started working for the OMS, he began making duplicate versions of the report: he'd leave King Street as early as he could and stop at his flat in Dorset Square and type up a new and slightly more abridged version of the same report, this time for a different master.

He became adept at tailoring his reports. It was simpler for The Annexe – more factual and more of a starting point for his face-to-face debriefs with Burton or Clarke, which took place at least once a week. For Osip, there was far more of what he'd describe as artistic licence, though he accepted that some may say it was closer to fiction.

To that end, he invented a cast of characters and realised they'd work perfectly in a new novel. They possessed an authenticity he could now see *The Jewels of Europe* lacked. Somehow, the reports rang true, with a heart and a flow which made the novel seem stilted in comparison.

He came up with a women called Barbara he claimed he'd encountered at a number of educational events and he wasn't sure if her surname was Hardie or Harvey and he thought she lived in Enfield but it could be Edgware and she spoke very good Russian and he'd overheard her saying she often travelled there and he was sure she had NKVD contacts... and then there was Piers, well-spoken and rumoured to be a minor aristocrat, who was a regular at meetings in Central London and was known to be very generous... and Malcolm, which he didn't think was his real name, surname possibly Stanley, but almost certainly a secret Trotskyite... and a young Indian man called Rajesh who he believed was a medical student at Barts... and a Jewish man called Gold-something or the other replete with a long nose and stooped shoulders and sallow complexion who Cooper thought couldn't be trusted but was very sharp – he thought Osip would buy that because his experience in Moscow had been that Russians didn't trust Jews, even though they made up half of the

Politburo – and half a dozen others, all with something about them which he hoped would intrigue the OMS.

And a couple of these – Barbara Hardie or Harvey in particular – had very good contacts inside King Street, which Cooper pointed out was the headquarters of the Communist Party. And here he added information he hoped Osip would be able to verify, thus putting him in a good light because it would show his reports were credible.

He listed all the people he could think of in King Street: he mentioned Cliff Milne in passing – he called him Clifford Mills, hoping that slight error would have more of a ring of truth about it – and said he was rather mysterious and there were rumours he may be involved with one of the Soviet Intelligence agencies. He even made an oblique reference to himself – a 'pleasant young man called Frank' who seemed to work for Mills, though after he handed that report to Osip, he immediately regretted it. It was frivolous and unnecessary.

And he wrote a long report on Sidney Dunn: possibly a Trotskyite spy, he said, connected with Mills and one of the Soviet agencies were rumoured to have killed him in his home in Stepney. He even provided the address and the date he was killed, but added that he couldn't verify this, it was just a rumour – but he knew Osip would check it out and find out most of the story happened to be true.

–

'You're making up for lost time, Bertie!'

They were meeting in an OMS safe house, a two-room apartment above a newsagent in The Broadway, a short walk from Hendon station. It had its own entrance down a dark alley and Osip clearly liked the place because their weekly meetings had been held there for three weeks in a row. Osip swore in Russian as he put money in the meter and after closing the curtains turned on the gas fire and a lamp.

Cooper took what the Russian had said as a compliment and nodded appreciatively.

'For almost eighteen months you do – nothing! Then less than two months ago I find you and since then – excellent!' Osip was tapping the report Cooper had given him the previous week. 'The information from inside the Party headquarters in Covent Garden is first-rate. It's almost as if you've been in there yourself.'

Osip laughed noisily and Cooper gratefully joined in.

'This Barbara Hardie—'

'It could be Harvey.'

'She seems very… very busy and well-connected. How often does she go into King Street and what does she do there?'

'I don't know exactly because I don't want her to become suspicious, but I believe she visits at least once a week. I get the impression that she may go there to collect money, which she then distributes to various Communist Party branches across London. I also get the impression that when she's there she spends some time in the building: she seems to know a lot of people.'

Osip was tapping the report once again. 'And the man you call Clifford Mills in the report: tell me more about him, tell me what he looks like.'

Cooper said he only knew what Barbara Hardie or Harvey had told him but he got the impression that he was very important indeed, but liked to keep a low profile, but – and this had only happened two days ago – he'd been with Rajesh, the Indian medical student, at a meeting in Camden and there was a man who came in on his own and stood at the back for a short while and then left and Rajesh said he believed his name was Cliff and he was something very important at King Street.

Cooper then described Cliff Milne and Osip looked pleased and said OMS in Moscow would be very pleased indeed when he told them.

'From the description and everything you tell me about this man, I believe his name is actually Cliff Milne, not Mills. I'm very pleased you mentioned him because the OMS believe he is NKVD. Does the name Molotov mean anything to you?'

Cooper shook his head.

'In terms of the hierarchy of the Soviet Union, Vyacheslav Mikhailovich Molotov is probably second only to Comrade Stalin. He's been out of favour recently but now he's back in Moscow again and there are all kinds of rumours as to what he's up to, including talk of him advocating stronger relations between the Soviet Union and Germany, would you believe?'

Cooper was doing his best to memorise what Osip was telling him.

'Cliff Milne was in Moscow around 1932 or 1933, and he became close to Molotov, who at that time was prime minister. We believe he has maintained that relationship with Molotov, which would explain his connection with the NKVD. This is very important information you've given us. But we require even more: we want to know everything you can find out about Milne. There was a reference in another report to a young man called Frank who may work for Milne? See what you can find out about him, too.'

—

Percy Burton was as delighted as Osip and he too wanted to know more about Milne.

The evening after his meeting with Osip, Cooper had written a new report for Burton, this one based substantially on what Osip had told him. He'd glimpsed a folder on Milne's desk, he wrote, which contained a typed letter in English, apparently from Moscow and the name under the signature was V M Molotov and he recalled two sentences:

> …may our personal friendship and comradeship continue to flourish and be productive… I am firm in my belief that a strategy of co-operation with Germany – as difficult as that is – will reduce the significant threat to the security of the Soviet Union and thereby…

Cooper had apologised if these two sentences meant nothing, but that was all he had time to see. He hoped it was nonetheless useful.

'And elsewhere in your report you say: "I'm increasingly of the belief that CM may have active links with the NKVD". What do you base this on?'

Cooper had anticipated this question as he'd failed to provide any evidence and he didn't think he'd get away with saying it was based on a gut feeling.

Or that Osip had told him.

'He's spoken approvingly of them recently – in terms of how they're the true guarantors of the Russian revolution. Maybe the language I used was possibly a bit speculative.'

'You mustn't worry, Cooper, the intelligence here is of the very highest standard – and I have to tell you that the information regarding Milne corroborates what we've understood about him from other sources, though not in such clear terms. I think now is the time to try Milne's safe.'

–

As February slipped into March, Cooper waited for a chance to try the safe. Cliff Milne was meticulous about keeping the second key on the chain round his neck. Not once did he see it anywhere else.

Percy Burton assured him he understood and said the fact that Milne was so careful pointed to the contents of the safe being important. He was to be patient. And in the meantime, he'd had a thought.

On the Thursday morning of the first week in March, Cooper was walking along the corridor of the second floor of King Street when a man emerged from an office. The corridor was lit only by a single light bulb so they only properly spotted each other when they were close and Cooper recognised the man immediately and going by his reaction, he did too.

The man was gaunt, with a heavy moustache and ears which stuck out and the last time Cooper had seen him was in the slide show at The Annexe when Burton had been showing him people to look out for. He'd seemed familiar then – though he was now tanned – and he seemed familiar now, but Cooper couldn't place him.

He discovered the man was called Douglas Marsh and he was talked of in reverential tones around King Street because, apparently, he'd been in Barcelona when the city fell to the fascists and he'd been a hero in the Civil War.

It would be a while before Cooper recalled where he'd last seen the man, and by then it was too late.

–

The night after he first saw Douglas Marsh in King Street, he met with Osip.

But this was no cosy meeting above a newsagent in Hendon. This time, Cooper travelled to Old Oak Lane station and headed towards Wormwood Scrubs and just as the prison came into view, he spotted Osip on the path in front of him clutching a bunch of flowers in his left hand, which was the signal that the meeting was on.

They joined a stream of people heading towards the Hammersmith Hospital – Osip had chosen a time to coincide with the hospital's visiting hours. He followed the Russian into the shadows of the land behind the hospital and prison.

'You have another report?'

Cooper handed over an envelope and apologised this one was rather short, but…

Osip didn't so much as glance at the envelope as he put it straight into his pocket and threw the bunch of flowers into the bramble.

'Are you all right?'

Osip didn't reply for a while and when he turned to face Cooper it seemed everything was apparently not all right. His face looked strained and even in the poor light. Cooper could see his eyes were bloodshot.

'Things are… difficult: it may be a while before we can meet.'

He was about to say something else but stopped himself and instead grabbed Cooper's hand and with his other hand clasped his forearm and looked him in the eye, uttering just one word before hurrying off into the night.

'*Tovarishch*.'

Chapter 27

Moscow
March 1939

Nikolai Vasilyevich Zaslavsky never failed to be shocked at the dramatically contrasting speeds with which events occurred in Moscow. Usually, change happened at a glacial pace: a decision which should have taken a matter of weeks at the most could take years, literally, as it worked its way through various committees at a speed a snail would consider slow. Some of the Five Year Plans took longer than five years to devise.

But at other times change occurred at a remarkable speed, as if in the middle of a bitter Russian winter's day warm sunshine suddenly bathed the city.

Nikolai Vasilyevich was particularly mindful of what had happened to Isidor Yevstigneyevich Lyubimov. Lyubimov lived in the same apartment block as him, close to the Kirov metro station, though the Lyubimov family were a few floors up and in a far superior apartment, as befitted his status as People's Commissar for Light Industry. Nikolai Vasilyevich was in awe of Isidor Yevstigneyevich. He was someone with impeccable credentials: a Bolshevik since the turn of the century, active in the revolution, a member of the Central Committee and the Presidium of the Supreme Soviet, recipient of the Order of Lenin.

Whenever he bumped into Isidor Yevstigneyevich and they exchanged polite if brief greetings he felt almost as if Comrade Stalin himself had spoken to him.

That was, until the end of September 1937, when Lyubimov was suddenly removed from his post and arrested, apparently for consorting with 'enemies of the people'.

Isidor Yevstigneyevich Lyubimov disappeared from the apartment block, though his family remained there awkwardly for a few more weeks, moving like ghosts on the rare occasions they were seen around the building. Two months later Lyubimov was dead: found guilty of being an enemy of the people and executed on the same day.

Nikolai Vasilyevich was shocked that a person could go from such a powerful position to being shot in a basement so quickly. If it happened to Isidor Yevstigneyevich Lyubimov, he thought, it could happen to anyone.

And now it appeared to be happening to him.

–

It was strange because at the beginning of March everything seemed fine at the OMS – the International Liaison Department of the Comintern. And then over a period of little more than twenty-four hours, it all changed.

Nikolai Vasilyevich turned up at work on a Monday morning – it was 6 March – and along with everyone else was diverted to a nearby hall because apparently the offices of the OMS had been flooded over the weekend. They remained in the hall during the day. Very early on it became apparent that something was not quite right. They were unable to leave without permission and if someone wanted to go to the toilet they would be escorted. During the day various people were called to another room and didn't return.

In the middle of the afternoon those remaining in the hall were called out one by one. A man with a Georgian accent who Nikolai Vasilyevich had never seen before checked his home address and said he was to go straight home and remain there until the following morning, when he was to report to the OMS office at ten thirty.

'The flood has been sorted, then?'

The man looked annoyed by what he saw as impudence. 'Don't be early. Or late.'

So, this is how it happens, thought Nikolai Vasilyevich. He'd often wondered about the people who'd been arrested and disappeared over the past few years and was confused why they didn't escape when they must have had an inkling of their impending fate. What was it about a man which made him such a compliant and accommodating prey? Now he himself appeared to be in such a position and could appreciate why they didn't leave. There was nowhere to go, and there was also a slim chance that there could be some misunderstanding and he'd have to settle for losing his job and maybe working in a factory or a state farm and he thought that on balance he'd prefer the latter.

A mood of grim resignation settled over Nikolai Vasilyevich as he arrived home earlier than usual and told his wife about the flood and he did wonder whether to tell her she may never see him again, but he couldn't bring himself to do that, and then thought about writing a letter, but he had no idea where to start and, in any case, if they raided the apartment in the early hours of the morning – which was quite probable – then the letter would be construed as incriminating evidence.

He hardly slept that night and got up at six to make himself a strong, black tea and sat in the tiny kitchen smoking, looking out of the grimy window at the traffic edging round the Boulevard Ring in the distance. When he finished his tea, he poured himself a vodka, which he never touched at this time of day, but he hoped it may settle his nerves. He then reached under the kitchen sink and opened his toolbox and removed the gold bracelet encrusted with diamonds, which had been hidden in a brown paper bag since he'd confiscated it during a raid eighteen months ago. He'd had it valued and it was worth at least half a year's salary and he thought if anything ever happened to him his wife would need this. He put the bracelet in the tin with a crude picture of Lenin on the lid where his wife kept the shopping money, along with the Slava wristwatch his father had bought him when he joined the Comintern and what cash he had in his wallet.

And then he left, with no expectation he'd ever return. For a while he paused in the doorway of his daughters' room and thought about kissing them, but he decided to leave them sleeping. Today would be a long one for them.

–

The man who met him on the landing outside his office was Emil, who'd worked for the NKVD in the past and the man who'd recruited the British agent, Archie.

'Come with me, Nikolai Vasilyevich.'

That certainly didn't sound nearly as ominous as it could have done and when they entered a side room one of the other people there wished him a 'good morning' and he was told to sit down and offered a cigarette.

'As of yesterday, comrade, the International Liaison Department no longer exists.'

Emil was sitting opposite him, flanked by two other men.

'From now on, the work of the OMS will be undertaken primarily by the NKVD. I will be heading the section responsible for this. The decision has been made that a small number of the most trusted OMS officers will be asked to transfer to the NKVD. A smaller number will join the GRU. The remainder are no longer required. Arrangements are being made for them.'

Nikolai Vasilyevich knew full well what 'arrangements' meant. He felt short of breath and was aware of gripping the chair.

'I am pleased to tell you that you are one of those transferring to the NKVD, Nikolai Vasilyevich.'

He nodded his head and said thank you three times and it was all he could do not to weep out of sheer relief.

'Eduard Vladimirovich in Berlin comes under you, does he not?'

He nodded. The man who'd recruited the Englishman Cooper: Bertie.

'He is no longer required. Arrangements are being made. And, likewise, Osip in London.'

'I would respectfully point out Osip controls two important English agents: Archie and Bertie.'

'Do you know Ivan Alexandrovich Morozov, the NKVD station chief in London?'

'I know of him.'

'He will now run Archie.'

'And Bertie?'

'I understand he disappeared until very recently?'

'We did lose contact, but he—'

'He is clearly unreliable, but we are undecided. But in any case, it has been decided he will be handled by the GRU. They have a new agent in London, an Englishman who's recently returned from Barcelona: he will deal with Bertie.'

Emil and the other two men stood up and Nikolai Vasilyevich did likewise and followed them into the corridor, walking as if in a daze. Along the corridor he heard shouting and from another floor, screams. Emil turned round to walk alongside him.

'I'm sure you realise how fortunate you've been, comrade. From tomorrow you'll be based in the Lubyanka. As for those for whom arrangements are being made, my advice is not to think about them. There'll always be victims. Someone has to pay the price.'

And as if to emphasise that, from a few floors below, the sound of a single gunshot rang out, its echoes lasting a good few seconds.

Chapter 28

London
March 1939

'Slow down, please!'

Cooper had just got off the number 74 bus and was crossing Gloucester Place and heading towards his flat in Dorset Square. He resisted the temptation to turn round, but slowed down once he was on the other side of the road to allow Osip to catch up with him.

'Didn't you hear me? I said slow down!'

It was the first time he'd seen Osip since their meeting on Wormwood Scrubs three weeks earlier when the Russian had seemed distracted and said things were difficult and it may be a while before they met. He was surprised because, as he understood it, the protocol was very strict: a controller wouldn't go anywhere near where an agent lived.

Or worked.

Or accost him in the street like this.

'What the hell are you doing here?'

Cooper was still walking and although they were now by the entrance to Dorset Square it occurred to him Osip may not know his actual address but had just followed him on the bus so he carried on walking, but Osip held him by the arm.

'Are you not going to your apartment? Number 33 Dorset Square, apartment four on the second floor? I'd prefer if we went there.'

When they entered Cooper's apartment Osip insisted he bolt the front door and then marched into the lounge, where he dropped into an armchair.

He looked dreadful: gaunt, pale-skinned and unshaven. His clothes were creased and when he removed his trilby – which Cooper always felt looked a bit too foreign, more like a fedora – his hair was greasy and unkempt.

'I'd like a drink, Bertie.'

'I can put the kettle on, Osip.'

'Get me a whisky and something to eat.'

Cooper watched as Osip quickly finished his whisky – which had been a generous measure – and then gestured for him to pass the bottle before pouring himself an even larger measure. They were sitting opposite each other with Cooper perched on the edge of the sofa.

'You have to help me, Bertie.' Osip looked flushed and as he stuffed the remainder of a sandwich into his mouth and chewed it he poured himself another whisky. He leant towards Cooper and indicated he should come closer. Cooper noticed how bloodshot the man's eyes were.

And there was something about his eyes, which Cooper had never seen before.

Fear.

'Terrible things are happening in Moscow.'

He paused to sip more whisky and Cooper thought about asking Osip how come it had taken him so long to discover that, but he thought better of it. Osip always told him it didn't pay to be too clever.

'They've turned on us, the bastards. Since 1921 the International Liaison Department has been the most effective arm of Soviet Intelligence, we make the NKVD look like amateurs. But now Stalin has decided he no longer trusts the OMS and has begun to dismantle it. There've been rumours, but I dismissed them because I assumed the OMS was indispensable and, in any case, Morozov – the NKVD resident here in London – told me not to worry because he said whatever happened in Moscow I'd continue in my job; it would just mean a transfer to the NKVD.'

Osip shrugged. 'And like a fool, I believed it until two weeks ago when I was at the embassy and Morozov called me into his office and said I was to return to Moscow, immediately. I'm no fool, I knew what that meant: the OMS is being purged and that includes me. I was trapped. I didn't have an opportunity to go back to my apartment and grab the bag I keep packed just in case and then disappear. Morozov told me he'd made all the arrangements.

'At that point, I knew the game was up. But a year ago I'd found a spare key for a fire escape at the rear of the embassy, so I told Morozov I understood, just needed to go to the toilet and he said to hurry up.

'If I'd been him, I'd have thought it was odd I'd not asked how I was going to get back to Moscow or put up something of an argument, but then we both knew how resigned people can be to their fate in these situations.

'I knew I had to move fast: I headed to the toilet but then ran up the stairs to the floor which I had the key for and straight down the fire escape and soon I was in the garden at the back. The guard on duty there was a comrade I knew well — he's from Leningrad, too. I told him I was going for a walk to clear my head and we both laughed and minutes later I was in Vicarage Gate where I hailed a taxi and told it to take me to Kings Cross. I then travelled on the underground for a few hours, found a cheap hotel in east London, moved to a different hotel every couple of nights and here I am, at last.'

'How did you find me?'

'That doesn't matter — what does matter is that I need your help now: don't forget, I'm a Soviet spy and you work for me. What do you think would happen if the British found that out?'

Osip leant forward again and pointed his cigarette at Cooper, allowing a long stub of ash to fall on the rug between them.

'But the NKVD in London — surely, they know about me?'

Osip shook his head. 'They don't know everything by any means; how to contact you, for instance, That's why they want me back in Moscow, so they can get everything from me before they dispose of me. If it was just a matter of eliminating me, Morozov would have taken care of that in London: I wouldn't be the first person he's killed here.'

Cooper needed time to think. He told Osip he should have a bath and a change of clothing while he made him a hot meal and the Russian said that was a good idea and, in fact, he was thinking of staying the night.

And as he stood in the kitchen preparing a meal for which he had no appetite, Cooper gathered his thoughts. As a British spy who was also working for the Soviet Union, Cooper was trapped. But the only person in London who knew he was a Soviet spy was lounging in his bath and about to eat his food and most probably spend the night in his bed.

If Osip returned to Moscow, then half the NKVD would know all about him.

And if he remained in London, then he dreaded to think what could happen.

It was an impossible predicament.

An almost impossible one.

–

Cooper left Dorset Square early the following morning after a sleepless night.

Leaving Osip in the flat he walked down to Bayswater Road and once he was sure he wasn't being followed took the number 12 bus to Acton. On the short walk towards Acton Central station, he checked he still wasn't being followed, and in Churchfield Road found a letting agency. They had just what he was looking for: a bedsit on the same road, close to the railway line, with a secure door to the side of the house, shared with just one other bedsit and that was vacant, a view over the street, which Osip would want, and it was clean enough. They agreed he could take it immediately if he paid an extra week's rent in advance and Cooper slipped the clerk an extra two pounds and thanked him for his trouble.

Osip travelled to the bedsit that afternoon by taxi. Cooper had packed a bag of food for him and promised to do what the Russian had instructed.

'Repeat it, please, Bertie.'

'I'm to go to Lloyds Bank in Baker Street and ask for the packet in the manager's safe in the name of Mr Drake.'

'Don't forget the number: they'll expect you to give it to them rather before they ask you for it.'

'9-8-7-9-4-4-4-3-0-2.'

'And they'll ask for an address.'

Cooper paused, trying to remember the name of the street. '17 Barber Street, Southampton. You're sure they won't want to see anything else?'

'My instructions to the bank were that the package should be released to anyone giving the correct code and address. As soon as you get the package, bring it to me here.'

'I don't understand why you haven't gone yourself?'

'It's too risky. I went to the bank two weeks ago to check on the papers and money in the envelope. Looking back on it, they were probably following me then. If that's the case, they'll be watching the bank now.'

Back in Dorset Square it took Cooper a while before he'd produced a letter he was satisfied with.

> Dear Comrade Ivan Morozov
>   This is a letter from a fellow comrade to inform you that the traitor Osip from the OMS is hiding in a first-floor bedsit at 2D Churchfield Road just by Acton Central station. Please be aware he has a gun. He is expecting a visit on Friday night.

Cooper wasn't sure how seriously Morozov would take it. But then he'd have been mortified at Osip escaping the previous week: he'd clutch at any straw to catch him.

There was one flaw, of course: what if they tried to take Osip back to Moscow and torture him there – or even attempt to do it here? If that happened Osip would almost certainly divulge Cooper's name, the man he would know betrayed him.

But Cooper decided this was a risk worth taking.

One risk not worth taking was to try and retrieve the package from the bank. There was no need.

He waited until the Friday lunchtime. Outside Notting Hill Gate station, he found a boy of around fifteen who looked at him incredulously when he offered him five shillings to run a simple errand. He followed the boy as he walked to the Soviet Embassy and watched as he handed the envelope to the guard at the gate before hurrying off – as Cooper had instructed him – in the direction of Kensington Palace.

–

Ivan Alexandrovich Morozov clutched the letter in disbelief. He'd been blamed for allowing Osip to escape the previous week and had been told unless he could find him quickly then he'd be the one returning to Moscow.

You can use the same ticket, they told him.

He needed to be sure this was genuine though. He travelled on his own to Acton, taking an embassy car into Oxford Street, spending an hour in Selfridges to lose his tail and after that a series of buses to Acton. He found 2D Churchfield Road easily enough. It was well chosen: its own side entrance and a good view of both the street and the entrance. He found a cafe diagonally opposite with a decent sight of the bedsit and gloomy enough for him not to be spotted.

Twice over the next hour a man appeared at the window, standing just far enough back for his face to be hard to make out, but glancing up and down the street in a professional manner and, as far as he was concerned, it certainly could be that bastard from the OMS and, if not, there was no harm in trying.

He returned that night with five of his men, all of them making their own way to a van parked behind Latimer Road station and it was nine o'clock when it arrived in Churchfield Road and parked well away from number 2D. The Georgian called Nikoloz had the entrance door opened in a matter of seconds and then remained on lookout, along with two of the others. Another two accompanied Morozov upstairs to the first floor. Morozov had decided he'd leave nothing to chance: he could have someone knock on the door and use an English accent, but he doubted Osip would fall for that. The other Georgian threw himself against the door, Morozov following in with his revolver drawn.

Osip was sitting on the bed, startled and reaching under the pillow. Morozov and the Georgian threw themselves at him, pinning him under them. The NKVD man's instruction had been clear: no guns unless absolutely necessary.

We don't want any embarrassment.

Osip was no match for the big Georgian. He struggled but Morozov slipped his long-blade knife into Osip's side, just under the rib cage as he'd been taught, and then twisted it around and moved it up and down.

–

Cooper read about the murder of the unidentified man in Acton in the following day's *Evening News*. There was a description of what he took to be him – as the man who'd rented the room – but it was suitably vague and described him as being in his forties and with a 'foreign accent', which was all very reassuring even though he had no idea where the rental clerk got that accent from.

Cooper's overwhelming reaction was a sense of relief. He was no longer committing treason by working for the Soviets: his connection with them had been severed.

Life ought to be a lot easier now.

Chapter 29

Archie had never liked Osip.

In truth – he realised that this was somewhat awkward given his relationship with them – he didn't like many Russians. He quite liked Emil, the man who'd recruited him in France nearly eight years before, and Nikolai in Moscow was decent enough, but they were more sophisticated and companionable sorts. As for the rest, they were either ideologues, peasants or Jews, none of whom he could abide.

Osip was a case in point: he reminded him of one of the gardeners at his parents' place in the country; large and malodorous, always giving the impression of being put upon and forever bending his father's ear about some problem or the other and he never understood why his father gave the man the time of day – or a job, for that matter.

Whenever they met, Osip was always complaining about this or moaning about that. He'd last met him in early March and this time the Russian said very little, other than that times were not good, and when he asked what he meant by that he'd shrugged and said it didn't matter, even though it quite evidently did. He told Archie it may be a few weeks before he saw him again, and when he asked if this was connected with things not being good, he'd shrugged again.

At first it suited Archie fine because frankly he needed a break from the subterfuge and constant strain of spying for the Soviets and forever having to lay his hands on new intelligence while at the same time avoiding coming under suspicion.

The good news was that, as far as he could tell, Phillips' hunt for him seemed to have run into a brick wall. The last he'd heard Phillips was suffering from what was euphemistically referred to as exhaustion but the rumours said he'd had a nervous breakdown. Apparently, he was in a clinic in Hampshire, not too far from where Archie had been at prep school, as it happened. Both dreadful places to be incarcerated.

On occasional moments of reflection – usually in the country at the weekend, late at night when everyone else was asleep and between his first and second Cognac – he'd acknowledge to himself that his feelings about people, which some could describe as prejudices – were possibly incompatible with his being a Soviet agent. But he never allowed these thoughts to develop into doubts or even preoccupations. As far as he was concerned, spying for the Soviet Union was a matter of having chosen which side to be on. Events in Europe showed the Continent was facing a stark choice between fascism and socialism, between war and peace, and there was no middle ground. He was more convinced than ever that he made the right choice, but that didn't mean he had to like the people whose side he'd chosen to be on.

And he was doing well at MI6. In December he'd been promoted, not quite to a senior officer but it was now only a matter of time before a promotion to that grade came through. He now had what the chief described as a problem-solver role, reporting to him, and that meant trips around Europe.

Which was what brought him to Paris, where the local MI6 station had got itself into a flap over all the intelligence it was receiving from different sources at the Quai d'Orsay.

This was all to do with a proposal from the Soviet foreign minister, or People's Commissar for Foreign Affairs, to give him his proper title, Maxim Litvinov. Litvinov was proposing a pact between the USSR, France and the United Kingdom in the face of the threat from Nazi Germany. For the time being, Litvinov had Stalin's ear, but there were those in Moscow who disliked

Litvinov and disliked his plan even more. And the British weren't keen on the plan either because they didn't trust the Soviets but there was more support for it in the Quai d'Orsay – the French Foreign Ministry – and this was the reason for the flap at Paris Station.

It seemed that they didn't know what to make of all the intelligence they were getting – the Quai d'Orsay was notorious for leaking like a sieve – and much of it was conflicting and there was a source in the private office of Bonnet, the French foreign minister, which said he was well disposed towards the proposed pact, but another source said he was minded to take the lead of the British and…

It took him a few days to make heads or tails of what was going on but finally he was making some progress, certainly enough to please the chief, and now it was a pleasant Wednesday afternoon and he'd just left the embassy on rue du Faubourg Saint-Honoré and was reflecting that there really was nowhere nicer to be than Paris in the spring when he became aware a man had fallen in step with him.

'Archie?'

Emil looked every inch the Parisian gentleman as he gently guided him across the road towards Avenue de Messine and into a small bistro, where the maître d' pointed to the stairs and followed them up to unlock a door into what appeared to be his office. He noticed that Emil was wearing what looked like the same cream suit with a blue-and-white-striped shirt and dark tie he'd worn when he'd first met him in Paris, nearly eight years before.

'I need to debrief you: I want to know everything you've been dealing with here in Paris. I presume it's to do with Litvinov's plan?'

'It is.'

'But first, I have a question. When did you last see Osip?'

'Five… six weeks ago?'

'Does it strike you that was an unusually long gap?'

'He said it might be a few weeks before we met again. I wondered if he'd gone back to Moscow, possibly.'

'Did he say anything else?'

'That things were not good.'

'Did he elaborate?'

'No, but then Osip never was one for elaboration.'

'The OMS no longer exists. You are now an agent for the NKVD, in which I am a senior officer. Comrade Nikolai Vasilyevich who you met in Moscow is now also with the NKVD. As far as you're concerned, you are to carry on as before. The view in Moscow is that your intelligence has been very good, but I think you will find that the NKVD is a more demanding master; it has higher expectations. Your controller in London will be our head of station there, Ivan Alexandrovich Morozov. I presume you've heard of him?'

'Of course. But what about Osip?'

Emil raised his eyebrows and pursed his lips. 'Osip is no longer with us.'

There was a long pause. Archie knew better than to ask Emil what that meant because he had a perfectly good idea. It was something of a relief, if he was honest.

'And these changes in Moscow, Emil, do I need to know what—'

'You don't need to know anything, Archie, but let me say this: for societies to function effectively, without descending into anarchy and chaos, they need to have people in power to control them. And every so often, there needs to be a change of power. The marginal difference between your society and mine is that in the West you have the charade of elections to effect a change in power. In the Soviet Union, we also experience periodic changes of power, but with us it is a matter of some organisations falling out of favour and individuals being no longer regarded as useful. It is a more efficient way of bringing about a change in power. These changes are still taking place, Archie; indeed, it is in connection with them that I need to know more about what the British and French views are on Litvinov's proposal. So, if you can—'

'Can I just ask one more question? There was another agent Osip was looking after. Osip said more than once that he wished me to get involved with him, whatever that meant.'

'As far as you're concerned, Archie, that agent is also no longer with us.'

Chapter 30

Nikolai Vasilyevich Zaslavsky considered himself a very fortunate man: not only was he still very much alive but he was also still free. He still lived in the pleasant apartment close to the Kirov metro station, and his wife and daughters still enjoyed the considerable privileges afforded to the family of a man in his position, and he still worked for Soviet Intelligence, which people in Moscow were fond of saying was the most efficient Soviet industry.

The difference was that since the OMS was shut down the previous month and most of its officers purged, Nikolai Vasilyevich – who'd feared he was going to be one of them – now worked for the NKVD.

He was based at the Lubyanka, the enormous yellow-bricked building on the eponymously named square, and notwithstanding his undoubted good fortune, he was finding it difficult to settle in. Although he was attached to the Foreign Intelligence Unit, the NKVD also looked after state security and internal espionage, which added an altogether new dimension to the work.

And then there were the factions: it wasn't that the OMS was above factions, but the NKVD was absolutely riven with them. There were factions that sprang up overnight, replacing other factions, and there were factions within factions and a newcomer like him was never sure whether he was in a faction or not and it was confusing and exhausting trying to keep up with it. The only thing the various factions had in common was a professed love for Stalin, in which they tried to outdo the other factions.

Nikolai Vasilyevich quickly learnt to keep his head down and avoid eye contact where possible — easier if you keep your head down — and concentrate on being amenable and efficient.

He could sense different people sizing him up, as if trying to make him out and decide if he was one of them, and one such person was a man called Yuri who worked for the Secret Political Department and seemed intent on testing him, asking him pointed questions about communist parties in other countries and their links to individuals in Moscow, and one day he asked him whether he'd ever got his hands dirty and Nikolai Vasilyevich talked about when he'd worked on a collective farm in Kostroma Oblast for a few weeks when he was a student, but Yuri stopped him and said he didn't mean dirty like that and to follow him.

He followed Yuri from his office on the fifth floor up to the basement, which sounded crazy, of course, but this was the Lubyanka, where anyone who didn't know the place assumed its notorious prison was in the basement whereas it was in fact on the top, windowless floor, hence the reason people who worked there talked about going up to the basement.

He followed Yuri down a narrow corridor dimly lit by bulbs encased in mesh holders, the rough brickwork interspersed every few yards by foreboding black steel doors and eventually they were let through a cage-type door and into another corridor and then to a brightly lit room where a petrified-looking man was strapped to a high-backed chair and blood was streaming from his face onto his naked torso.

Yuri explained that this was Sergei Pavlovich and Sergei Pavlovich was the Party secretary in Podolsk, an industrial town on the Pakhra River, just south of Moscow, and Sergei Pavlovich had evidently confessed to a shocking litany of disloyalties and all that needed to be resolved now was what had happened to the Party funds from Podolsk and would Nikolai Vasilyevich care to question Sergei Pavlovich accordingly?

Two hours later, he could see what Yuri meant by getting his hands dirty. It was worse than that, it was as if he'd immersed himself in a sewer. He'd been gentle at first with the Party secretary from Podolsk – *please tell me about the funds... maybe there's been a misunderstanding* – but then Yuri had taken him into the corridor and told him not to be so soft because people respond best to threats or violence, which is how he found himself telling Sergei Pavlovich that if he confessed to stealing the Party funds then the life of his wife would be saved and his children would not be sent to a state orphanage with different names.

It was as simple as that.

Sergei Pavlovich sobbed as he signed his confession, phlegm dripping from his nose, blood oozing from the cuts on his face, his naked chest streaked with lines of dried blood, making him look like a wounded animal.

The following day Yuri informed Nikolai Vasilyevich that his initiation into the NKVD was not quite complete and to please follow him once more. This time they descended to the real basement of the Lubyanka, where the execution chamber was situated behind thick walls and an enormous padded door.

Just before they entered the room Yuri handed him a Nagant revolver.

Sergei Pavlovich was standing handcuffed against the far wall as if none the wiser to his fate.

He smiled when he saw Nikolai Vasilyevich but the smile quickly faded as he listened to one of the guards read out his death warrant... crimes against the state, political deviancy, corruption, et cetera, et cetera... and then Yuri said Nikolai Vasilyevich should go ahead and it was only then that the erstwhile Party secretary from Podolsk understood these were his last few moments on earth and he started shrieking and when Nikolai Vasilyevich pulled the trigger his hands were shaking so much his first shot missed and struck the wall, the second one caught Sergei Pavlovich in the shoulder and the third one in the chest, but he was conscious when he crumpled to the floor, groaning in agony as the dark blood flooded around him, and Yuri said they may as well not waste any more bullets.

A week later, Emil asked to see him.

'I understand you passed your initiation test!' He looked pleased, and Nikolai Vasilyevich said thank you.

'It won't have escaped your attention, Nikolai Vasilyevich, that there's a tendency here in the Lubyanka for people to gather in groups of people they trust.'

'Factions?'

'You may have observed too that some of these factions, as you describe them, are associated with politicians: members of the Central Committee and Government ministers all want a power base within the NKVD.

'But being in a faction can be dangerous: as you know, politicians can suddenly fall out of favour and that can have disastrous consequences for those associated with them in the NKVD and elsewhere.

'One finds oneself drawn into a faction rather than requesting to join it and I have to tell you I've recently become involved with a faction associated with Vyacheslav Mikhailovich Molotov. There is growing concern in parts of the Kremlin about the activities of Maxim Maximovich Litvinov. With all this talk of a war between Germany and Great Britain and France, it appears that the People's Commissar for Foreign Affairs has been suggesting a defence agreement between the Soviet Union and Great Britain and France.'

'Really?'

'I'm pleased to see you're shocked, because that is the correct reaction. For us to be drawn into a war in Europe would be madness... it is not in the interests of the Soviet Union to be involved in an imperialist war, but Litvinov is a Jew and thus ill-disposed to Germany and he also has the ear of Stalin and, very worryingly, Stalin is backing Litvinov's plan.

'This is where Comrade Molotov comes in: he is the leader of the faction in the Kremlin that opposes a pact between this country and Great Britain and France and as part of his campaign against it, he has gathered a group of us here within the NKVD.'

'Opposed to Stalin? Surely—'

'Opposed to Litvinov, not Stalin. There's a very strong belief that Comrade Stalin's support for Litvinov is waning and he'll soon cease backing that plan. But, certainly, there is a risk.'

'And what's the point of us being associated with any faction?'

Emil stood up and strolled over to the window, pulling back the curtain to study the square below. 'You ask pertinent questions, Nikolai Vasilyevich. I would answer that there is little to be gained from wandering alone in the middle of a street. One has to show the courage of one's convictions, because if we back the right camp then considerable advantages will accrue to us in terms of our future intelligence activities. For instance...'

Emil turned round and pulled up a chair next to him. 'Molotov is very smart: he has a network of associates overseas and there's even talk of him being in favour of a pact with Germany—'

'With the Nazis? Surely not!'

'A non-aggression pact, nothing more than that... but that's just Kremlin gossip. But we need to be on the right side.'

Chapter 31

London
June 1939

An enduring memory from his childhood in Dorset.

Every August a funfair came to town, which his mother insisted was an event quite beneath them and yet she'd – reluctantly – relent and allow him to go. The memories were of the smells and the sounds, the excitement of the arcades and thrill of the rides.

But the most enduring memory was of a stall operated by a scowling man unseasonably dressed for summer in a heavy coat with a thick scarf and woollen gloves, along with a cloth cap pulled low over his face. The idea was to throw a weighted cloth bag at a puppet and if you knocked it over then you'd win a prize, yet every time he hit the puppet another one would spring up with the man insisting he'd missed.

Eventually, the young Cooper cottoned on to the fact that the man was operating a lever to enable the other puppet to pop up.

But that was the memory: one puppet falling down, the prize within his grasp, only for another puppet suddenly to appear and snatch it away.

It was funny how apparently innocuous childhood memories could come back to haunt you so many years later.

–

For months Cooper had been waiting for an opportunity to break into Cliff Milne's safe, but to do that he needed access to Milne's second key – which he always kept on a chain round his neck.

There had been a plan of sorts which involved Cooper going into King Street on a Sunday and staying behind until late at night to let in through a rear entrance an expert safe cracker who The Annexe had used before and he'd proceed to break into the safe.

But the plan was abandoned, not least because the King Street building was always well-guarded, even at weekends and especially at night. Their distrust of the British state ran deep.

Then Pamela met up with a trusted police contact who put her in touch with an equally trusted locksmith who worked for the police, even on occasions when the work could be described as not entirely legal – in fact, especially on such occasions.

And this led to Cooper and Pamela knocking on the door of a darkened basement in a back street of Fulham one wet afternoon in early May. It took a while for someone to come to the door.

They were hurried in and the door shut and bolted behind them and now they found themselves inside the locksmith's work-shop, which was a small, low-ceilinged room with no windows and work benches filled with all the tools of the locksmith's trade.

He was called Ronnie and Ronnie said there was no need for them to give him their names because, of course, he quite understood the need for confidentiality and discretion and he understood there were some photographs?

Cooper had taken photographs of the safe the previous week, as requested by Ronnie. There were a dozen photos: the front of the safe, a close up of the make, model and serial number, the sides of the safe and then of the two locks, the one for which the key was hidden behind the safe and the one that Milne kept the key for. For the second lock, Cooper had attempted a close-up of the keyhole and he'd angled a lamp to illuminate it.

Ronnie studied the photographs for a good ten minutes, holding them at different angles and occasionally nodding – which was promising – and then tutting, which sounded more ominous.

'Are you any good with your hands?'

'In what way?'

'Are you dextrous rather than clumsy? Good at odd jobs and the like?'

Cooper said he supposed he was average.

'It is possible to make a replica key for this lock, but it's a lengthy and tricky process: if I had the safe in here with all my tools around me like they are now, it would take me quite a while and there'd be a lot of trial and error involved. But, as I say, it is possible. It's not going to happen in one go either: you'll need to return to me a few times before we get it right. But we'll get there! Now, why don't you sit down and I'll explain.'

It took weeks and Ronnie turned out to be a patient and helpful tutor and Cooper came to regard his workshop in the basement in Fulham as something of a sanctuary: calm and quiet with Ronnie's record player playing jazz in the background and plenty of cups of tea to keep them going and every time something was not quite right Ronnie would say that was fine because you didn't make an omelette without cracking an egg, did you, and Rome wasn't built in a day and they'd both laugh.

The process began with Ronnie selecting a blank key, which he said approximated as closely as he could get to that particular safe and that keyhole. He sharpened the long shank, coating it in a fine layer of what looked like soot and a thin layer of wax and told Cooper to place it inside the keyhole and then carefully try to turn it.

'It won't open, of course, but as you try to turn and twist and wiggle it, the internal mechanism of the barrel will make tiny marks — scratches — on this part of the key, which is called "the bit". Bring it back to me and I'll use those to fabricate another version of the key and you repeat the process. We may need to repeat that process half a dozen times, possibly even more.'

It took until the end of May because Cooper had to wait until he could be sure Milne was away from the office and no one was likely to disturb him. But on the last Sunday in May and to the accompaniment of Count Basie, Ronnie spent far longer than usual on another duplicate key and when he finished it, he held it up to the light as if it were a valuable diamond and invited Cooper to study it and announced that if this one didn't work then they'd have to resort to a stick of dynamite!

There was no need for dynamite.

The replica key slipped into the lock with an ease none of the other versions had and as he turned it there was an audible click and when he pulled the handle the door of the safe opened smoothly.

Cooper remained crouched on the ground without moving for a full minute, alert to the slightest sound. He studied the inside of the safe carefully, memorising the exact position of its contents because it was quite likely that Milne had placed them in a particular order so he'd be able to spot if anything was moved.

On the top shelf was a considerable amount of money: a bundle of fifty £1 notes held together with a paper clip, an unsealed envelope containing twenty £5 notes and a roll of other banknotes, tightly held together with a knotted piece of string. On the second shelf was a brown folder full of newspaper cuttings, while on the bottom shelf were four thick folders, each containing dozens of closely typed sheets of paper, some in English, others in Cyrillic.

Cooper moved a lamp from Milne's desk and placed it on the floor and then photographed half a dozen pages from each of the four folders, a mix of those in English and Cyrillic.

By the time he left King Street he was emotionally exhausted.

At least Burton would be pleased.

It was the Wednesday after he'd broken into the safe.

Cliff Milne had telephoned the office on the Monday to say he'd be away all week as he had important business 'elsewhere' and Cooper resolved to photograph more of the documents, even though he'd yet to hear back from Burton on what he'd made of the first batch.

He'd just returned to his office after his lunch break when he realised someone had followed him into the office and closed the door behind him.

It was Douglas Marsh.

'We'll go into Milne's office.'

'He could be back at any time.'

'You know full well he's away all week.' Marsh stood by the inner door to Milne's office and held out an open hand for Cooper to pass him the key. When they entered, he sat behind the desk and indicated Cooper should sit opposite him.

'I'm curious as to how long you're going to persist in pretending you don't know me?'

There was a long silence and Cooper was aware of the faint ticking of a clock he was sure he'd never heard before. He must have looked genuinely puzzled.

'You don't recall me from Moscow... from the Lux Hotel... Sova?' As he said this the man stroked his eyebrows and it was then he realised who Douglas Marsh was.

'Harry – Harry Moore!'

And that was when Cooper finally recalled who the man was who'd appeared at King Street earlier in the year and was reputed to have been in Barcelona when the city fell to the fascists. He'd only seen him occasionally since then and now he was less gaunt and he'd lost his tan and shaved off his moustache and with the help of his name he did indeed remember him from Moscow.

He repeated 'Harry!' as if he was genuinely thrilled to be meeting an old friend and felt the urge to ask him whether his real name was Harry Moore or Douglas Marsh, but the man addressed that issue first.

'None of us are who we seem to be, are we? I see you're now Frank Reynolds, though in Moscow we established that whoever you were, you certainly weren't an Irishman from Rathmines in Dublin called George William Hobson.'

Cooper had no idea how to respond.

'I'm correct, aren't I?'

He nodded.

'And you really didn't recognise me?'

'I do now.'

'I know a lot about you, Reynolds – or Hobson – a lot that could get you into a considerable amount of trouble: I know you were an agent for the OMS and I'm not sure who you're working for now and I know that you're very good at somehow pretending to be someone else, someone who's very adept at appearing to be an ordinary chap, a hard-working comrade, but there's clearly a lot more to you and I'm determined to find out exactly what that is. My guess is that neither Reynolds nor Hobson is your real name and you're certainly something more than a well-meaning clerk volunteering here. I can't imagine that Milne knows all this about you, does he?'

Cooper shifted awkwardly and recalled his training on how to act during an interrogation.

Never volunteer any information.

Let the person questioning you exhaust what they have to say. That way, you'll have an idea of the extent of their knowledge about you.

'You're not going to tell me, are you?'

'Tell you what?'

'Tell me who you're working for and what you're up to?'

Cooper shrugged and said he honestly wasn't sure what he was getting at because he was really quite unimportant, no more than a clerk really and he wasn't up to anything and—

'If you're so unimportant, how come you were staying at the Lux and had that bogus Irish identity in Moscow and now have a different name, eh? George William Hobson hasn't become Frank Reynolds for no reason.'

Marsh raised his eyebrows to make it clear he was expecting an answer.

'There's something about you I can't work out. You're obviously no longer OMS, because that no longer exists, but you're up to something and I'm not sure what it is. You're working for someone... maybe NKVD like Milne, but possibly some other group. Maybe you're an infiltrator – who knows? But I'll find out – and from now on you'll work for me. You'll do what I say, because you know that if you don't co-operate, I can make life very difficult for you. Imagine what Milne and the others will make of you, eh? And the British authorities!'

And that was the moment when Cooper remembered the funfair; the puppet who was knocked down only to be replaced by another one. He'd got rid of Osip, who he thought was his last remaining threat.

But now, up popped Douglas Marsh, and he was faced with an even greater threat.

But he didn't panic. He assured Marsh that he was happy to co-operate with him, but all the while he knew exactly what he was going to do.

–

'It's chaff!'

Cooper asked Burton what he meant, and Burton said surely you know what chaff is and Cooper said, yes, but they were talking about the documents he'd photographed from Milne's safe, not what you found on a farm.

'Don't be clever, Cooper, you know full well what I mean: the documents are all run of the mill stuff, they're not top-class intelligence. This is all internal Communist Party nonsense, some mildly interesting stuff on who's in favour in Moscow and who's suspected over here of being a Trotsky supporter and a few names we'd been unaware of – not unhelpful or uninteresting by any means, but not... not what we were hoping for, certainly not after waiting all this time.'

'I'm sorry. I did my best.' Cooper couldn't hide his disappointment. Burton could have been more grateful.

'Don't take it personally, Cooper. We need you to stick at it though. The feeling is that Milne is the person in the Communist Party with the closest links to Moscow, certainly now that Litvinov has been booted out and replaced by Molotov. Just keep looking: sooner or later you'll find something.'

—

It was a year since the debacle in Brussels and since Murray had found him in Regent's Park, promising to help if he ever needed him, and then proceeding to tell him how to make contact.

The Seven Stars in Holborn, an elderly barman called Bernard.

Cooper was a good deal more worldly now than he'd been then – certainly than he'd been two years before when he'd been tricked into going to Moscow – and as a result he was somewhat sceptical when he entered The Seven Stars in Carey Street on a Thursday evening in June, the day after meeting Douglas Marsh.

A sign over the entrance announced that the pub had first opened in 1602 and that just added to the surreal nature of his visit: it all felt quite unlikely that this visit would lead to him meeting Murray.

He doubted he'd ever see Murray again.

But it was as if he was following a script. He wandered through the pub and in a downstairs snug spotted an elderly barman who said indeed he was when Cooper asked if he was Bernard by any chance.

'And how can I help you, sir?'

'May I ask if you have any Island malts?'

'We do indeed, sir: may I ask which one you'd prefer?'

'A Talisker, perhaps?'

The slightest of pauses from Bernard, a brief pursing of the lips as if allowing himself time to think, and then a pleasant smile and a suggestion that if sir wished to wait at that table in the corner he'd go to the upstairs bar and bring a Talisker down for him, no trouble at all, sir.

Five minutes later Bernard appeared at the table and placed a large whisky in front of him and drew up a chair.

'I took the opportunity of telephoning our acquaintance...'

'Mr Murray?'

'Indeed, sir, though one does try to avoid names. He would be happy to meet you. He suggests tomorrow night, in this very bar, at six o'clock.'

—

They'd exchanged pleasantries and spoken briefly about the weather, of course, and each drank half a pint of mild before Murray suggested they go for a walk, which took them through Lincoln's Inn and past the barristers' chambers and the neat lawns and pairs of barristers walking along in their gowns and their clerks behind them burdened by files they were taking back to their office.

When they reached an isolated bench, Murray asked what he wanted and to keep it as brief as possible and said it went without saying that if anyone approached, he was to change the subject.

Cooper hesitated.

'Let me help you: you want someone killed?'

Cooper nodded, shocked at the avoidance of any euphemism. He explained that the man's name was Douglas Marsh but he was also known as Harry Moore and he couldn't be sure of which was his real name, but he worked for the Communist Party and was based, for want of a better word, in their headquarters in King Street and—

'Where does he live?'

'I'm not sure.'

'Not sure or you don't know?'

'The latter, I'm afraid. If it's any help, he was in Moscow in 1937 and stayed at the Lux Hotel and I understand he was in Spain earlier this year and may have been in Barcelona in January.'

Murray nodded and said that was helpful but, ideally, he'd need more to go on and Cooper said of course.

'Preferably a photograph. Deliver what you can in an envelope to Bernard, as early as possible next week. We have no direct contact from now on. I don't expect to ever hear from you again.'

'Of course, I quite understand.'

Murray stood up and straightened his jacket and said there was a surprising chill in the air.

'Apart from anything else, the world is changing very fast and one often wonders which side one is on.'

He paused and looked at Cooper for a moment as if he was about to say something else but then turned sharply on his heels and headed off, walking briskly and within moments had disappeared into the shadows of Lincoln's Inn.

–

He'd found a photograph of Douglas Marsh from the sheet Burton had given him in The Annexe and another from a 1934 edition of the *Daily Worker*, a bit grainy but it was a decent enough resemblance. He wrote a detailed description, a key feature of which was the brown jacket with leather elbow patches that Marsh always wore, along with the information that when he left the office, he always headed south to cross Waterloo Bridge.

He'd delivered the envelope to the obliging Bernard in The Seven Stars on the Tuesday evening and worried he'd hear back that this wasn't good enough and when he heard nothing, he assumed that if anything were to happen to Marsh it certainly wouldn't be for a while.

But the following Monday he sensed that something was up in King Street; the atmosphere even more conspiratorial than normal. There were more closed doors and huddled conversations than usual and Cliff Milne said he wasn't to be disturbed and

Cooper knew better than to draw attention to himself by asking what was going on.

He found out soon enough though when he bought his copy of the *Evening News* on his way home from work.

Tooting Man Dead in Horror Fall

Police in Tooting say they are investigating the death at the weekend of a forty-nine-year-old local man.

The body of Douglas Marsh of Furzedown Road, Tooting, was found at the foot of a flight of steps behind Tooting Bec Road in the early hours of Sunday morning.

Police say that at this stage in the investigation they do not suspect foul play and believe that intoxication was contributory to the cause of Mr Marsh's fall.

Chapter 32

It was a small envelope, taped to the underside of the shelf in Cliff Milne's safe, and Cooper only came across it by accident more than anything else. He hadn't spotted it on any of the four occasions he had broken into the safe since the beginning of June, but then he hadn't looked or felt under the shelf.

Opportunities to get into the safe had been few and far between and even when he'd got into it and photographed documents Percy Burton had been notably less than enthusiastic about the results. They were 'fine' he said, 'quite useful... interesting enough in their own way', English upper-middle-class code for saying they were disappointing and not quite what he was hoping for.

'But do keep digging, Cooper, you're bound to strike gold sooner or later!' He'd deliver that in a manner which barely masked his disappointment.

It was the August Bank Holiday – the 7 August – and Milne was in Devon for a few days. It was too good an opportunity to miss.

He'd only come across the envelope – which measured some four inches by six – because under the shelf was a larger envelope, full of newspaper cuttings, and as he pulled it out his hand brushed the envelope.

He removed it carefully, making a mental note of how it had been attached under the shelf, and placed it on the floor and then remained still, listening out for any sound beyond the office.

There was Cyrillic writing on the cover:

Молотов, Вячеслав Михайлович

And below it, in smaller writing: *Molotov, Vyacheslav Mikhaylovich.*

Molotov, the new Soviet foreign minister.

Cooper felt his heart beat faster and his hands trembled as he opened the envelope. Inside were four sets of very thin paper, each folded into very small squares.

He opened each one carefully, as if handling a valuable stamp. They were four letters, all typed in English.

17 April, 1939
Moscow
USSR

My dear comrade!

I hope this letter reaches you safely: this courier is one of the very few people I trust wholeheartedly.

I returned to Moscow at the beginning of the month and I'm not sure whether that was a wise move: one can never be sure as to how safe one is. I hope I still retain the trust of Comrade Stalin, though many comrades who've been arrested and punished no doubt thought the same.

My main concern is the undue and damaging influence Maxim Maximovich Litvinov currently has. Did you imagine Jews like him think that by changing their name they suddenly become proper Russians? Almost everyone of influence in his Ministry of Foreign Affairs is a Jew, along with ambassadors such as Maisky in London and Suritz in Paris.

As you and I have discussed on a number of occasions, Litvinov is actively pursuing a military and diplomatic pact between the Soviet Union and France and Great Britain. This has considerable support in France, less so in your country and there's no doubt that one or two well-placed agents have helped to encourage a lack of enthusiasm in London for Litvinov's crazy plan. Their role – and yours – in undermining it has been crucial.

But all is not good, my dear comrade. Litvinov remains the People's Commissar for Foreign Affairs and as a Jew he's unquestionably hostile to Germany and also retains the ear of Comrade Stalin and for as long as that is the case then the prospect of a disastrous pact between the Soviet Union and France and your country remains a very real one.

I will continue to do what I can to undermine this and to turn Stalin against Litvinov. But this is not without very personal considerable risk. Should anything happen to me then you must take every precaution to ensure your own safety. It is known within certain circles in Moscow that you and I go back a long way and should I be arrested then our representatives in London or opponents in your headquarters may use that as a reason to move against you.

In the meantime, I am relying on you to do what you can to continue to ensure Litvinov's proposed pact receives minimal support in London – and I look forward to reading more information from you as to what progress or otherwise he is making.

Should this be the last time you hear from me, that, comrade, is the fate of a revolutionary.

Stay strong!

MBM

The next letter was shorter.

8 May, 1939
Moscow
USSR

My dear comrade Sova!

This is the briefest of letters – for reasons which will very quickly become apparent.

Litvinov has gone and since last Wednesday I am the new People's Commissar for Foreign Affairs!!

My only disappointment is that Comrade Stalin is of the view that it is sufficient to have dismissed Litvinov from his post. I'd hoped he'd be arrested and eliminated by now, but sadly that has not happened.

I am now doing my best to disentangle the Soviet Union from Litvinov's proposed pact with France and Great Britain. I cannot thank you enough for the work you have done in ensuring such a negative attitude to the proposal in London. Agent A seems to be very effective and very well placed.

In the meantime, discussions with Berlin are tentative but positive.

Your friend and comrade,

MBM

Cooper now felt all of his senses heightened. Reading these letters felt as if he had his hands on history.

8 July, 1939
Moscow
USSR

My dear comrade!

It is two months since I last wrote to you and there is much to catch up on.

The most important news from here is we are still stringing France and Great Britain along, letting them think that we are interested in a military pact with them. But I'm reassured that Comrade Stalin is furious those two countries entered a pact with Poland, which he sees as a hostile act towards the Soviet Union. For this reason, he is now leaning — rather too cautiously, one has to say — towards my plan of a rapprochement between us and Germany.

I've been making the point that Europe is heading to war and we cannot be on the side of the capitalist and imperialist so-called 'democracies'. If we have to choose which side to be on — and, as you know, I believe we do have to make a choice — then it is in our interests to side with Germany.

At the moment we are negotiating a commercial agreement with Germany, which is very much in their interests: they are in desperate need of our raw materials. I'm optimistic we can extend our co-operation beyond this and look to negotiate something more substantial.

And this is where you come in, my friend. I cannot stress too strongly how confidential and top secret is the possibility of a wider pact between us and Germany. However, in anticipation of it, we do need to address one especially critical issue — namely how we counter and eliminate any dissent to a possible pact within the Communist Parties of Western Europe?

It would be too dangerous for you to do anything at the moment, but I urge you to start thinking about how to exercise control and discipline over the British Party in the event of an announcement of a pact with Germany.

In comradeship,

MBM

Cooper could only imagine how delighted Burton would be with this. And there was one more letter.

1 August, 1939
Moscow
USSR

My dear comrade!

This letter is being brought back to London by Ivan Alexandrovich Morozov: he speaks highly of you and also of another agent — A — who has been of so much help to us.

Since becoming People's Commissar for Foreign Affairs I've learnt more about the extent of our intelligence operations abroad and I'm astonished at their scope and their sophistication. I worried the dismantling of the OMS could have an adverse effect on our overseas operations, but I'm pleased to see that the NKVD, the GRU and the embassies have maintained their effectiveness. The role of people such as yourself and of secret agents such as A is vital.

Morozov told me we have another British agent in London who he refers to as B and with whom he's lost contact, which is a clear source of embarrassment to him. There seems to be a good deal of confusion as to who was running this agent, and it may well be he was one of those being run by the GRU. Morozov was a bit too guarded and vague for my liking on this: evidently there was a connection between Agent B and Harry Moore, who I think was known as Douglas Marsh in London? Morozov tells me Marsh died in an accident in June: have you heard anything and would you have any idea who this B could be?

Much progress is being made with Germany. We expect to finalise a commercial agreement with

334

them soon and although there's still much to do, I'm hoping that this will be but a brief prelude to an announcement before the end of August of a more substantial agreement of a military nature, the news of which will set the world on fire!

I read your very helpful letter of 12 July with much interest. I think you are right to anticipate some disquiet in the British Party at any announcement of a pact with Germany. However, people need to remember what democratic centralism means: if the Soviet Union decides that it is in its interests to enter a pact with Germany, then that must be accepted without discussion or equivocation. There can be no room for any reservations, let alone dissent.

I count on your help in this respect.

I note what you said about three or four possible dissidents within your Central Committee, but I cannot be more emphatic: there is no room for dissent and I expect all twenty-four members of your Central Committee to endorse any agreement we make with Germany.

Your friend and comrade,

MBM

In the margin beside the final paragraph were a number of initials written in Cliff Milne's handwriting:

HP?

WGMP?

JRC?

But Cooper was too distracted to give any thought as to what or who those initials stood for. At first, reading the letters his mounting emotions had been a heady mixture – elation at how thrilled Percy Burton would be with what was undoubtedly, to use his description, gold, and also fear at what the letters revealed – a possible pact between the Soviet Union and Nazi Germany.

But these emotions had evaporated as soon as he came to the second page of the letter written on 1 August. The agent referred to as 'B' was unquestionably him, not least because of the Morozov connection and the link with the now dead Douglas Marsh.

He couldn't possibly alert The Annexe to the existence of agent B, which meant he couldn't let Burton or anyone else see the second page of the final letter.

As a British agent he was staring at the most revealing and dramatic intelligence imaginable.

Yet it was now clear he'd be unable to share the most important part of it.

He was lost in his thoughts until the sound of a car horn brought him back to his senses.

He turned on the lamp and began to photograph the letters.

He had a plan, of sorts.

–

'I'm confused with all this, Cooper...'

Charles Cooper nodded. He'd expected Burton to be confused.

Percy Burton was sitting at his desk in The Annexe headquarters on Bryanston Square. Spread out in front of him were nine photographs – the first three Molotov letters and just the first page of the final letter, the August one.

'I fail to understand why Milne took the precaution of concealing this highly sensitive correspondence from Molotov in his safe, but only included the first page of the August letter?'

'Maybe he lost the rest of it, sir, as I suggest in my report?'

'But Molotov isn't anyone, is he, Cooper? He's the Soviet Foreign Minister and the letters incriminate Milne: it is not the kind of correspondence one leaves lying around on the bus or on the kitchen table! One would have thought that either Milne would keep every scrap of that correspondence under lock and key or else destroy it. But not lose part of the correspondence, that makes no sense!'

'But those letters there, sir, they're very important, surely?'

'I don't dispute they're interesting, but I'm not sure they're as interesting as your report would suggest. You rely too much on speculation. I've made the point to you before, Cooper, when studying intelligence one must distinguish between informed analysis and speculation. In your report you state that you believe that Cliff Milne is operating in a clandestine manner on behalf of the Soviet Union. That is a reasonable supposition. Some would say it is stating the obvious – after all, there is a specific reference to his helping undermine a pact with the Soviet Union.

'However, you go on to say in your report, where is it… let me find it… ah, here we are: *Based on a careful reading and analysis of the letters I believe that the Soviet Union may be using its commercial negotiations with Germany as a cover for entering into a full-scale military pact with them.*'

He dropped the report onto the desk and waved his hand melodramatically.

'Where is the evidence for that, Cooper, eh?'

Cooper knew he couldn't reply that the evidence had been on the last page of the August letter. Instead, he shrugged and said he could see what he meant.

'Of course, if there was any firm evidence to that effect, it would be of the utmost importance and His Majesty's Government would act accordingly and urgently, but this is too speculative. If I were to alert the Foreign Office to this they'd dismiss it out of hand. As it is we need to keep an eye on Milne: sooner or later something more substantial may emerge.'

'We may not have enough time, sir?'

'Why ever not?'

'Because I believe that if there is to be a pact between the Soviet Union and Germany that could take place before the end of this month.'

'As you say in your report. More speculation. How do you know that, Cooper?'

Burton leant back, lifted his eyebrows and stared quizzically at Cooper, who opened his mouth and began to reply before stopping. He could hardly quote from the last page of Molotov's last letter, of an announcement 'before the end of August'.

'An informed guess, sir.'

'There we are, Cooper – a guess. Speculation. And there's another thing, Cooper: in your report you talk about possible opposition to such a pact from within the Central Committee of the British Communist Party and you go so far as to actually name three people. I can't find their names…'

'Harry Pollitt, the General Secretary of the Party; Willie Gallagher, the Communist Member of Parliament for West Fife, and JR Campbell, the editor of the *Daily Worker*.'

'Yes, thank you, Cooper – how do you know these three are likely dissidents, tell me?'

Cooper said, yes, he saw the point, he accepted this was speculation and it was based on his knowledge from inside—

'I suggest, Cooper, that you get back into that safe as soon as you can and find me something more substantial. I don't deny what we have here is interesting and certainly more interesting than anything else you've dug up, but I'm loathe to pass it on and make a fool of myself.'

'But what if it turns out to be true, sir?'

'What if what turns out to be true?'

'The Soviet Union going into a military pact with Germany?'

'You really have got that bit between your teeth, haven't you, Cooper?'

'I have a very strong feeling, sir: after all, if I have interpreted Molotov's letters correctly, and you were to share that, it would be quite something, don't you think?'

He expected another lecture about speculation or even impertinence, but Burton paused and seemed to be having second thoughts.

'I'll tell you what I shall do, Cooper: I shall send round a memorandum to alert people to the possibility without creating too much of a flap. And there is another point, we've not established the provenance of the letters, have we – or even whether Molotov speaks English?'

He stood up in a manner which made it clear that was the end of that and although Cooper now felt emboldened by Burton's promise to send a memorandum, he didn't feel emboldened enough to point out that surely the situation was urgent enough to merit more than a memorandum.

—

Percy Burton was a worried man after Cooper left.

He liked to think he was decisive and a good judge of character, but both those qualities were failing him now.

Even though it was only four o'clock he poured himself a whisky and asked his secretary to bring through the file on Charles Cooper and when he'd finished reading it was nearly six o'clock and he asked Pamela Clarke to come and see him.

'When was it you first spotted Cooper?'

'Early last year, sir – March, if I remember correctly?'

'And was there anything about him at the time or subsequently which would make you doubt him?'

'Doubt him in what way, sir?'

'I think you know what way!' He'd raised his voice and immediately apologised and said it had been a long day and maybe he was somewhat under the weather, but what he meant was could she be absolutely certain that he was as innocent as he seemed?

'We checked him out, sir, didn't we? There was nothing to arouse any suspicion. After all, I was the one who persuaded him to go to a Communist Party meeting and that was how it all started. He wasn't a walk in and we didn't turn him.'

She knew better than to ask what was causing this doubt because that wasn't done, but she found it hard to resist asking if everything was... all right.

'I do hope so, Pamela, but I can't make up my mind about Cooper. I find it hard to decide whether he's exceptionally good at what we ask him to do, or whether he's very lucky or whether he's at times perhaps too well-informed or whether... I don't know, I can't always make him out. Maybe he seems a bit too good to be true is what I'm trying to say.'

Pamela smiled and asked if maybe she could have a whisky too and Burton apologised and said it had been quite remiss of him not to have offered and she suggested they sit down on the comfy chairs as he called them.

'What you've just said about Cooper, sir, isn't that the point?'

'Eh?'

'Isn't that the point you always make about agents, that at some point or the other you're not sure about them, that you can't always make them out? You've said that about every agent I've been involved with and I daresay you had those doubts about me too. We're not bank managers or shop assistants or foremen in a factory or any other predictable and routine job. There's always going to be an element of doubt about all of us, sir: we're not ordinary people. We're enigmatic. We're unpredictable. The world we operate in is neither ordinary or predictable, is it? We practise deception every day and rely on our intuition – and our nerves. That's bound to cast us in a suspicious light from time to time.'

Percy Burton leant back and looked less tense now and said he supposed she may be right.

'Has Cooper done anything wrong, sir?'

'Wrong? No, I don't think so... I certainly hope not. In fact, on the contrary, he may well have unearthed something...' And then he stopped himself and Pamela nodded in a way that showed she quite understood and he didn't need to say any more.

'Perhaps you ought to be getting home, sir?'

'I have a memorandum to write first.'

Chapter 33

London
August–September 1939

The full impact only truly registered with the Foreign Office towards the end of the week and by lunchtime on the Friday – 25 August – it was clear that the department's traditional early departure of diplomats and other senior officials to the country for the weekend was in grave doubt.

By early afternoon, no one dared leave their desks.

It was the same at the War Office on the other side of Whitehall and at the headquarters of MI6 in St James's.

Civil servants senior enough to be in the know, but not senior enough to be considered responsible in any way, commented it was as if a giant tidal wave had struck Whitehall, leaving victims reeling and numb with shock.

At Number 10 Downing Street the atmosphere began as one of bewilderment, soon turning to rage.

Who knew about this?

Someone must have known?

Find the person who knew!

At first, it was impossible to find anyone who'd admit to knowing anything. Officials shook their heads and insisted this was the first they'd heard of it and were as shocked and surprised as the next person.

And then an official on the French desk at the Foreign Office called Milton admitted seeing a memorandum the previous week. He'd been puzzled by the fact that it was sent from 'Burton,

Special Office' and he recalled asking his boss what 'Special Office' was and whether 'Burton' was a person or the town on the river Trent, only to be told it didn't matter because the memo was a load of nonsense anyway.

And that was the beginning of the end for Percy Burton.

–

Percy Burton had met with Cooper on the Thursday, 10 August, three days after Cooper had photographed the Molotov letters from Cliff Milne's safe in King Street. The memorandum was a compromise of sorts, the standard civil service way of covering one's back.

It was typed on pale blue paper with Burton's carbon copy on a pale-yellow sheet.

MEMORANDUM

From: Burton, Special Office
To: Germany Desk, Foreign Office
Date: 11 August
Subject: Moscow manoeuvres

Unconfirmed and yet to be corroborated reports from a hitherto reliable SOURCE suggest talks currently underway between the Soviet Union and Germany regarding a commercial agreement, may be a cover for a more substantial agreement between the two countries which may extend to full-scale military pact.

SOURCE indicates this may be announced before end of the month. SOURCE indicates this is being driven by Soviet Foreign Minister MOLOTOV.

MOLOTOV understood to be hostile to proposed pact involving Soviet Union, France and this country, which he has been seeking to undermine since replacing LITVINOV in May.

SOURCE reports MOLOTOV anticipating some dissent in Communist Party of Great Britain to a pact with Germany and is insisting on unanimous support from Party's Central Committee.

It went in the internal post late on the afternoon of Friday the 11th, which Burton knew full well meant it was highly unlikely anyone would see it before Monday and even then it would not be top of anyone's in-tray because he'd avoided marking it 'Most Urgent' or 'Top Secret' and unlike most memoranda, it only had one recipient, the chronically over-worked Germany desk.

Conveniently, that Saturday was the 'Glorious Twelfth', the start of the grouse shooting season, which meant fewer people than usual would be around to see the report.

And as it was, no one on the Germany desk at the Foreign Office looked at it until Wednesday the 16th when it ended up on the desk of a rather put-upon chap called Travers who was indolent with resentment after having recently missed out on the third secretary job in Lisbon so he did nothing until the Thursday when he sent copies to the Soviet and French desks and hoped that would cover his back.

Milton on the French desk did read the memorandum on Monday the 21st and thought it was interesting and certainly tallied with his own understanding that the proposed pact between the United Kingdom, France and the Soviet Union was floundering so he drafted a telegram to Paris to that effect and arranged to see the head of French desk the next day to clear it with him, because his back needed covering too.

It all started that Monday, really, building up to the crescendo on the Friday. First there was the news from Moscow over the weekend that the commercial agreement had been signed and then on the Monday came the news the Soviets had suspended the tripartite talks with France and the United Kingdom. On the Wednesday the German Foreign Minister von Ribbentrop arrived in Moscow 'for talks' and by the Thursday a Non-Aggression Pact between Germany and the Soviet Union had been announced and among the flurry of telegrams from Moscow was one from the Hon. Milo Smart quoting an article in *Pravda* which talked about improved political relations between Germany and the Soviet Union.

On the Friday there was a terribly worrying telegram from the MI6 station in Berlin, which was the cause of that tidal wave in Whitehall. A German diplomat called Hans von Herwarth had told the American ambassador in Berlin, Charles Bohlen, that that the Soviet–German pact contained a secret protocol allocating different spheres of influence between the two countries.

They were dividing Europe up between themselves.

–

If Percy Burton thought he'd been clever in covering his back with a memorandum, which he could say showed he had made some effort to share his knowledge of the Nazi–Soviet pact, then he was horribly mistaken.

Everyone wanted to find someone to blame for London not knowing about this serious development. MI6 had soon heard about the Burton Memorandum, as it became known, and were furious he'd not shared this intelligence with them. The Foreign Office were furious it had been sent just to one desk and without the sense of urgency it so obviously merited. And Downing Street was furious with everyone, so Burton was called into Downing Street that weekend where it became very apparent very quickly this was an audition for a scapegoat and he'd got the part.

How could he have sat on such vital intelligence?

Did he not appreciate the significance of this?

When he did share it, why did he do so in such a lacklustre manner?

Who was his source?

Percy Burton was no fool: he knew he was most probably about to be sacrificed so as to satisfy the almost animalistic urge to find someone to blame, someone whose fault this could all be. And he was tired, too: The Annexe had been established in 1931 as what he'd always understood was a one- or two-year project at the most and he'd done the job for eight years and that was a pretty decent innings.

He did say he wasn't sure it would have made any difference had they all known about the pact earlier, but when one of the private secretaries said in a pointedly sharp manner that wasn't his judgement to make, Burton realised it really was all over. There was no point in resisting.

So, he said he acknowledged he'd underestimated the significance and indeed importance of this intelligence and was prepared to accept responsibility... and if a gentleman's agreement could be reached then he'd be prepared to tender his resignation.

'What, here and now?' said one of the private secretaries sitting in judgement on him. He sounded incredulous.

Percy Burton nodded.

'And the gentleman's agreement?' The private secretary could barely conceal his sheer relief that this unpleasant business could be sorted so quickly and so amicably without having to resort to anything unpleasant.

'If I were to be allowed to resign without any blemish on my character or record and retain my full pension, of course.'

'Of course!' The private secretaries spoke in a chorus and stood up and hands were warmly shaken and the man who was there from MI6 announced perhaps this was the opportunity to close The Annexe and subsume its functions into the Service.

Percy Burton was escorted back to The Annexe's offices in Bryanston Square to collect a few personal possessions, unlock his safe and hand over the main Annexe codebook and his master list of contacts.

And that was that. A Service car took him to his London apartment where he was finally able to reflect on matters. He was upset, of course, at the rapid turn of events, but not a little relieved at the same time. But most of all, he was shocked that in their haste to get rid of him the private secretaries had failed to pursue answers for the questions they'd originally asked, not least who the source for this information was.

He did wonder how Cooper would get on now, because in these circumstances the staff who worked for The Annexe would be absorbed into MI6, but agents were cut adrift.

Percy Burton had taken precautions though. When it became apparent earlier in the week that something was up in Moscow, he did anticipate that he could be in some kind of trouble, so he'd taken Cliff Milne's Molotov letters and the negatives from The Annexe and quite contrary to every rule in the book, placed them in a bank security deposit box under an assumed name.

One never knew when one would find intelligence like this to be useful.

—

Cooper had been oblivious to the events of that last weekend in August. He'd followed the news closely, of course, and his reaction to the Ribbentrop–Molotov Pact, as it was being called, was one of vindication. He knew Burton would be delighted and probably quite apologetic and he waited for a message to come to The Annexe.

But no message came.

In those last days of August, the atmosphere in the King Street headquarters of the Communist Party was as tense as he'd ever known it: more meetings behind closed doors and furtive conversations in dimly lit corridors.

Cliff Milne acted like someone who'd suffered a terrible bereavement. He looked pale and drawn, hardly spoke and spent much of the time in his inner office with the door locked. He left in a hurry on the Thursday afternoon, carrying two briefcases and wearing an overcoat, which struck Cooper as odd as it was such a warm day and it also struck him as out of character when he paused to shake Cooper's hand before leaving.

Cooper waited an hour and then broke into the safe.

It was empty, apart from a solitary ten-shilling note on the middle shelf.

It was obvious something was up, and Cooper realised he too had to leave King Street quickly.

Rather than returning to the safe house in Willesden he headed to Dorset Square and feeling the need to be even more careful than usual, walked all the way to Park Lane to catch the number 74 bus, stopping en route at a telephone box in New Bond Street to dial a Pimlico number.

It was the first time he called it.

It was only to be used in an extreme emergency, Burton had told him. 'If you think your life may be in danger,' Pamela had added, and although he thought that may be going a bit far, he sensed something serious was up and certainly the fact he'd heard nothing from The Annexe for a week now, despite the grave international situation, was most worrying.

A man answered the phone, saying 'how may I help you?' in a bored manner and this took Cooper aback because for some reason, he'd expected a woman to answer the phone and rather more urgently.

'I am in town for a couple of days and would very much like to meet with my Uncle Robert.' He hoped he'd got the message exactly right because otherwise the call would be aborted.

'And is that his nephew, Alan?'

'No, it's Alan's brother, Graham.'

'Very well, I shall pass the message on.'

And that was that. It should all be fine now.

—

But nothing happened. He returned to Dorset Square and expected to hear back from The Annexe within a couple of hours or certainly that evening but the phone remained silent and he went to bed at midnight and hardly slept until dawn when he eventually dozed off and when he woke up it was gone eleven o'clock and the phone was still silent and he had no idea what to do other than remain in the flat and wait.

At noon he turned on the radio to catch the midday news.

Germany has invaded Poland.

Five German armies including tanks and cavalry units have crossed the border.

Over one million troops taking part in the invasion.

Fierce Polish resistance.

Warsaw and other Polish cities have been bombed.

The British and French governments have issued an ultimatum.

He was so shocked he turned off the radio and for some reason closed the curtains, only to find himself spending the next hour peeking out of them and then decided he couldn't stay in the flat and wondered about going to The Annexe, but planned instead to head to the safe house in Willesden where there'd most probably be a message waiting for him. Maybe he ought to have headed there in the first place.

But the house in Willesden appeared to be abandoned. No one answered the door, there were no lights, and this was unusual because it was very rare for Mr Meldrake to leave the house, and now Cooper was very worried because none of this felt right and, if he was honest, he was rather frightened.

He returned to Dorset Square and after pacing around it for the best part of an hour decided his best course of action would be to go to The Annexe after all.

He'd get it sorted there. After all, he'd provided first-class intelligence and had been proved right. Maybe the message to the Pimlico number hadn't been passed on. No doubt with the Soviet–German pact and Germany invading Poland everyone was rather busy.

He had a bath and got changed and felt better and decided to open the curtains but before doing so peered out of the gap.

He stood frozen in terror, gripping the curtains so hard it seemed they may come off the rails and his heartbeat quickening as a cold fear wrapped around him.

Below him in the square was the unmistakable figure of Murray, pausing to light a cigarette and casually looking in the direction of his apartment and then at his watch.

It took Cooper a whole minute to regain his composure and then another five minutes to throw a few things into an overnight bag, including all his papers and his cash.

He slipped out through the rear of the building, worried Murray may have someone covering it, but then remembered he preferred to work on his own. There was a small wall to clamber over then a narrow alley leading into the mews and from there into Linhope Street, trying to walk as calmly as possibly, skirting Regent's Park and north towards Primrose Hill, where he found a pleasant-looking small hotel and booked a room in the name of Dickens and when asked for his first name for some unaccountable reason he said 'Percy' and he couldn't believe he'd been so stupid and the fact that Percy was on his mind was hardly any kind of an excuse.

—

He remained in his room for most of the Saturday and Pamela Clarke found him the next morning, the Sunday.

Soon after he'd come down for breakfast, he heard a woman's voice behind him ask if he minded her joining him and before he could answer she'd sat down and said well done for choosing a table in the corner and would he mind passing the sugar?

She looked exhausted, like someone who'd not slept in days, and when she lit a cigarette her hand was trembling.

'How on earth did you find me?'

She didn't answer for a moment, the narrowing of her eyes indicating she wasn't in the mood to discuss it. 'That really doesn't matter, though it ought to be a lesson to you as to how careful you need to be.' She drank from her teacup with the same hand which was holding the cigarette and Cooper found himself thinking that looked quite stylish, almost Continental.

'I don't have long, Cooper, so you need to listen most carefully. Don't ring the Pimlico number ever again. Under no circumstances are you to go anywhere near Bryanston Square or your apartment or the house in Willesden. You must not visit or telephone your mother. Do not return to King Street. Do not have any contact with anyone from the Communist Party.'

'And what about Murray because—'

'Forget about Murray and forget about Burton.' She poured herself another cup of tea and said he ought to eat some breakfast and act normally.

'The Annexe no longer exists. For the time being you are in great danger. That applies to a number of us, myself included.'

'How long is for the time being?'

He'd expected her to be annoyed at the question, but she replied in a business-like manner.

'There's an envelope here with some cash and a new identity for you. Check out of this hotel after breakfast and leave London and then disappear for a few weeks. There's a telephone number in the envelope. You're to ring that number in the first week of October, not before then. You're to say you have a violin to be repaired and the person who answers will ask you what is the problem and you're to say the bridge is broken. They'll give you an address to bring it to. You're to go there.'

'And if no one answers?'

Pamela was standing up now. Her hair was loose and when she ran her hand through it she looked as pretty as she had done that foggy February afternoon outside Aldgate station and Cooper couldn't help thinking what would have happened had he not stopped then and taken one of her leaflets.

'If no one answers? Then God help you. There's something I need to ask you before I go.'

She hesitated for a moment or two and leant closer to him, her face just inches from his. He could smell the cigarette and perfume.

'Does the name Archie mean anything to you? I need to know if it does.'

Cooper was unsure how to answer. Burton had told him about Archie a year previously, but he didn't know whether he should admit to that. After all, she'd just told him he should forget about Burton.

'No, I don't believe so… may I ask in connection with what?'

She shook her head and then tapped the brown envelope on the white tablecloth before sweeping out of the room.

He went up to his room to pack and decided he'd walk to Chalk Farm Road and catch the 639 bus to Kings Cross. He'd take the first train north he could get on and he'd keep moving and maybe everything would be fine.

When he went down to reception it was approaching a quarter past eleven and he asked if they could prepare his bill because he was checking out, but the receptionist seemed distracted, so much so that he asked if she was all right and she pointed to the lounge, which was full of guests and staff gathered round a radio set.

'The prime minister is about to make an announcement sir.'

Cooper stood at the back of the warm room, crowded with people looking like mourners awaiting the start of a funeral service.

The silence was broken by the voice of Neville Chamberlain.

'*This morning the British ambassador in Berlin handed the German government a final note stating that, unless we heard from them by 11 o'clock that they were prepared at once to withdraw their troops from Poland, a state of war would exist between us. I have to tell you now that no such undertaking has been received, and that consequently this country is at war with Germany.*'

There were gasps in the room and the sound of soft weeping and muffled coughing and an elderly man said, 'Good God!' and someone else turned up the radio.

Cooper was in such a state of shock that much of what the prime minister subsequently said didn't register, apart from his final words.

'*It is the evil things that we shall be fighting against – brute force, bad faith, injustice, oppression and persecution – and against them I am certain that the right will prevail.*'

Author's Note

Every Spy a Traitor is a work of fiction and therefore any similarities between the characters in the book and real people are unintended and should be regarded as purely coincidental.

There are some obvious exceptions to this – historical figures such as Stalin and others who are referred to in the text, though not appearing as characters in themselves. The one person who does feature as a character is Vyacheslav Mikhailovich Molotov, who as the People's Commissar for Foreign Affairs from May 1939 was the Soviet Foreign Minister and the man behind the Soviet Union's notorious pact with Nazi Germany.

Likewise, Maxim Litvinov. He was the People's Commissar for Foreign Affairs from 1930 until being replaced by Molotov in 1939. He was regarded as an opponent of any pact with Germany and when he was dismissed, Stalin said: 'The Soviet Government intended to improve its relations with Hitler and if possible sign a pact with Nazi Germany. As a Jew and an avowed opponent of such a policy, Litvinov stood in the way.'

Despite this, Litvinov survived: he was Soviet ambassador to the United States from 1941 until 1943 and died in 1951 at the age of seventy-five.

The Nazi–Soviet Pact – also known as the Molotov–Ribbentrop Pact – is referred to from Chapter 29 onwards. For readers interested in finding out more about it, I highly recommend *The Devils' Alliance: Hitler's Pact with Stalin 1939–1941* (Vintage, 2016) by my friend Roger Moorhouse.

The details about the events leading up to the Pact in the Molotov letters (Chapter 32) are accurate, though the letters themselves are fictional. Likewise, the antisemitism alluded to in this chapter was certainly an aspect of the Soviet Union under Stalin.

Isidor Yevstigneyevich Lyubimov in Chapter 27 was also a real person.

Currencies and their relative value are always a bit of a minefield – if that's the right metaphor – but if it helps, £10 in 1937 would be the equivalent of £560 today, which equates to $700 (US) and €640.

Goslitizdat, or the State Publishing House of Fiction, referred to in Chapter 10, did exist, though of course its role here is fictional, in keeping with their chosen genre. In Chapter 7, the quote from a guide book about 'fruitless Parliamentarianism' and 'the reawakening of race-consciousness' is taken from an original 1936 edition of the Baedeker Travel Guide to Germany.

I do try to ensure that when I refer to a place by name – be it a town or a city, a railway station or a street or hotel or even a restaurant – then that place would have existed at the time. My sources are a mixture of original research and contemporary guide books and maps.

All the intelligence organisations featured in *Every Spy a Traitor* are genuine. The one exception is The Annexe, which is completely fictional – as is its location in Bryanston Square and the hiring of assassins.

As a general rule – though not an absolute one – characters in my books are always fictional unless I state otherwise or they're obviously historical figures. On the other hand, readers can assume that places are genuine.

One of these places is 16 King Street in the Covent Garden area of Central London, which in *Every Spy a Traitor* is infiltrated by Cooper. It was the headquarters of the Communist Party of Great Britain during the war and indeed up to 1991. Many of the Communist Party leaders referred to in the book were real people: Pollitt, Gallagher, Campbell, Dutt, Rust, Klugman and Springhall. Pollitt, Gallagher and Campbell were the only